1992

Although rationality is a central topic in contemporary analytic philosophy and in the social sciences, literary scholars generally assume that the notion has little or no relevance to literature. In this interdisciplinary study, Paisley Livingston promotes a dialogue between these different fields, arguing that recent theories of rationality can contribute directly to literary enquiry and that literary analysis can in turn enhance our understanding of human agency. The result is a work that helps bring literary studies into a more productive relationship to the human sciences.

Livingston provides a broad survey of the basic assumptions and questions associated with concepts of rationality in philosophical accounts of action, in decision theory, and in the theory of rational choice. He challenges prevalent irrationalist and mechanistic conceptions of human motivation and gives examples of the ways in which rationality is involved in the writing and reading of literary works, ranging from Icelandic sagas to Beckett, Dreiser, Kafka, Lem, Poe, and Zola. Livingston's critical analyses show how theoretically oriented readings of literature can contribute to the formation of hypotheses about the dynamics of human action and interaction.

LITERATURE AND RATIONALITY

LITERATURE AND RATIONALITY
Ideas of agency in theory and fiction

PAISLEY LIVINGSTON

Professor, Department of English, McGill University

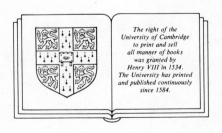

*The right of the
University of Cambridge
to print and sell
all manner of books
was granted by
Henry VIII in 1534.
The University has printed
and published continuously
since 1584.*

CAMBRIDGE UNIVERSITY PRESS

Cambridge
New York   Port Chester
Victoria   Sydney

Published by the Press Syndicate of the University of Cambridge
The Pitt Building, Trumpington Street, Cambridge CB2 1RP
40 West 20th Street, New York, NY 10011–4211, USA
10 Stamford Road, Oakleigh, Victoria 3166, Australia

First published 1991

Printed in Great Britain at the University Press, Cambridge

British Library cataloguing in publication data

Livingston, Paisley
Literature and rationality
1 Literature. Rationality.
1. Title
801

Library of Congress cataloguing in publication data

Livingston, Paisley, 1951–
Literature and rationality / Paisley Livingston.
p.   cm.
Includes bibliographical references and index.
ISBN 0 521 40540 8
1. Literature – Philosophy. 2. Knowledge, theory of.
3. Literature and science. 4. Science – Philosophy. 5. Reason.
1 Title.
PN49.L545 1991
809′.93384–dc20   90–22179   CIP

ISBN 0 521 40540 8 hardback

to my parents

Contents

Acknowledgements

Part of the research for the present study was conducted while I enjoyed a year as *chercheur étranger* at the *Centre de Recherche en Épistémologie Appliquée* (CREA), at the *École Polytechnique*, Paris. I thank Jean-Pierre Dupuy and André Orléan for their generous support during my stay there. I am also pleased to acknowledge financial assistance received from the Social Sciences and Humanities Research Council of the Canadian government. Suggestions and comments made by Jon Elster, Thomas Pavel, and an anonymous reader helped me to improve the manuscript.

Introduction: literature and rationality

The idea that 'man' may be defined as the rational animal is surely an outdated philosophical fiction, a singularly .Western prejudice, perhaps even *the* Western and sexist prejudice par excellence. Does not the evidence of history – or of even a moment's introspection – flatly refute the notion that human beings are rational? Rationality is the 'crystal palace' mocked by Dostoevsky's underground man; real people live in Babel. We can no longer believe in the grand old thesis that human history as a whole is animated by Reason; nor do we have any good reason to think that the preferences of even the most enlightened and lucid modern individuals correspond to the models of rationality invented by neo-classical economics, such as the subjective expected utility model and the theory of rational expectations. It would seem to follow that the concept of rationality does not embrace much of either collective or individual reality, and should therefore be abandoned.

Moreover, even if one were to grant that rationality is a notion having some restricted value in the human sciences, this would not necessarily imply that it has any great relevance to literature. Rationality may seem a particularly inappropriate concept to bring into a discussion of literature: the prevailing tendency today is to associate literature with madness, dreams, and passion, not with reason. The *homo sapiens* of the sciences, then, is contrasted to the *homo demens* of literature, particularly in the age of romanticism. Thus, although in bibliographies of philosophy and the social sciences, 'rationality' and cognate terms are headings for countless entries, in the comprehensive bibliographies published annually by the *Modern Language Association*, the subject heading 'rationality' is followed by a mere handful of items.

It seems clear, then, that the conjunction of the terms 'rationality' and 'literature' in my title is likely to evoke two kinds of questions. One concerns the veracity and importance of the very notion of rationality; the other challenges the relevance of this concept to literature. Responding to these two issues in this introduction will allow me to set forth some of the main assumptions and goals of the present study.

A review of some of the most salient facts about human history, as well as a few moments of honest introspection, should suffice to demolish any belief that people have ever inhabited the crystal palace of perfect rationality – or that they are ever likely to do so. This is a very important point, the implications of which are anything but trivial. Yet the very same evidence also supports the idea that it would be a mistake to describe human beings as creatures who totally fail to satisfy any and all norms of rationality. People are not perfectly rational, it is true, but nor is their behaviour totally incoherent or random. Being neither omnipotent nor impotent, they sometimes behave in ways that effectively realize their goals; being neither omniscient nor totally ignorant, they sometimes achieve a measure of knowledge. This domain of possible knowledge and effective action, a domain that falls between the extremes just evoked, is explored by the various theories of bounded and moderate rationality that have been developed in the human sciences.[1] Rationality, then, is not a concept that we want to discard, even if we think it important to criticize the unrealistic assumptions that make up *homo oeconomicus* and other overly idealized social science fictions.

Arguments for the value of concepts of rationality can be based on a number of theses that are not subject to any reasonable, non-sceptical forms of doubt. For example, it is plain that in their daily affairs, women and men constantly interpret themselves and each other as persons having conscious desires, beliefs, and intentions to act. People think that it is often possible to distinguish between cases where someone does something intentionally and cases where behaviour is not under intentional control.[2] Moreover, these attributions of mental states to other agents are not tentative and purely speculative, but involve serious practical commitments. Every time we take a flight in an aeroplane, or step into the cross-walk before an approaching automobile when the traffic signal has just given us the right of way, we are implicitly wagering that other people's behaviour will conform to any number of complex constraints on perception, inference, and action. For example, we may be tacitly assuming that the other person's beliefs, desires, and actions will conform to a 'practical syllogism' of the following form: if you want a certain state of affairs to obtain and believe that a certain action will bring it about, and if you moreover have no good reasons for not doing so, then you should perform this action. In relation to the example of the pedestrian standing at the crosswalk, this schema could be applied roughly as follows: the pedestrian wants to cross the street and assumes that the driver of the approaching automobile has a certain amount of practical knowledge about traffic regulations and about how to control an automobile; the pedestrian can also ascribe to the driver a basic desire to avoid an accident, which means that the driver is most likely to want to stop and let pedestrians cross the street when they have the right of way. This ascription of beliefs and desires leads to the prediction that the driver will bring the car to a stop only a few feet away from the white line.

It is an indisputable fact that human beings are often able to predict each other's behaviour: witness the many instances where people manage to keep a rendezvous with each other, meeting at the agreed place at the right time, in spite of the complex contingencies involved. How are such things possible? It is clear that people do not manage this sort of everyday co-ordination of behaviour by thinking about each other's neurophysiological processes, neural nets, or the stimulus–response correlations postulated by behaviourist psychology. Nor do they achieve these remarkable feats of co-ordination by means of radical philosophical thinking about the status of this or that morsel of *Dasein*. They do not reckon in terms of social totalities, rhetorical systems, discursive formations, or 'desiring machines'. The way people in fact manage to understand and predict each other's behaviour is by relying on certain kinds of attributions of belief, intention, and desire. In other words, they reckon in terms of what the other person may be assumed to think and want. Moreover, as I shall argue below, this kind of intentional explanation of other people's behaviour relies on some very basic assumptions about the rationality of the agent: if we did not assume that there were any regularities or systematic connexions of some sort between a creature's behaviour and some of the intentional attitudes that we might attribute to that creature, then there would be no point in trying to explain this being's behaviour in terms of such attitudes. Thus, assumptions about rationality come with, and are in fact presupposed by, the general framework of intentional explanation, or in other words, the language of agency, with its talk of action guided by reasons.

My argument, then, is that we have good reasons for believing in the validity of working within the very general framework of intentionalist psychology, and that assumptions about rationality are a necessary and important part of that framework. Yet it is by no means being proposed here that intentional explanations of individual action provide a satisfactory total explanatory framework for the human sciences – far from it. Some of the explanatory limits of this perspective will be discussed below. Moreover, it is not my contention here that the framework of intentional understanding gives us some kind of infallible knowledge of others. Attributing rational connexions of some sort to people's beliefs, desires, and actions may be reliable a lot of the time, but the predictions and explanations we produce in this way remain fallible, and there are many cases where they go wrong. Quite obviously, I may attribute a certain intention to another party and thereby profoundly misunderstand her action, which was in fact oriented by quite a different attitude. Or again, I may misunderstand someone's behaviour by wrongly assuming it to be linked to a particular attitude, when in fact no attitude whatsoever was responsible for this behaviour. Yet when one intentional explanation falters, we often try to make sense of what happened by continuing to think in terms of rational agency, looking for another, more viable intentional explanation. For example, if the driver sped through the intersection instead of stopping, we are likely to ask ourselves – that is, if we were lucky enough to survive – what other goal the person was trying to pursue in driving in such a manner. We look for some other intentionally meaningful connexion between beliefs, desires, and action, asking what kind of beliefs and desires could have made the behaviour seem appropriate to the agent. 'Where's the fire?' is a folk saying that is sometimes uttered on such occasions, suggesting that the motorist's criminal behaviour should be compared ironically to the fireman's legitimate and purposeful dangerous driving. It may be, then, that the conceptual framework relative to rational action – very broadly defined – is a heuristic that we keep on employing until we encounter evidence that it simply does not apply to the case at hand. For example, we look for the driver's reasons for ignoring the traffic signal until we learn that she suffered a stroke and lost control of the vehicle as a result of purely physical causes.

In short, some very general and basic assumptions about rationality may constitute a privileged but fallible heuristic, which amounts to the operating assumption that at least some of the time we will be able to understand and explain people's behaviour in terms of their reasons – the beliefs, desires, and intentions that guided their activity. This rationality heuristic is privileged for the following reason: even if we knew for certain that human beings most often diverged from the constraints of rationality – and this even on some fairly mild definition of those constraints – it would not follow from this fact that assumptions about rationality could not be an important conceptual tool; they could still be an indispensable method of exploring human behaviour, a method we keep trying to employ as long as we grant human organisms the status of agents. The rationality heuristic is fallible because human rationality is indeed limited and imperfect: our thinking about ourselves and others is neither omnipotent nor omniscient.

I turn now to the second objection evoked above. Are the kinds of issues that surround pedestrian notions of practical reasoning particularly relevant to literature? Is it not possible to grant what has just been said about certain concepts of rationality while denying that they play any important rôle in literature and its analysis? Responding to this complex question is the object of chapter 2, where I delineate a number of different ways in which conceptions of agency and rationality are relevant to literature and to literary scholarship. Basically, I defend two theses. The first is that it is highly unreasonable to deny that at least a significant subset of literary phenomena are purposeful activities comprehensible in terms of the rationality heuristic that I have just evoked, and it follows that assumptions about rationality can play a rôle in at least some forms of literary enquiry. I also present some arguments in support of a much stronger thesis, which is that assumptions about agency and rationality are in fact essential to *all* literary phenomena and hence to all adequate literary enquiries.

Some of the broad strokes of the former contention can be conveyed in the present context by referring to a particular example, which will also help to give the reader a better sense of what is meant by my references to a rationality heuristic. In *Egil's Saga*, an Icelandic family saga written around 1230, the modern reader encounters a description of some behaviour that is likely to be a bit puzzling.[3] The protagonist Egil, we read, has learned that his father Skallagrim has passed away during the night and has been found 'sitting on the edge of the bed, dead and so stiff that they could neither lift him nor straighten him out'. What does Egil do when he arrives on the scene? Stretching his father's corpse out flat, he plugs the nostrils, ears, and mouth with wax. The text continues:

Next he asked for digging tools and broke a hole through the south wall. When that was done, he got hold of Skallagrim's head while others took his feet, and in this way they carried him from one side of the house to the other and through the hole that had been made in the wall. Without delay they next carried the body down to Naustaness, and pitched a tent over it for the night. The following morning, at high tide, Skallagrim was put into a boat and taken out to Digraness. Egil had a burial mound raised there on the tip of the headland, and inside it Skallagrim was laid with his horse, weapons and blacksmith's tools.

As is characteristic of the narrative style of the sagas, this passage gives the reader descriptions of actions, but provides no explicit information about the actor's motives, goals, intentions, or other states of mind. Egil makes a hole in the wall and carries his father's body out through it, but no reason for this behaviour is explicitly given. How are we to understand this? One way in which a reader can understand the passage is by trying to fill in the missing intentions. In other words, we try to connect the particular gestures that Egil performs to a meaningful plan or scheme of action, the assumption being that some such connexion was implicit in the narrative. We make sense of the behaviour reported to us by linking it to attitudes, such as belief and desire, that might have motivated it. Since these attitudes are not overtly stated, we can only infer their presence, and in so doing, readers must draw on their own background and contextual knowledge. In the case of the saga, modern readers may lack the background knowledge that would make it possible for them to find a plausible connexion – especially if they read an edition without notes and lack the advice of a specialist. Why does Egil break a hole in the wall of his father's house and remove the corpse through it, instead of simply carrying him out through the door? Why does he block the corpse's nostrils, mouth, and ears? These may seem like totally inappropriate or senseless things to do. Some modern readers may be led to conclude that Egil is not at this point in the story a plausible character at all, but a marionette who has been made to move about crazily by the author, in which case they may try to infer what the author's reasons for writing the story that way could have been. And indeed there are many points in the sagas where readers are wise to give up looking for plausible psychological motivations of a character's actions and to think instead in terms of the other kinds of effects the writer may have been after. Following one well-informed hypothesis about the pragmatic context in which the Icelandic family sagas were composed and read, it is simply wrong to assume that their authors were always trying to convey undistorted truths about people and their psychology.[4] Yet it is often possible to make some plausible inferences about the other sorts of desires and beliefs that guided the composition of a saga.

Many aspects of Egil's behaviour are readily intelligible to most readers: in all cultures people typically bury their dead and perform some kind of funeral ceremonies, and this is clearly what Egil and his helpers are doing when they erect a mound, even though the Viking trappings may seem somewhat peculiar (one may well wonder what motives there were for inhuming the corpse with a horse, weapons, and blacksmith's tools). Yet Egil's other actions are not in fact totally bizarre or senseless; they have at the very least an internal intelligibility that can be grasped once the reader possesses certain background information. Breaking the hole in the wall makes sense once we know that it was thought that ghosts returning to haunt a house could only enter it the way they came in. Although the text does not say so, we may assume that Egil plans to repair the hole in the wall once he has taken the corpse out, thereby preventing his father from getting back into the house later. The action of breaking the hole in the wall thus belongs to a larger plan that links a present intention to a decision to do something else in the future, the actions being related in a structure of means and ends. Similarly, Egil's other gestures involve planning and problem solving. A corpse's orifices were blocked because it was thought that this would prevent the dead man's spirit (*hamr*) from getting out.[5] Thus the actions described by the text become intelligible against a background of religious beliefs. Knowledge of these

beliefs makes it possible for readers to grasp the nature of the
fictional character's implicit practical reasoning in a particular
situation. The religious beliefs in question form a complex network
that includes such items as a distinction between two ways of being
dead – one in which the deceased party undertakes the journey to
Hel, the other in which he comes back from the grave to pester the
living. The network of beliefs includes various ideas about how one
may effectively deal with a ghost (*draugr*) – such as the method
adopted by Egil. One of the most striking features of the network of
beliefs in question is the fact that in the Old Norse judiciary system,
it made perfect sense to file a legal suit against a corpse.

The example shows how a very basic conception of rationality
can play a rôle in the intelligibility of narrative: we understand
crucial aspects of the narrative by thinking in terms of the character's practical reasoning. More specifically, we fill in meaningful
relations between the character's actions and such intentional
attitudes as beliefs, desires, emotions, and intentions. In the example at hand, the desire is a matter of Egil not wanting his father's
ghost to come back and haunt him; the belief is the idea that
carrying the body out through the window and fixing the hole in
the wall afterwards will prevent the ghost from returning; Egil
forms an intention to perform a certain action as part of a plan, and
acts on it – all of which follows appropriately from Egil's desires
and beliefs. Thus, what may seem like a strange and irrational
superstitious practice can be understood as manifesting a basic
syllogism of practical rationality: very generally, a certain course of
action follows from the actor's beliefs, desires, and intentions. And
the practical syllogism that is implicit in the action is also implicit
in our understanding of the description of the action: given the
gestures, we infer the plan (or means–end schema) of which they
are a part.[6] It would seem, then, that understanding narrative
depictions of action requires that we apply a basic rationality heuristic, meaning simply that the reader makes inferences about
coherent and meaningful connexions between an agent's actions
and intentional attitudes.

A number of contemporary literary critics and theorists do not
share the view that the language of rational agency is directly
pertinent to our comprehension of literary phenomena. Roland
Barthes expressed the contrary point of view when he wrote that 'in
narrative, what deliberates over action is not the character, but the

discourse'.[7] Barthes grants that what he calls the 'code' of action and psychological verisimilitude is an important part of literary discourse, but he insists that the determinations of this discourse are none the less not intentional, that is, not to be understood in terms of the practical reasoning of any agent or agents. Yet such claims are dubious. One may very well doubt that a discourse can really do any deliberating, and I return to this objection below. Yet suppose we accept the idea that what deliberates over action is the discourse and not the character. It would still be the case that in order to understand the discourse's deliberation, readers would have to grasp what this discourse says about the character's deliberations, which means they would need to apply a rationality heuristic. For example, if we are to understand Oedipus as a mere pawn or function of the *muthos* of tragic discourse, we must first of all think about him as an agent of purposeful action and try to understand him in such terms. Only then is the reader in a position to measure the distance that is created in the discourse between the intentions and the real consequences and causes of the tragic hero's actions. To eliminate any and all reference to Oedipus's plans, beliefs, and desires would make it impossible to identify tragedy's *dissoi logoi*, which contrast the character's attitudes and efforts to the other conditions and forces that determine what happens to him. More generally, there is good reason to believe that in all discourses where there is any form of psychological verisimilitude (which means all or almost all literary works, and certainly all genuine narratives), making sense of the discourse requires, at the very least, that the reader take some fairly long detours through an understanding of what the characters are doing *qua* intentional agents (albeit fictional ones). Developing intentional understandings of the characters' actions, then, is a necessary (but not a sufficient) condition of the comprehension of most literary works. If assumptions about rationality are a necessary feature of all intentional understandings – a point to be defended in chapter 1 – then it follows that these same assumptions about rationality play an important rôle in the understanding of literature.

In chapter 2 I also advance arguments supporting a stronger thesis, namely, that concepts of agency are necessary to all forms of literary enquiry. Briefly, I contend that there are good reasons to think that it is impossible to understand and explain literary phenomena adequately without relying on the assumption that intentional agency is not reducible to textual processes and codifications. In this regard it is significant to note that in spite of Barthes's explicit proclamations in favour of a thoroughgoing textualist stance, there is still a psychology subtending the theory of discourse and codes that he advances in *S/Z* and other texts – Lacanianism, which is a psychology that tries to reduce agency to language. It is anything but self-evident that this attempt is successful. In chapter 2 I argue that it is a mistake to assume that texts, discourses, and works of art are autonomous entities or functional systems capable of engaging in effective practical interventions in the world; it follows that it is literally impossible for a discourse to 'deliberate over action' or to engage in any other sort of purposive activity. I also explore arguments to the effect that the very identification of symbolic artefacts as such depends on a number of important assumptions about the activity of sentient agents, beginning with the writers whose efforts are indispensable to the existence of literary works. Critics' ability to individuate literary works of art may require reference to the action of relevant agents and not merely to features of texts. One of the central theses of the theory of minimal rationality is 'no rationality, no agent', and I propose and defend a related dictum: 'no agency, no textuality'.

The two lines of argument that I have just evoked jointly suggest that critics can hardly afford to dispense with the rationality heuristic: concepts of agency and rationality may very well play a fundamental rôle in all understandings and explanations of literary phenomena, and they *certainly* play such a rôle in many of them. A point that should be stressed here is that my claim in what follows is not that applying a rationality heuristic to the actions depicted in texts is all that there is to our understanding and appreciation of literary and other narratives – for indeed it is not. What is more, it is not my assumption that literary enquiry should be limited to the appreciation and explication of literary works, for even when these goals are successfully achieved, other aspects of literary history remain to be explained. In what follows I shall argue that concepts of rationality can play a valuable rôle in a number of distinct varieties of literary enquiry, no one of which should be taken as the sole end of the literary disciplines. What is more, although I shall be arguing that the rationality heuristic has a privileged status in relation to literary-historical enquiry, this status does not entail the erroneous view that everything in literary history can be explained in terms of the conscious intentions and practical reasoning of individual authors. My stress on concepts of agency and rationality does not amount to a rehabilitation of what is known as the 'intentional fallacy'.

There is another way in which I motivate my conjunction of the terms 'literature' and 'rationality' in the present study. Not only can we ask how concepts of rationality can be applied to the understanding of literature, but it is also possible to ask how literary works illustrate, challenge, and complexify various conceptions of rationality advanced in the social sciences. What contributions can the critical analysis of literary works make to the formation of hypotheses about the patterns of rationality and irrationality in human action and interaction? In what ways can the reading of literary texts lead to the refinement of contemporary hypotheses about rationality, irrationality, and the framework of intentional explanations? Such questions lead us to explore the value of the analysis of literature within the context of a research problematic of central importance to the human sciences. In such an approach, literature is not an 'object' to which a social scientific concept is applied in cookie-cutter fashion. Instead, 'rationality' and cognate terms are better understood as standing for an important constellation of issues and hypotheses, the value of which is to open up lines of enquiry. One of my central goals in what follows is to analyse aspects of literary texts with the aim of contributing to our understanding of the kinds of questions raised by rationality, irrationality, and intentional explanations. I am seeking, in this manner, to draw on the heuristic value of the critical analysis of literary works.

In the second part of this book, then, I interpret a number of literary works with the aim of working on questions pertaining to hypothetical models of rationality and agency, a particular point of focus being motivational concepts. I begin in chapter 3 with a discussion of basic questions about agency and rationality raised in the naturalist fiction of Theodore Dreiser, arguing that his documents clarify the shortcomings of reductive views of motivation. In spite of Dreiser's proclamations to the contrary, the models of agency in his narratives grant a significant rôle to complex intentional attitudes in the generation of motivational states. Chapter 4 mobilizes a reading of aspects of Dreiser's *Sister Carrie* in relation to a distinction between atomistic and agential models of rationality. The same text makes possible a clarification of the question of the rationality of desire, and allows me to trace some of the limits of intentionalist explanations. In chapter 5, I discuss Émile Zola's *La Joie de vivre* in terms of the place of long-term planning in a theory of agent's rationality. Reference to the complex episodes presented in this narrative makes it possible to propose a hypothesis about a source of irrational planning, namely, a species of social influence in which the agent adopts an unreasonable imitative strategy. Finally, chapter 6 discusses Stanislaw Lem's *His Master's Voice* in relation to the issue of the rationality of social situations, focusing in particular on the text's depiction of the epistemic and practical rationality of a scientist engaged in a collective research project.

In proposing these particular literary readings, it is not my ambition to exhaust the meanings of the works involved or to survey all possible literary texts that are potentially relevant to the theoretical questions being raised. Even less do I claim to have written comprehensive author studies or a detailed and realistic specimen of literary history. In my view these are complementary avenues of enquiry that move on different tracks. Rather, my aim is to explore the heuristic value of a number of texts in relation to problems raised by a few central concepts pertaining to rational agency. If my choice of texts and topics manifests any form of rationality, it is of the bounded and minimal variety.

PART I

Theories and questions

CHAPTER I

Rationality: some basic issues

In this opening chapter I delineate a number of issues related to concepts of rationality and irrationality, and identify some of the assumptions and questions that are carried forward into the rest of this study. My goal is to formulate the issues as explicitly as possible in an effort to clarify the lines of enquiry that could potentially be taken up in analyses of literary phenomena. The question of the relevance of the issues surveyed in this chapter to literature will remain open until chapter 2. I hope that it is clear that my goal in the present work is not to provide a detailed treatment of all of the issues broached in this initial survey of topics.

A very basic background assumption that subtends the full range of particular theories of human rationality and irrationality holds that an important subset of human behaviour may be accurately characterized as purposeful action. In other words, it would be pointless to raise the issue of rationality in relation to any entity or events deemed to be devoid of intentionality and purposiveness.[1] Thus, anyone who lends credence to some notion of human rationality may be expected to think that the latter two notions may rightly be applied to human beings, and anyone who does not lend any credence to intentional attitudes, or who thinks they play no effective rôle in human life, can hardly deem the notion of rationality necessary. The assumption required by the concept of rationality does not specify that all human doings must involve intentional attitudes: it is acknowledged that people are frequently moved by non-conscious or organic processes and that sometimes their behaviour is not coherently linked to deliberations or controlled by intentions. The assumption, however, is that an important subset of human behaviour is aptly described as intentional or voluntary behaviour, or as what various philosophers refer to as 'action'. Action is often defined as behaviour that is engaged in for a reason, where 'reason' is used as a very general term designating the various intentional attitudes that may contribute to the motivation and orientation of behaviour: desires, preferences, goals, choices, present-directed intentions, mental states such as deliberate 'trying' or 'endeavouring', various beliefs about the environment, as well as beliefs about 'ways and means' or the possibility of achieving certain ends in this or that manner. To say that action is behaviour engaged in for a reason is to stipulate that it is these reasons that bring about the action, generating or perhaps even causing it in a certain way.[2] In short, we speak of action when an agent's attitudes of wanting, believing, desiring, intending, and so on, are oriented teleologically towards future states of affairs, and when it is these attitudes that effectively control behaviour.[3] We speak of an intentional explanation when we explain behaviour by viewing it as action, that is, by linking it to the attitudes that were the operative reasons behind it.

Rationality, then, is a concept that is only meaningful in relation to the framework of action and the intentional explanations that are appropriate to it. In other words, no action or no intentionality, no rationality. Someone who did not believe in any such thing as attitudes of believing, knowing, desiring, preferring, and so on, surely would have no use for a concept of rationality, which defines a type of regularity or privileged relation – a *ratio* – holding between such items. Nor would such a person be warranted to speak of irrationality, a notion that presupposes the possibility of rationality as a background.[4] Rather, it would be more appropriate in that case to speak of the non-rationality or a-rationality of human affairs. Thus a first, and perhaps the most basic, issue that may be raised in regard to the concept of rationality has to do with the status of this kind of prior assumption about behaviour. We may refer to this topic as the question of agency, which can be broadly formulated as follows: what basic assumptions about agency must be made if concepts of rationality and irrationality are to be applicable to behaviour? Are these assumptions warranted? What would it mean to do without them?

Rationality, I have just suggested, implies intentional agency, as opposed to various other options, such as a physico-chemical determination of the individual agent's behaviour. What of the converse argument? If we lend credence to the language of intentional agency (that is, if we believe this language is adequate or appropriate in describing some significant category of human doings), does it follow that we must hold any assumptions about rationality? This issue may be called the question of the rationality principle. The response may be negative, in which case we might ask whether some other kinds of basic assumptions, having nothing to do with rationality, are required to make intentional explanations work. We may refer to this issue as the question of a-rational agency: what plausible models of agency and intentional explanation can be constructed in the absence of assumptions about rationality? If, on the other hand, the response to the question of the rationality principle is affirmative, then we must ask which assumptions about rationality should be adopted, an issue that is complicated immensely by the fact that there are different candidates for the rôle of the most basic principle or heuristic of rationality.[5] This issue may be referred to as the question of rationality assumptions, as it is a matter of asking which assumptions are necessary and/or sufficient to the elaboration of intentional explanations and a viable model of agency.

I shall now clarify this first cluster of issues before introducing some more. My remarks on the basic question of agency will at this point be brief, for I consider concepts of intentionality and action to be necessary to the description and explanation of significant aspects of human behaviour. Yet many post-structuralist theorists claim to be interested in a radical questioning of such an assumption. They thus entertain the possibility that all notions of human agency are products of some purely contingent and factitious ideology or discourse, behind the back of which are the unknown – and perhaps forever unknowable – forces. As this story goes, the concept of individual agency is basically a theological hangover produced by the Enlightenment which, drunk on reason, sought to secularize the notion of God's divine will. Yet, as no human agent could ever really attain the status of the unmoved mover, what we need is a historical perspective on the emergence and future disappearance of what is taken to be the 'problematic philosopheme of agency'.[6]

My own stance on this issue is that sceptical doubts about the veracity of the language of action and agency can indeed be coherently entertained, but reasoned proclamations of their global inappropriateness and falsehood cannot, for such efforts are self-defeating. An example is Barbara Herrnstein Smith's comment that human activity 'could be seen as Brownian motion, Heraclitean flux, or Nietzsche's pure "play of forces" '. She adds in a note: 'The evocation of a totally disassembled or nihilistic perspective on human activity or all activity has its purposes in certain theoretical discourses, and it is evidently thus that Derrida would restate and thereby conserve the value and productivity of Bataille'.[7] Although statements of this sort may have the merit of challenging naïve beliefs in the perfect freedom and autonomy of the individual, such exaggerations only blunt this purpose. If human activities were really seen as Brownian motion, they would be totally unpredictable. How, under such conditions, could the labels 'Derrida' and 'Bataille' be made to correspond to sets of activities having anything like 'purpose', 'value', or 'productivity'? To speak of an activity having a purpose is already to speak within the framework of action, and indeed Derrida is referred to as a purposive agent in the cited phrase, for he is said to be engaged in the actions of restating and conserving. The totally 'disassembled' perspective is evoked, then, and not achieved, and there is a tension between the evocation and the achievement. It is strictly incoherent to enjoin someone to abandon all beliefs in agency when such a gesture presupposes the veracity of the very thing that one enjoins the other person to abandon: 'Stop believing in beliefs!' says the contemporary Cretan, implying that others both have – and should go on believing in – beliefs. Moreover, we are ostensibly given reasons why we should not believe that people are capable of fixing their beliefs in function of reasons. Similarly, it is incoherent to urge someone to decide to stop using the language of purposeful action, intention, and decision, for implicit in the exhortation is the idea that the speaker and listener are intentional agents capable of making a decision and of acting on it.

Some of the proponents of the position in the philosophy of mind known as 'radical eliminativist materialism' have contended that the argument that I have just adopted is question-begging: in their view, the *reductio* takes for granted the validity of intentional attitudes, which is precisely what they wish to challenge.[8] The real issue, then, is a matter of deciding what would constitute a truly successful challenge to so-called 'folk psychology', with its talk of beliefs, desires, and actions generated by reasons. Is there any reason or definitive proof why there could never be a fully non-intentionalist model of human behaviour? Perhaps not, but one thing is clear: the successful challenge cannot be a matter of self-defeating proclamations of the end of intentional attitudes, but must take some genuinely alternative form. Perhaps such an alternative could be realized one day by means of accurate descriptions of the neurophysiological processes that make possible and determine human behaviour and experience; perhaps it could even take the form of a sub-symbolic, massively distributed, connexionist computer program, capable of aping human cognitive capacities – and of dispensing with a natural language laden with inaccurate psychological conceptions. In that manner, the language of intentional agency would be replaced the way modern chemistry replaced alchemy. Perhaps. But at the present time, the materialist eliminativist's projections and promises along these lines have no compelling implications for researchers in the humanities, who may remain committed to working with an intentionalist psychology based on a non-reductionist form of materialism. Eliminativism sometimes looks like a project for the radical reform, and not merely the scientific description, of human agency. It may be impossible to prove that such a reform cannot be achieved, but it is certain that contradictory essays in literary criticism are not capable of bringing it about.

Many contemporary statements to the effect that the concept of intentionality is illusory are self-defeating in that they implicitly rely on the very notion that they purport to reject. An analogous problem plagues at least one version of an instrumentalist attitude towards the language of intentionality. This language is said to be a 'stance' that is optional in the sense that one can choose to adopt it or not in regard to particular items, but the very notion of such a choice implies a prior adoption of the intentional stance, at least in regard to the kinds of items that are supposed to be able to do the choosing.[9] Intentionality would seem to be a kind of framework fact, a basic feature of our attitude towards significant aspects of human behaviour; as such, it cannot be globally rejected or suspended in a coherent manner. I return to the possibility of developing viable alternatives to the entire framework of intentionality in chapter 3, where I discuss the shortcomings of one such approach in detail. For now, I turn to the separate issue concerning the relationship between assumptions about agency and rationality.

Do intentional explanations have to rely on any assumptions

about rationality? It may be argued that we do not go about the everyday business of trying to explain and predict other people's behaviour in terms of its relationship to intentions, beliefs, desires, and the like unless we have at least an implicit stance or prejudice about how these kinds of items are typically related to each other. There has to be a certain level of confidence that the enterprise of intentional explanation is going to work part of the time, and this confidence rests on some very basic attitudes about what kinds of connexions there are likely to be between other people's motives, thoughts, and actions. Perhaps the 'thinnest' or most minimal way of putting this basic stance or principle is to say that we necessarily assume that the relation between people's attitudes and actions is not purely random. This 'non-random' assumption, which need not be conscious, does seem to be a necessary 'zero degree' condition of the framework of intentional explanations. If one thought one's neighbours had various beliefs, desires, and intentions, and that their actual behaviour was only randomly related to these attitudes of theirs, then there would be no incentive for trying to understand or predict their doings in terms of these attitudes – in which case one would be well advised to look for some other factors. One might very well perceive certain behavioural regularities – for example, one observes that the neighbours almost always open the curtains when it is light outside and close them when it gets dark – but there would be no good reason to assume that these doings were linked to any particular beliefs or desires in any coherent or systematic way: for example, the regular gesture of closing the curtains when night falls would not be connected to a desire for privacy or even to some idea about social propriety, for such behaviour might just as well have been generated randomly by any other notions or preferences – or by none at all. This example has the modest virtue, I think, of suggesting that any model of intentional agency that is going to have a chance at being even slightly plausible will need to involve constraints or conditions that move us significantly away from this sort of randomness and in the direction of heuristics involving at least a moderate form of rationality.

Yet not everyone agrees that to say that the hypothetical connexions must be non-random is necessarily equivalent to saying that they must be rational. Perhaps I could successfully explain and predict my neighbour's actions a lot of the time if I assumed that this person's behaviour was systematically connected to certain desires and beliefs in some highly idiosyncratic and non-rational way. In that case there would be a principle or regularity that makes a kind of intentional psychology of this agent possible, but there would be no reliance on any principles or assumptions having to do with rationality. A proposal along these lines has been made by Janet Levin, who argues as follows:

> we would be willing to ascribe intentional states to a creature as long as it meets the following, extremely weak, conditions: first, the putative beliefs we ascribe it are states that arise systematically from perception – either directly, or by means of principles that govern the generation of new beliefs – and its putative desires are states that arise systematically, again, either directly or indirectly, from its goals and needs; second, these putative beliefs and desires interact to produce behavior according to (sufficiently) stable and lawlike principles; and finally, the principles linking perception, belief, desire, and behavior make essential use of the semantic structure of the beliefs and desires, and of the perceptual situation and behavior as described.
>
> According to these conditions, however, perceptual beliefs need not be *reliable*, inductive procedures need not be even minimally *truth preserving*, and the principles that describe the influence of belief and desire upon action need not approximate the canons of decision theory. Nor must these principles be adaptive, or evolutionarily sound. True enough, beliefs and desires must be ascribable in a way that gives stable, coherent, and systematic explanations of behavior, but in no (interesting) sense of the term 'rational' must they 'rationalize' the actions they produce.[10]

Levin illustrates her thesis by evoking a number of creatures whose antics are said to be explicable in intentional, but a-rational, terms. One of them is a being that consistently engages in self-defeating behaviour. For example, this creature – that Levin does not characterize as a 'person' – has an overarching desire to meet Greta Garbo and believes that going to a certain party is the only way to do so. What is more, the creature has the opportunity and ability to go to this party, and knows it. Yet the creature does not go to the party and thus fails to satisfy its desire to meet Garbo. This episode is wholly typical of its behaviour, for whenever this strange, self-defeating being becomes aware of one of its desires, it does something meant to guarantee that it will not get what it most strongly desires. Levin proposes that this being's behavioural pattern instantiates the following generalization: if this creature most strongly desires q and believes that p brings q about, and if this creature believes that it desires q, then it will refrain from doing p.

Applying this principle, we can explain the creature's behaviour, and in so doing we do not have to rely on any principles or assumptions about rationality.

Levin's proposal is at once bold and challenging. Her arguments are particularly significant in the present context because I shall be assuming, *contra* Levin, that intentional descriptions and explanations do necessarily rely on a rationality principle, which I consider to be a fallible heuristic. In other words, my stance on the question of a-rational agency will be that a-rational models are incorrect and not workable. Thus a response to Levin's position is in order. We may begin by observing that a key feature of Levin's proposal is that although the semantic content of the agent's beliefs and desires must be taken into account in understanding their systematic links to action (which implies that it is still a matter of intentional explanations), it is not assumed that these links must take the form specified in definitions of rationality. Note, however, that in order to argue for the possibility of this model of a-rational agency, one still requires an understanding of what a rational kind of behavioural disposition would be, so as to be able to contrast it to the other kind of non-random mental arrangement that would still make intentional explanations possible. Thus Levin refers to the 'canons of decision theory' and to other assumptions about rationality. It is clear that to get anywhere with what I have called the question of a-rational agency, one must also have some stance on the question of rationality assumptions.

Levin occasionally supports her basic contention about the viability of an a-rational conception of agency by referring to rather stiff rationality assumptions – those of decision theory. I explain some of the basic insights of the latter below; suffice it to say for now that if the question of a-rational agency hinged on that particular theory, Levin would probably be right. Yet it seems to me that the most basic and difficult issue that Levin's text raises has nothing to do with the canons of decision theory, but concerns instead the possibility of developing intentionalist explanations of behaviour that do not rely on far more modest and minimal assumptions about rationality. Along these lines, the minimal assumption that Levin discusses is the basic practical syllogism that I evoked in my introduction: if one desires q and believes that p brings about q, and if one is able, and believes oneself able, to do p, then one does p.[11] Associated with this syllogism is a basic rationality heuristic: given the behaviour *p*, one makes sense of it by inferring the desire(s) and the belief(s) that generated it. What I want to argue is that Levin's claim that an intentionalist explanation can do without this principle is not very plausible; moreover, it is not clear to me what methodological implications would follow even should the plausibility of her claim be granted: it would not necessarily follow, for example, that those working within an intentional psychology should stop relying on the minimal assumption about rationality that Levin identifies. In other words, even if we could suspend such assumptions, which is dubious, it does not follow that we should do so.

Although Levin's systematically self-defeating creature is in some sense intelligible, it seems wrong to think that this intelligibility in no way relies on the basic practical syllogism that she evokes. On the contrary, the alternative behavioural principle that Levin proposes remains parasitic on the practical syllogism as she defines it. Levin states that her a-rational creature systematically avoids satisfying a desire of which it becomes aware, either by refraining from doing what it can do to satisfy its desire, or by taking steps to ensure that it never gets what it most strongly wants. Yet what grounds could anyone (the creature included) have for attributing any desires at all to such a being? If the creature's behaviour really exemplified Levin's alternative syllogism, what reason could we have to believe that what the creature most desired was to meet Garbo? Levin's answer to that question reveals her reliance on the practical syllogism that was supposed to be suspended in her example. She refers to the agent's 'avowals and stated goals' and to various other items of behaviour that are supposed to suggest that a fascination with Garbo is in fact a ruling passion of the creature, a passion that gets thwarted when it is time to go to the party. Levin tells us that the creature collects pictures of Garbo, sees all of her movies, avows its adoration of the star, and otherwise behaves like a starstruck fanatic. Yet Levin's interpretation of these antics relies on the basic practical syllogism, for she has assumed that going to see Garbo films was undertaken by the agent in order to satisfy a desire to see Garbo films, and not, following the alternative principle, in order to thwart some other desire. Otherwise, why would the agent's filmgoing habits provide any evidence for a desire to meet the idol? Why not assume that the creature goes to Garbo films in order to avoid satisfying some other desire, such as a desire to see some other star's films, or to stay home and read a book? It will not do here to say that the creature was unaware of desiring to see Garbo films and could thus successfully act on that desire: how could anyone selectively choose to see Garbo films without ever being aware of any desire to do so? Similar remarks hold in regard to the creature's 'communicative' behaviour. Levin's a-rational behavioural principle implies that when the creature 'avows' a desire to meet Garbo, we should *not* assume that this utterance was genuinely motivated by the creature's desire to avow the nature of its desire, which implies in turn that we should not rely on the utterance's content in trying to fathom the strange creature's motives. But Levin relies on the contents of the avowal in a straightforward way in claiming that the utterance provides evidence of the creature's desire to meet Garbo.

My point, then, is that in order to attribute motives consistently at all, we have to work with the assumption that at least some of the time the agent's behaviour actually is undertaken with the goal of satisfying, not thwarting, the agent's strongest wants, for in the absence of such an assumption, we cannot even begin to make any systematic hypotheses about correlations between behaviour and such items as desires, beliefs, and intentions. The practical syllogism that Levin evokes is just such an assumption about rationality, for it allows for inferences from behaviour to wants and beliefs. Levin implicitly relies on this same schema in order to be in a position to claim that the self-defeating fan engages in some instances of irrational behaviour. Thus I echo Donald Davidson's claim about rationality assumptions being a condition of attributing any thoughts, desires, or other attitudes at all to a creature.[12]

In what follows I shall indeed assume that intentional explanations require the application of a basic rationality heuristic. My idea is not that people always behave rationally, but that the irrational and rational dimensions of human agency are made intelligible by working with this heuristic. Such a claim leaves many issues unresolved, beginning with the question of what working with a rationality heuristic involves. In this regard, some important features of rationality assumptions may be identified by referring to a proposal advanced by Christopher Cherniak in his *Minimal Rationality*. This author sets forth a general, minimal rationality condition, which runs as follows: 'If *A* has a particular belief–desire set, *A* would undertake some, but not necessarily all, of those actions that are apparently appropriate.'[13] It is further specified that the agent will not attempt too many of the actions that seem inappropriate given the belief-desire set. An action performed by an agent is said to be 'apparently appropriate' if and only if according to that particular agent's beliefs it would tend to satisfy that agent's desires. Note that this is a very weak (and vaguely framed) constraint on the systematic relations between a person's beliefs, desires, and actions. The 'fit' between the different cognitive items is only specified in terms of a subjective notion of appropriateness (which could vary wildly in actual cases – nothing is said about which of the agent's desires the agent must believe will be satisfied; nor is anything specified about what the agent must believe on the topic of how these desires are to be satisfied). Cherniak indeed specifies that 'Appropriateness here again must be evaluated relative to the agent's beliefs, not the objective facts, since it would be an unacceptably extreme idealization to assume the agent's beliefs are always correct. However, we have seen that these beliefs are subject to an "objective" consistency constraint' (p. 139 n. 6). Yet Cherniak's objective consistency constraint is also rather minimal. Here is what it requires: 'If A has a particular belief–desire set, then if any inconsistencies arose in the belief set, A would sometimes eliminate some of them' (p. 16). This clause is totally remote from the idea that an agent's beliefs must match the ideally rational principles of logic, and that the agent must add, delete, and alter beliefs so as to maintain global coherence or validity (deductive closure). The minimally rational agent will fail to make many of the sound inferences that follow from his or her beliefs, and will make some invalid ones; such an agent must have some, but not ideal, logical ability: 'it cannot be the case that a minimal agent is able to make no inferences, but the agent can be unable to make any particular one' (p. 28). Cherniak's proposal thus allows for any number of contradictions in the agent's belief system, particularly those holding between beliefs stored in the agent's long-term memory. In Cherniak's view, long-term memory is compartmentalized and obeys less stringent rationality constraints than does short-term memory or focal awareness. Presumably, the agent cannot have an occurrent or focal belief that p and not-p, whereas the agent can be said to believe p as well as not-p as long as both beliefs have the status of dispositional attitudes, such as long-standing attitudes not actively recalled at the same moment.

Cherniak's model is a theory of rationality that places us at quite a distance from those views on human agency that many thinkers associate with the concepts of personhood and The Subject, which involve highly idealized standards of unity and the conscious integration of the individual's experience.[14] Cherniak's proposal has basically two facets. The most original is a quantitative loosening of a rationality requirement that in some respects resembles Karl Popper's 'rationality principle' (on at least one reading of the latter).[15] Roughly, Popper's principle stipulates that we should assume that every human action is subjectively rational in the sense that it is deemed 'appropriate' by the agent who engages in it. Popper acknowledges that such an assumption is false if taken as a universal empirical law about human behaviour, yet he none the less describes this very principle as the necessary basis of situational analyses (essentially, analyses that explain an agent's doings in terms of the agent's desires and beliefs about that situation). The basic intuition here is that we have explained someone's action when we have described the beliefs and desires that made that action seem appropriate to the person who performed it. A major problem with Popper's proposal is that nothing precise is said about what it means for an action to be 'subjectively appropriate' for the agent, the result being that it is impossible to evaluate the empirical or methodological status of the crucial clause. Popperians have found it difficult to square the master's insistence on the rationality principle with the rest of his strictures about scientific enquiry: the principle would seem to have empirical content and looks like a false generalization that should be eliminated from the body of scientific theory, yet the principle can also be construed as a false but useful methodological rule, or even as one of the basic, and essentially metaphysical, assumptions constitutive of a research programme. It is not clear to me which of these options Popper's laconic remarks were meant to defend, and my view is that the debate over the precise status of the principle in Popper's thought cannot be settled because some of his key formulations are hopelessly vague.

Although Cherniak does not say so, his proposal concerning minimal rationality responds quite precisely to a complaint that has been levelled against Popper's notion, namely, the idea that in examples of *akrasia* (and perhaps in other forms of irrationality), agents do not always do what they themselves deem appropriate.

Cherniak's notion is that the rational fit between action and desire and belief, however it may be defined, does not always have to obtain in all particular instances: not everything people do is appropriate to their beliefs and desires, and they neither conceive nor execute all of those actions which these beliefs and desires potentially entail as being appropriate. Similarly, in regard to the rationality of belief, Cherniak loosens the unrealistic requirements written into many of the formal models developed in epistemic logic.[16] Thus, Cherniak's global constraint holds without it being stipulated that all of an agent's actions and beliefs have to be rational. This implies as well that the hypothesis concerning the global constraint is only falsified in regard to a particular agent if we cannot find some cases that satisfy its loose definition of appropriate belief–desire–action connexions – and 'not too many' that violate that norm. This is clearly a tall order: if the general minimal rationality condition is a thesis about an individual agent, it could only be falsified at the end of that agent's life, for at that point one might have some small chance of determining whether the agent has performed enough subjectively inappropriate deeds to violate the clause about 'not too many' inappropriate actions. If, on the other hand, the thesis is about people's behaviour in general, then it is clearly unfalsifiable, for until we happen to experience the *Dies irae*, it will be strictly impossible to establish whether humanity has satisfied the rather vague clause about performing enough subjectively appropriate actions and 'not too many' inappropriate ones.

Although this facet of Cherniak's proposal for necessary (but not sufficient) minimal rationality conditions of agency may have its merits, I shall be returning to it below so as to discuss some ways in which it might be challenged and improved. Yet I turn first to the second facet of his proposal, which is much more fundamental. Here it is a matter of his fairly laconic and undeveloped rendition of what is a basic feature of every definition of rational action, namely, the specification of a relation of adequacy or appropriateness between an action and certain intentional attitudes, such as a belief and a desire. As we have already seen, in Cherniak's version – as is quite common – the appropriateness of an action is a purely subjective affair, determined only in relation to the agent's beliefs and desires. More specifically, the appropriateness of an action involves the agent's belief that it would 'tend to satisfy' the agent's desires.

Following Cherniak's account, then, a particular action is subjectively appropriate – and can thus potentially contribute to the agent's overall rationality – if the agent thinks performing it will tend to satisfy (some of) his or her desires. This is a deceptively simple idea, one that has the task of responding to a question of no small complexity. Although there is no precedent in the literature for doing so, I shall call this problem the question of atomic practical rationality, for it is a matter of asking under what conditions we may ascribe rationality or irrationality to an individual unit of action, as if it could be understood and evaluated in isolation from all other actions performed by the agent. 'All other things being equal,' this question goes, 'when is it rational for an agent to do x?' where the emphasis is on the x, not on this particular agent's doing x in the context of that agent's personal history. We may already anticipate that this question will have an analogue in relation to belief, the question of atomic rationality of belief, for people sometimes ask under what conditions we may ascribe rationality or irrationality to the holding of a particular belief.[17] Furthermore, it may be noted that the question of the rationality of belief branches into at least two different issues: on the one hand, there is the question of atomic epistemic rationality, which is a matter of asking when it is rational, in regard to purely epistemic ends, to have a certain belief; and on the other hand, there are questions about the rationality of this or that belief relative to other, non-epistemic ends.[18]

These basic questions about atomic rationality are anything but simple and involve various subsidiary problems, such as that of defining the various highly loaded terms that necessarily figure in answers to them. Note as well that they tend to be closely interrelated in so far as beliefs are a necessary ingredient in practical rationality, and certain forms of action and inaction (such as actively seeking information, or declining to do so) may have direct consequences for the rationality of a belief. Let us briefly consider the relation between Cherniak's answer to the question of atomic practical rationality and some of the others that have been proposed in the literature. To begin, here is a very similar statement of the basic clause about the rationality of a particular action: 'if agent x desires q and believes that action p will enable him to get q, he is practically rational in choosing p. How he came to believe that p leads to q is not relevant.'[19] Note that the condition concerns any agent, x, and that it involves only a particular relation between the action and two other factors, a belief and a desire. This kind of proposal may be contrasted to various other positions.[20] Various perspectives on the basic ingredients of an 'atom' of practical rationality may be constructed by weighing additional requirements on the elements figuring in the basic schema just cited. Such perspectives, which may have both a descriptive and a normative thrust, range along a spectrum defined by two extremes: on the one hand, there are theories in which the rational 'fit' between action, belief, and desire is established by a very broad constraint, and on the other, theories that require a far more stringent and restrictive constraint on this relation. Thus one author suggests that action is rational when it can be understood 'as one which the actor in some way apprehends as a means to an end', so that the rationality of a particular action is synonymous with its instrumentality.[21] Another makes rationality synonymous with teleology, so that any act, viewed narrowly as an act that is determined by some want, is rational.[22] Note that Cherniak's idea of appropriateness, which is charged with the crucial function of singling out cases of a rational derivation of actions from beliefs and desires, is totally subjective: all that is required for an action to be 'apparently appropriate' is that the agent believe it will 'tend to satisfy' that agent's desires. If the agent is wrong, or if the desire in question is self-destructive, the individual action may still be rational. I could have the most deluded ideas about myself, other people, and the external world, but as long as it seems to me that my actions follow appropriately from these beliefs and desires a lot of the time, I qualify as being a 'minimally' rational agent. This means as well that in order to be rational, actions do not have to succeed: the agent may believe that p is an effective means to q, but this belief can be false, and q may in fact never follow from the agent's rather accomplished performance of p. This kind of purely subjective conception of rationality is common in the literature. As one author cogently states it, 'Nothing can count as an error of reasoning among our fellow adults unless even the author of the error would, under ideal conditions, agree that it is an error.'[23]

Moving along the spectrum towards stiffer constraints on rationality, we find ourselves in the context of debates over the distinction between 'optimizing' and 'satisficing'. Does the action chosen have to be estimated by the agent as the very best possible solution? Or does rationality merely require that the choice represent one among various viable solutions, or again, a choice satisfying some internal standard or criterion that may not be selective enough to single out what is objectively the optimal solution? In what terms are the different available means to a given end to be evaluated? Such topics are taken up in Herbert Simon's discussions of the differences between 'procedural' and 'substantive' rationality, as well as in his famous distinction between optimizing and satisficing (although it is not always clear in Simon's texts whether these four terms refer to a single dichotomy or to two different distinctions). Simon's concept of bounded rationality may suffer from a basic ambiguity in so far as it either refers to a form of rationality that is weak relative to an objective standard of perfection, or to a form of rationality that is perfect relative to the agent's limitations and situation. The issue of the nature and extent of Simon's distance from the mainstream model of optimization hangs in the balance.[24] It should also be noted that Simon's choice of terms in speaking of 'procedural' and 'substantive' rationality may be especially misleading for those who are more familiar with the language of the Weberian tradition. Simon's distinction, it should be noted, does not correspond to Max Weber's opposition between 'instrumental' and 'substantive' rationality (*Zweck- und Wertrationalität*).[25] The latter distinction concerns the difference between two very different ways of construing rationality, not to two different stances on the question of what constitutes an appropriate relation or 'fit' between means and ends. It is important to note that many definitions of rationality focus uniquely on the latter issue: as Geoffrey Mortimore observes, 'It is common to identify rationality in action with choosing the appropriate means to attain one's ends.'[26]

Here we may anticipate the possibility that the definition of appropriateness figuring in Cherniak's proposal will be judged far too minimal or 'thin' to express any of our more robust intuitions about practical rationality, epistemic rationality (or more generally, the rationality of belief), and agency. In this regard, Jon Elster clearly distinguishes between 'thin' and 'broad' theories of individual rationality, making the following important point: 'I suggest that *between the thin theory of the rational and the full theory of the true and the good there is room and need for a broad theory of the rational.*'[27] In this direction we encounter the debate between externalist and internalist (or objective and subjective) criteria of rationality. In terms of the formula introduced above, this means that one may turn one's attention to the desire for q, asking whether it is in itself a rational desire (and thus we broach the question of atomic motivational rationality, which concerns the rationality criteria to be applied to desire and other motivational states). One may similarly interrogate the agent's belief about the means–end relationship between p and q, requiring that this belief itself be rational in some sense, such as 'justified', 'warranted', or even 'true' (which suggests that such versions of atomic practical rationality imply an answer to the problem of atomic epistemic rationality). Putting these different elements together, one may generate such options as the following: 'if agent x desires q, and if the desire for q is rational, and if agent x rationally believes that action p is a good means of getting q, he or she is practically rational in choosing p'. Along these lines, Richard Foley describes (but does not defend) what he calls the 'radically objective' conception of rationality: 'All else being equal, it is rational for S to bring about Y if he has a goal X and Y is an effective means to X' – and note that here, it is not the agent's belief about the instrumental relation between the x and the y that counts, but the fact of the matter.[28] An even stronger constraint is proposed by Martin Hollis, who requires not only that the action chosen be 'likeliest' to realize the agent's goal, but that it actually be in the agent's 'overall real interest' to realize the goal in question.[29]

Yet this is only the beginning of the complexities involved when we begin to examine the question of atomic rationality in some detail. Not only is there the problem of finding terms in which to evaluate rigorously the rationality of such items as beliefs and desires, but it is also necessary to confront the question of whether these two items are themselves necessary and/or sufficient for specifying the basic intentional configuration of an atom of rational action. (The term 'atom' may be particularly appropriate in this context: like its physical counterpart, the basic unit of rational action has a way of splitting up into smaller and smaller components, the ontological status of which may be subject to debate.) For shorthand, we may refer to this group of issues as the question of the components of intentional explanation.

What, for example, is the place of the concept of desire in intentional explanations? Does the notion play a necessary rôle in such explanations, or need it only figure in some of them? Could it be eliminated entirely? A sizeable literature surrounds even these most basic issues, and I shall now briefly present some of the broad strokes, as these matters will concern us in subsequent chapters.[30] In recent times, the central discussion in this regard has been identified as the debate between 'Humean' and 'anti-Humean' positions, or again, as the debate between what are called the 'cognitivist' and 'conativist' stances on the rôle of desire in intentionalist psychology. Conativism has been characterized as the view that at least one desire is an essential component in any explanation of an intentional action; desire, then, is a necessary but not a sufficient condition of the latter. Typically, cognitivists do not assert the logically opposite thesis, but the idea that in some cases, belief may be sufficient to move an agent to act, which would imply that the explanation of the latter need not always involve any reference to desire.[31]

This debate leads quite directly to a discussion of the different senses of 'desire'.[32] Two very basic senses may usefully be identified: on the one hand 'desire' is understood as a term that designates some kind of sensuous longing for some state of affairs; on the other hand, there is the more general and formal sense of desire as a kind of generic motivational state: 'whatever tends to move the agent to act.' When one is hungry and *gourmand*, one is likely to have a desire in the former sense (as well as in the latter) for one's dinner. Although dutiful soldiers deeply dread being killed or wounded, they none the less desire – in the latter sense but not in the former – to take their place on the field of battle, which is one reason, perhaps even the determinant reason, why they do not desert. Conativists, then, consider that desire, in one of the two senses, if not both, is a necessary element in any action. Even when people do things that they are loath to do, there is a sense in which they desire to do it, for the action must be motivated by some genuine desire – which may be a reluctant attitude to the effect that this thing is the lesser evil, or what duty requires.

Yet cognitivists retort that the conativists are equivocating: not everything people do is motivated by desire in the genuine sense of the word, which as far as cognitivists are concerned, is the first sense mentioned above. In other cases, this argument runs, the motivation needed to propel action is derived from beliefs, such as beliefs about one's duty, or the belief that any other course of action would be disastrous. Some soldiers may indeed desire combat and are moved by some bellicose passion, but many soldiers have no real desire to fight and are effectively motivated to participate in ghastly battles only because they either believe it is the right thing to do or because they see no way out: what puts them on the 'path of glory' is the prospect of facing a firing squad. In such cases, belief alone leads to action. Yet here the conativist responds that the deliberative process will be endless unless some overarching desire – in the broad sense – puts a stop to motivational regress. Dutiful soldiers must desire being dutiful more than they desire the other possibilities they contemplate, for otherwise they would never form any decisive, present-directed intention to act on one belief as opposed to another. They may very well believe that they should be dutiful instead of seeking to save their own hides, but this belief cannot be determinant and produce action unless such people have a decisive desire to do what they believe they should do, as opposed to something else.

Is the debate between cognitivists and conativists that I have just rehearsed purely a matter of arbitrary stipulations? Not if it is a matter of choosing between the two unacceptable extremes that the two positions are sometimes taken to represent. One extreme conjures a rather philosophical image of a humanity that is capable of being moved to action by pure beliefs and arguments. The hearts of these bloodless beings are composed of syllogisms of the following sort: 'It is good to be willing to sacrifice one's life for one's country, I should do the good, therefore, I shall sacrifice my life . . .' The other extreme paints a portrait of an egotistical and sensual individual, driven by a handful of primitive appetites, and then generalizes this portrait to all human beings. Yet these two extreme versions are in fact shunned by many of those who argue for cognitivism or conativism. Thus cognitivists may freely recognize that many actions are motivated by desires, and conativism should not be confused with psychological hedonism, or the idea that people are ultimately only moved by the prospect of pleasure or the satisfaction of their sensuous longings. If the conativist insists on the necessity of desire as an ingredient in action, the 'desire' in question is a generic motivational state, a rough-grained concept that obscures fine distinctions between the varieties of what Davidson has called 'pro attitudes', such as needing, wanting, preferring, longing for, lusting after, and so on.[33] These distinctions may be reintroduced at a second stage of the analysis. Conativists may define desire, then, as a necessary (but not sufficient) precondition to action, which means that without desire, there will be no effective motivational state. Conativists, then, should recognize that a given desire does not necessarily entail action (given that we do not act on all of our desires). Desire may in that case be understood as standing for a disposition to form the intention to act with the aim of realizing a certain state of affairs, the latter being the object of the desire. Desire does not entail action, but an action does entail desire. The conativist position is more plausible in those versions of it that are not committed to the erroneous view that beliefs play no rôle in the generation of effective motivational states. Desire is not said to engender these motivational states all alone, but works in conjunction with belief. Thus the agent may have the most urgent appetitive and sensuous longing for some state of affairs, but does not act on this longing in the absence of all beliefs; for example, the agent has to have a belief that p is an effective way to realize the particular q that is so hotly desired. Desire is necessary but not sufficient to action, and there may be good reason to assume that the other conditions include beliefs as well as some effective motivational state. Similarly, cognitivists need to distinguish the latter sort of motivational state from beliefs in general, for they surely want to recognize that not all beliefs effectively lead to action.

Thus, if at first glance it would seem that both camps want to make their favourite item the essential and determinant ingredient in action, it turns out that neither desire nor belief can really be expected to play that rôle, as both are better viewed as attitudes that together contribute to the generation of effective motivational states. It looks as if the upshot of the debate between cognitivism and conativism is that both positions must recognize that intentional explanations cannot work simply with notions of belief and desire, however their respective rôles might be construed. Moreover, the idea of an effective motivational state may not be reducible to some special combination of beliefs and desires. Thus some theorists hold that the explanation of intentional action requires other terms, such as 'present-directed intention', 'trying', 'endeavouring', and 'willing'.[34]

Above, I evoked the following basic formula figuring in discussions of practical rationality: if agent x desires q and believes that action p will enable him to get q, he or she is practically rational in choosing p. Note that this formula includes not only a belief and a desire, but also a 'choice': the right kind of belief, coupled with the right kind of desire, dictate a rational choice of p, which then presumably leads to an action, or the actual doing of p. And note too that in Cherniak's formula for minimal rationality, reference is made to the agent 'undertaking' action. Here we detect the shadow of yet another term that may need to figure in a basic account of action, namely, intention, in the sense of a present-directed intention to perform some action that the agent may successfully or unsuccessfully execute. This notion differs from both belief and desire in that it stresses the rôle a present-directed intention plays in controlling – as opposed to potentially influencing – present conduct. Intention, in this sense, is not reducible to the agent's overarching or predominant desire, for we do not always act on even our predominant desire. Michael Bratman notes: 'As a conduct controlling pro-attitude my intention involves a special commitment to action that ordinary desires do not . . . a predominant desire does not ensure either volitional or reasoning-centered commitment.'[35] We will see in what follows (especially in chapters 4 and 5) that strong arguments have been developed for taking the attitude of intention, in its different senses, into account in any theory of the way in which intentional attitudes combine to produce rational action. The basic unit of practical rationality, it may be argued, is not a particular link between an action, a belief, and a desire, but a link between beliefs, desires, intentions – the latter taken in several distinct senses – and action. To signal additional issues to the reader, it may be noted that some authors argue that emotions are yet another constellation of attitudes, irreducible to either belief or desire.[36]

In the foregoing remarks, I have only begun to introduce some of the issues involved in the question of the elements of atomic rationality. We may now begin to complexify our schematic presentation of the problems by drawing on the vast literature known as 'decision theory'. Very generally, decision theory tries to make accurate models of the ways in which wants and beliefs combine in the formation of rational decisions.[37] Many theories of decision work with two main types of factors: (1) the agent's wants or desires, determining the 'value' or 'utilities' of the possible outcomes of his or her decisions; and (2) the agent's information or beliefs about what the world is like and about how his or her possible actions are likely to influence the world. These beliefs, it is assumed, determine the probabilities of the possible outcomes of actions. Thus in the elementary situation constructed by these theories, the decider is situated within a 'decision matrix' having the following components: (1) the set of alternative actions from which the agent is to make a choice; (2) the set of possible states of the world that the agent associates with each possible course of action; (3) the 'utilities' or values that the agent associates with each of the outcomes. Thus, to construct the most minimal 'decision' situation, we would imagine a case where the agent believes there is only one possible course of action, a_1, and believes that this action can only have the result of producing a single state of affairs, s_1, the value or utility of which, for the agent, is u_{11}. Thus, if the agent really wants to realize the value associated with u_{11}, the agent 'has no choice', and performs action a_1. This rather impoverished 'decision matrix' would be written as follows:

	STATE
ACT	s_1
a_1	u_{11}

Before we move on to complexify this situation, note that even in this impoverished set-up, the agent's decision involves various beliefs, including a belief that a_1 is the only alternative, as well as a belief that if a_1 is performed, s_1 will occur. The agent also has a 'want' or 'preference', expressed in an evaluation of the state of affairs s_1.

A slightly more complicated basic decision situation involves a choice between two possible courses of action, having two different expected outcomes, the respective utilities of which must be determined by the agent:

	STATE
ACT	s_1
a_1	u_{11}
a_2	u_{21}

Thus if the agent chooses a_1, state of affairs s_1, having utility u_{11}, is the expected result. Now the agent has the problem of deciding which of the two possible outcomes is most valuable, which is certainly not a trivial problem in many cases, where the different attributes of the two states of affairs may not be commensurable in any obvious manner. Such situations are frequently evoked in literary texts, where the narrative disequilibria often arise from a protagonist's difficulty in reconciling disparate goals and values.

In the standard models of decision theory, particularly those having an essentially economic orientation, the problem of the commensurability of states of affairs is typically assumed to be solved, so that the wants and preferences of agents are plotted on a scale of 'expected utilities'. Thus the assumption is typically made that an agent's evaluation of the different outcomes figuring within a particular decision matrix can be accurately identified by a utility measure associated with these outcomes. According to the principle of maximizing subjective expected utility, which is the fundamental decision rule of Bayesian theory, the rational agent should choose the alternative with the maximal subjective expected utility (or if there is more than one such alternative satisfying the constraint, then the agent should choose any one of them).[38]

Let us now see what kinds of additional complexities are introduced into the models of decision making at the heart of the standard Bayesian theories. Quite generally, it is a matter of introducing an element of 'risk': the agent must choose between several different possible courses of action, and the agent no longer knows for certain what state of affairs will result from any given alternative. In a typical example, we imagine an agent who must choose between making two different bets. On the one hand, the agent may choose wager a_1, having two possible results, s_1 and s_2, with which are associated the outcomes or payoffs of \$0 and \$100 respectively. Wager a_2's two outcomes, s_1 and s_2, yield \$0 and \$100 respectively. This basic decision situation would then be represented as follows:

ACT	STATE	
	s_1	s_2
a_1	\$0	\$100
a_2	\$0	\$100

Thus if the agent chooses a_1, and if the possible state of affairs s_2 is what happens to be realized as a result, the utility (u_{12}) won by the agent is \$100. So far in this simple example, the agent has no reason to prefer either alternative, for in either case the agent has the same chances of winning \$100. Typically, in Bayesian models of decision, additional complexities arise from two sources. Quite obviously, the payoffs could differ. For example, if a lucky win on the first bet promised \$1000 instead of \$100, the first bet would be the rational preference. Yet even if the payoffs were the same, there is another possible basis for a rational preference. Suppose we change the situation by having the agent believe that the gamble represented by the first choice is more likely to result in a win than the second gamble. Suppose, for example, that the agent believes that the odds on the second bet are 50–50, while the odds on the first one are 80–20 in her favour. Given this change in the situation, a new calculation of the utilities that may be associated with the two possible choices is possible. According to the standard Bayesian theory, we now evaluate the options in terms of the agent's subjective estimation of the likelihood of the respective results, as well as in terms of the agent's preference for one kind of outcome as opposed to another. In the example at hand, the 'subjective expected utility' of the first bet is obviously higher than that of the second one (for a_1, $.2 \times \$0 + .8 \times \$100 = 80$; for a_2, $.5 \times \$0 + .5 \times \$100 = 50$), so the first bet is the rational choice, all other things being equal.[39]

The kind of decision matrix just evoked is a schematic example of what is referred to in the literature as a situation of decision making under 'risk', for the simple reason that the agent has no guarantee that the real outcome will be the most advantageous one (note that although choosing the first bet is most rational, the agent could still be unlucky and come up with $0, instead of a $100 prize). Decision making under risk is typically distinguished from decision making under 'uncertainty', where 'risk' refers to cases where the agent is able to make quantitative estimations of the probabilities of the states of affairs associated with a particular course of action. The agent is said to be in a situation of 'full' information. This does not mean, however, that the agent knows exactly what will happen; rather, it means that the agent has an exhaustive list of the relevant states that may result from a particular decision, as well as a mathematical probability for each one, so that the sum of these probability estimates is one. If the agent has no such information, the decision situation is said to be one of 'uncertainty', which means that the agent cannot assign probabilities to the different possible states, or cannot even formulate what he or she considers to be an exhaustive list of them.[40] Behind one door there is a lady, and behind the other, a tiger, but no calculation of the respective probabilities is possible.

In the schematic models of decision introduced so far, various beliefs held by the agent have an indispensable rôle. In many cases, it is useful further to complexify the model by taking into account the agent's beliefs about those beliefs. Thus, models of decision making may be further complexified by taking into account the agent's second-order beliefs about the first-order probability estimates that go into a standard decision matrix.[41] Let us alter our first example a bit to make this point tangible. Imagine the situation of an agent who must choose between placing a bet on one of two different sporting events. Suppose the two bets between which the agent must choose are of a very different nature. The first bet is one where the agent knows a great deal about the two teams that are about to compete, having followed their careers carefully and observed their previous matches with each other. If asked to assign a numerical probability to the forthcoming match between these two teams, our agent would have to say that the odds are about 50–50. The second wager is quite different. The agent knows little about the two teams and would have to give them 50–50 odds, this judgement being based on ignorance. Yet the agent has heard it said that the general wisdom is that the two teams in question are in fact quite unevenly matched. The agent has no reason to doubt this popular wisdom, but does not know which team is favoured, and thus would have to fall back on the 50–50 judgement in making any real decision on that bet. Such are the two bets. As before, the agent can choose between them, and if the agent wins on either one she gets $100, and if she loses, she pays nothing. Thus, the standard decision theory would tell us that the agent has no reason to prefer one bet to the other. Yet here we may wonder if other factors should not be considered. For example, does the agent consider that the two probability estimates are equally reliable and equally well-founded? What are the agent's beliefs about the reliability of the beliefs expressed in the first-order calculation? The expectation formed in relation to one of the possible choices is supported by no detailed information whatsoever about the events that will determine the payoff, and could, as far as the agent knows, be quite wrong. Perhaps one of the teams is much stronger than the other, and those in the know would never accept a bet on the match at 50–50 odds. On the other hand, there is a bet that is supported by quite a lot of information. Thus the agent could reckon that it is more rational to choose the first bet over the second.

Thus, the agent's beliefs about his or her own information about the situation may play a crucial role in a decision.[42] Similarly, rational choice may engage the agent in difficult estimations of what to do in cases where the information presently available is held to be less than optimal. Another example may be used to illustrate one dimension of this kind of problem. A consumer wishes to purchase an expensive commodity, but does not have complete information about the prices at which the same kind of item is sold in various places – although the consumer does have some reason to believe that the price could vary significantly from place to place. The consumer may satisfy the desire to buy this commodity by going to any one of a number of different merchants, and clearly an 'effective' means of satisfying this desire is to go to any merchant who carries the commodity and settle the matter right away.

Assuming that money is no object for the consumer in question, any such solution is an 'optimal' solution, for there has been no ranking of them. Yet what if the consumer desires not simply to buy the item, but to acquire it at the lowest possible price? Now there is an objective ranking of solutions, determined by the situation on the market, so, in principle there is an objective solution to the problem. If the consumer has complete information about all of the prices at which the item is sold, the choice of the most efficient means to the goal is again a problem having an objective and univocal solution. Yet what if the agent's information is incomplete, as is so often the case? Is it optimal to engage in a protracted and costly search to find out which merchant sells the item at the lowest price? What if there is a merchant in a remote city who sells it at a significant discount? Investigating this possibility might bring a large payoff, but again, it might not: the consumer might make a costly investment in order to obtain the information about the prices offered elsewhere, only to learn that the discount to be had at the end of this process does not even equal the cost of obtaining the information. Buying from any merchant instead of investing in a costly search for information would have been the most cost-efficient solution, yet the agent could not know this in advance. This kind of example underscores the basic fact that the information upon which decisions are based itself has a cost, and may be the object of additional decisions.

Decision theorists who are concerned primarily with the complexities of Bayesian models sometimes give the impression that uncertainty is only, or is primarily, a matter of being unable to assign exact probability estimates to the anticipated outcomes of actions. However, reference to the other elements figuring within even a schematic model of the basic decision situation shows that this is a one-sided perspective. The agent, we have just said, may not know what probabilities to assign to the elements in the set of possible states of affairs that may ensue from a given alternative. This is indeed a first potential source of uncertainty, but there are others. For example, the agent may not, when pondering the possible effects of a given action, have a clear sense of what all of the relevant consequences may be, in which case the agent's beliefs about these consequences do not constitute a closed or well-defined set at all. Similar considerations may hold in relation to the agent's beliefs about possible alternative actions: the agent faced with a decision to make may not be able to get a clear sense of all of the alternative courses of action, and it seems reasonable to assume that successful problem solving often hinges on the ability to discover and identify such alternatives. Still another source of uncertainty is involved when the agent cannot readily determine the relative values of different possible outcomes: the 'utilities' to be attached to particular outcomes are unclear, and it is not obvious in what terms their respective 'weights' are to be judged. Finally, an even more radical and global form of uncertainty should be considered, namely, one in which the agent doubts that his or her entire framework for thinking about possible outcomes will be valid in the future: the agent considers that the present expectations about possible outcomes fall within a paradigm that may itself prove to be invalid, yet it is impossible to predict the future knowledge that will be available in the new paradigm.[43]

So far the conceptions of rationality that have been evoked in my survey of the issues have all centred about the evaluation of individual actions and decisions, taken in isolation. Another budget of problems is encountered when we raise the question of the wisdom of what we have called the 'atomic' approach to the criteria of rationality. Does such an approach really promise to express our most robust intuitions about the rationality and irrationality of the ways in which preferences and beliefs conspire to produce decisions, effective intentions, and actions? Are the basic assumptions about rationality which make possible intentional explanations reducible to assumptions about connexions between discrete cognitive items and acts? Are these assumptions applied in complete isolation from any prior identification of the particular agent involved?

In regard to these issues, it may be useful to return for a moment to Cherniak's proposal for a minimal theory of rationality. His minimal rationality condition specifies that rationality is a matter of so many discrete or atomic calculations in which actions are generated out of a pool of beliefs and desires. These atomic productions are then subjected to a global, and purely quantitative evaluation: there must be some 'appropriate' derivations, and not too many 'inappropriate' ones. This may be a very dubious assumption to build into a model of agency, an obvious danger being that one of the subjectively appropriate actions undertaken by the agent may in fact be quite harmful to that agent's long-term interests, which suggests that rationality is not reducible to a global quantitative standard applied to a collection of isolated elements.[44]

As Bratman argues in his *Intention, Plans, and Practical Reason*, agents with limited capacities for calculation and deliberation, who need to co-ordinate their own and each other's actions, cannot afford to weigh and measure all possibilities at every discrete instant, dealing with each new situation or problem without carrying over any previous policies, long-term plans, or prior intentions. In other words, the bounded rationality of minimal agents cannot afford to be atomic. In Bratman's words, we are not 'frictionless deliberators' or 'time-slice agents', that is, 'agents who are always starting from scratch in their deliberations'. Instead, 'we settle in advance on prior, partial plans and tend to reconsider them only when faced with a problem'.[45] Yet Cherniak's proposal fails to offer any provision for exploring the ways in which the purposeful thinking and behaviour of human beings involve complex temporal relations as well as cases where intentions and actions are linked in hierarchized, means–ends schemata, extending across time in structures of planning. If actions and intentional attitudes are organized in this manner, their rationality should probably be evaluated in terms of these connexions most of the time, not in terms of some global evaluation following which there are either 'enough' or 'not enough' rational atomic actions.

Some of the very general questions that are raised here may be formulated as follows: what is the relation between the rationality of actions and the rationality of agents? Do long-term intentions and plans play a special rôle in both? How do these trans-temporal relations between particular instances of practical deliberation alter the criteria that may be used to assess the rationality of ensuing action? How is the rationality of a particular intention or action related to the long-term satisfaction of the agent's desires as a whole? How is the rationality of one belief related to that of a larger system of beliefs? Let us refer to this latter constellation of issues as the question of agent's rationality, which concerns the criteria of rationality to be used in the assessment of the attitudes and actions of a temporally extended agent. I shall be discussing these matters in relation to literary examples in chapters 3 to 5, where I illustrate some of the advantages of an agential perspective on rationality.

Finally, to evoke one last constellation of issues, it should be pointed out that everything that has been said so far concerns only concepts of rationality applied to the doings of individual agents. Surely we need also to raise the question of collective rationality, which asks under what conditions interpersonal relations, interactions, joint-actions, institutions, and the like may be deemed rational or irrational. I shall return to these matters below. In the next chapter I evoke some of the basic insights of game-theoretical analyses of strategic interdependency; in chapter 6 I focus on the relation between individual and collective rationality.

To sum up this schematic overview of the issues, I shall gather up the basic questions that have been isolated along the way. The question of agency, I have said, concerns the basic assumptions about human agency that must be made if concepts of rationality and irrationality are to be applicable to human behaviour at all, and asks whether these basic assumptions are warranted or can be coherently denied. I discuss this issue at some length in chapter 3. The question of the rationality principle asks whether any assumptions about rationality are necessary to intentional understanding and explanation. If a negative answer is adopted, one must then deal with the question of a-rational agency, which concerns the models of agency and intentional explanation that can be constructed in the absence of assumptions about rationality. I have argued in favour of a positive response to the question of the rationality principle. If that conclusion is adopted, we are led directly to the question of rationality assumptions, which concerns the specific nature of our assumptions and intuitions about rationality. The question of atomic pratical rationality is a restricted facet of the latter issue. It is a matter of asking under what conditions we may ascribe rationality or irrationality to an individual action, taken in isolation. Similarly, the question of the atomic rationality of belief asks under what conditions we may ascribe rationality or irrationality to the holding of a particular belief, while the question of atomic motivational rationality does the same in regard to desire. The question of the components of intentional explanation introduces additional complexities, among which is the problem of understanding the complex relations between beliefs, desires, and intentions. Moreover, the latter question takes us away from isolated actions to the relations between the various attitudes and actions of a particular agent, until we encounter the question of agent's rationality, which involves us in an investigation of the ways in which rational agents engage in long-term planning and extended deliberation, in an hierarchical organization of intentions and actions. Finally, there is the question of collective rationality, which involves the application of concepts of rationality and irrationality to interagential relations, interactions, and collective objects, such as institutions, conventions, customs, practices, and the like.[46]

Not all of the issues just surveyed will be discussed in detail in what follows, nor do I pretend that my ensuing analyses remain neutral in regard to them. I assume, first of all, a particular stance on the most general question of agency. I do not posit the framework of action and agency as a synthetic *a priori*, but allow that it is conceivable in principle that it could possibly be rejected, e.g. the day someone actually provides a workable alternative approach to understanding human behaviour without reference to agents' reasons. In my view, the chances for this sort of non-self-defeating alternative to the entire framework of agency are rather slim, and I thus think the burden of proof is on the shoulders of those who denigrate what they call 'folk psychology' in the name of such a possibility. On the question of the rationality principle, I assume that a positive response is warranted: assumptions about rationality are a necessary part of the framework of intentional psychology. I consider these assumptions to amount to a basic rationality heuristic having the status of a *privileged but fallible* approach to the understanding and explanation of human behavior. The heuristic involves a first, rather minimal assumption to the effect that people's mental attitudes and behaviour are connected in a non-random manner; working with the heuristic also involves the assumption that at least some of the time an agent's behaviour is explicable in terms of that agent's subjective reasons for engaging in that behaviour, where these reasons are not necessarily restricted to a single instant in time or to any one type or combination of attitudes. Beyond this I shall not go at the present moment; my additional claims about the nature and status of rationality assumptions and criteria will emerge in the course of the study.

A final comment should be made about the normative connotations carried by all concepts of rationality, even those that are most subjective and all-embracing. Although judgements of rationality are sometimes meant to be purely descriptive, they often carry normative weight, and the reader will observe in what follows that I am interested in the ways in which actions can be evaluated in terms of the agent's rationality and irrationality. Yet many modern thinkers hardly prize the ideal of rationality and even consider that it is bound up with values that are in fact anything but admirable. An example is the following passage, signed by two dozen professors of literature:

what passes for 'rationality' in a particular historical moment is likely to look irrational from the perspective of another . . . affirmations of shared attributes often mask oppression based on unexplored assumptions of hierarchical difference . . . many dreadful thoughts and brutal deeds have compelled the assent of people fully convinced of their own rationality and the irrationality of a cultural other. The view that 'science' and 'rationality' can comprehend 'complex factors in human development' without the messy intrusion of 'gender and ideology' is an Enlightenment dream, long since turned to nightmare.[47]

This passage raises the question of the relationship between values and norms associated with rationality, on the one hand, and a broad range of other values, on the other.[48] I shall return to this question below, but shall make one brief remark at the present moment: it should be clear from my previous arguments that many of the people who lash out at what they take to be a wholly pernicious Enlightenment ideology in fact rely upon, and should want to defend, certain basic assumptions about the rationality of all women and men. That they do rely upon them is implicit in the language of their attacks against hypocritical and reified concepts of rationality, for it is a language of action. That they should rely upon these assumptions about rationality is the case because many of the values that they wish to promote, and which they seem to think are diametrically opposed to all conceptions of rationality, in fact could never exist in the absence of certain basic forms of rational action. Rationality, it may be argued, is a necessary but not a sufficient condition to these other values, so that even if one believes in the absolute priority of certain norms of social justice – as opposed to the ideal of a 'rational society' – it may be that values associated with rationality are a necessary ingredient to their realization. It also follows that engaging in rationality assessments of the right sort can be an invaluable means of critique. In short – and to be as clear as possible – rationality is not assumed, in what follows, to be the only and highest value. Yet it does not follow from this point that strident condemnations of rationality, in both its epistemic and practical dimensions, are a good way to promote any other values, which is why it is important to try to engage in a careful and detailed examination of the complex issues that surround the question of the value of rationality. It is crucial to understand that theories of moderate rationality do not entail the absurd idea that rationality is an ethical and political panacea. They do suggest that moderate forms of rationality are a crucial element of people's ability to achieve some degree of co-ordination in their actions and interactions. A moderate form of rationality, then, may be a necessary element in intentional explanations; it is also likely to be an indispensable means to the creation and preservation of other values.

CHAPTER 2

Agency, rationality, and literary knowledge

Having surveyed a number of questions related to the notion of rationality, I turn now to the issue of their pertinence to literature, my primary goal being to identify a number of distinct avenues of literary-critical enquiry. Clarifying the basic orientations and assumptions of several different approaches to literary phenomena will make it possible to define the particular aims of the analyses presented in the rest of this study, as well as to identify topics for future research.[1]

The question of the relation between concepts of rationality and 'literature' is complicated by the vagueness of the latter term. Literary scholars have never been able to agree over the boundaries of their object domain, which remains extremely open-ended, embracing whatever items a variety of traditions happen to have preserved under the rubric of 'literature'. The term evokes any number of multi-faceted items as well as a broad range of phenomena that are in one way or another thought to be significantly related to them. As a result, the literary field is an ontological *auberge espagnole*, for it houses past and present agents, actions, and events, mental states and attitudes, types of physical artefacts, institutions and conventions, symbolic inscriptions and utterances – as well as the aesthetic qualities of any of the above. It is not uncommon for literary critics to debate over angels, demons, and vampires. Moreover, critics' approaches towards this vast and variegated object domain are not on the whole particularly disciplinary, for the open-ended collection of literary phenomena can be examined following any number of perspectives, notions, and interests.

Some literary scholars, it is true, have sought to give their field a more sharply circumscribed disciplinary basis, and although such tendencies are an important vein of literary pedagogy and research, their status is still a matter of much debate.[2] Essentially, the attempt to orient research towards the 'specificity of literature' has typically amounted to trying to discover and emphasize what may be loosely identified as the aesthetic qualities of literary works; by focusing on the latter, it is sometimes thought, we study literature as literature. Yet the many attempts to apply this basic approach remain highly problematic and have not converged on any single methodology or coherent disciplinary self-understanding. Briefly, many of the aesthetic notions depend on various assumptions (at once philosophical and ideological) that many scholars today feel inclined to reject. For example, many critics no longer feel confident that analyses based on the doctrine of aesthetic autonomy can embrace the full range of processes that have actually been at work in the writing and reading of literary works. What is more, the attempt to erect an aesthetic framework of literary analysis has a way, not of erecting disciplinary boundaries, but of leading, on the contrary, to additional interdisciplinary borrowings, which has the effect of making the question of the foundations of literary research depend on that of the foundations (and non-foundations) of other fields. For example, the concepts and assumptions of aesthetics are not purely literary; what is more, there is good reason to think that the aesthetic properties of literary works of art bear an essential relation to meaning; consequently, the critic or scholar who tries to analyse literature's aesthetic properties ends up taking at least an implicit stance on a number of topics – such as the nature of 'reference' – that the students of language tend to group beneath the rubrics 'semantics' and 'pragmatics'. It is unsurprising, then, that the attempt to probe the specifically aesthetic qualities of literary works of art has typically led critics to have recourse to various non-literary linguistic and/or rhetorical concepts.[3] It is accurate to say, then, following Richard Miller, that literary studies figure among the 'self-questioning' fields, that is, those lacking 'foundations' in the sense of reliable descriptions of a collection of relevant domain-specific causal processes.[4]

The diversity of criticism's approaches to the literary domain can be illustrated by referring to a sample of the kinds of statements that critics might make and defend in reference to what would appear to be an uncontroversial example of a literary item – the play *Mascarade*, by Ludvig Holberg:

(1) *Mascarade* is a typical comedy of intrigue influenced by the Italian *teatro delle maschere*.[5]

(2) In writing *Mascarade*, Holberg used half of a play by Joachim Richard Paulli as his basis.

(3) While writing *Mascarade*, Holberg intended to create a play that would express his idea that society should allow a 'reasonable freedom' (*en fornutftig Frihed*) to its members; this intention was linked to his desire to oppose the state's repressive policy of prohibiting masquerades and gambling.

(4) *Mascarade* is Holberg's unintended expression of his unconscious Oedipal ambivalence towards his father, represented in the figure of Heronimus; other figures represent facets of Holberg's psyche, including contrasting rebellious and obsequious sons.

(5) *Mascarade*'s representation of the carnivalesque dimensions of masquerades exemplifies Bakhtin's emphasis on the critical and revolutionary dimensions of popular festivities.

(6) *Mascarade* conveys Holberg's philosophical belief, also expressed in his Epistle 347, that masquerades and carnival rightfully express the natural equality of master and slave.

(7) *Mascarade* has had an important political and social function in the constitution of the national literary culture of Denmark.

(8) *Mascarade* manifests the essential instability of language, for in its incessant displacements, tropisms, and figural processes, it paradoxically subverts the Subject's claim to coherence and grounding.

(9) *Mascarade* is not particularly original: its style is clumsy and uninspired, and the plot clearly reflects Holberg's slavish imitation of Molière. Perhaps its greatest merit was to have served as the inspiration for Carl Nielsen's lovely opera of the same name.

(10) Early in 1724, Holberg composed the script for *Mascarade* at his home on the Kømagergade in Copenhagen. The play was first performed in late February, 1774, at the Lille Grønnegade Theatre, and was first published in 1731 in *Den danske Skue-Plads*.

(11) In its belated neo-classical form and thematics, *Mascarade* reflects an illusory bourgeois ideal of Enlightened freedom based on an adequation between reason and nature.

Although this list certainly does not represent all possible types of critical assertions, the kinds that it exemplifies do appear quite frequently in literary-critical publications. Thus the list quite faithfully illustrates the fact that the topics of critical enquiry are much more diverse than restrictive definitions of 'literariness' allow, for critics are interested not only in a literary work of art's aesthetic qualities, but in its psychic, social, and linguistic conditions and consequences. Given the complexity and heterogeneity of the object domain in question, this is as it should be: an insistence on purely aesthetic topics in the name of disciplinarity would amount to a mutilation of literary history, which is not reducible to the creation and experience of the aesthetic qualities of a corpus of literary artefacts, utterances, and performances. In this regard, it is at once appropriate and highly significant that the essays included in a recent literary history have been organized around a broad variety of events, actions, and artefacts, including the following: 'Four Years after Writing the Pléiade's Manifesto, Joachim du Bellay Goes to Rome and Repines', 'Rousseau Writes his *Essai sur l'origine des langues*', 'Prosper Mérimée Publishes *La Vénus d'Ille*', 'Louis-Napoleon Bonaparte, President of the Second Republic, Becomes Emperor Napoleon III of the Second Empire', and 'The 500th Program of "Apostrophes" is Broadcast on Antenne 2'.[6]

With these remarks in mind, we may now turn to the issue of the relevance of concepts of rationality and agency to the literary field. The present study defends a dual hypothesis: not only are the concepts and issues related to rationality and irrationality directly relevant, and indeed, essential, to enquiries concerning literature, but literature in turn has genuine cognitive value in relation to questions of human rationality and irrationality. The task of the present chapter is to defend the former claim; the latter claim is introduced at the end of this chapter and is defended at length in my subsequent chapters.

As I argued in my introduction, my belief that concepts of rationality are valuable tools for literary enquiry should not be understood as entailing the view that literary activities conform to some rigid and idealized standard of Rationality; even less does it entail the idea that literary activities should be *evaluated* in such terms. In my view it seems safe to assume that the canons of Bayesian decision theory are not applicable to the kinds of choices, preferences, and actions that may be associated with literature: the theory's classic assumptions are already problematic in relation to the actual preferences agents have in regard to a quantified commodity such as money, and this within particular kinds of economic contexts, and thus it is unlikely that this theory could be expected to tell us anything about agents' attitudes towards the relative merits and significance of features of poems and plays. Yet the SEU model hardly exhausts the concepts and issues that may be associated with rationality. My contention is that even if one's working hypothesis were that 'literature' is intimately linked to unreason in all of its forms – madness, perversion, weakness of the will, wanton desire, self-defeating behaviour, the primary processes, self-deception, ambiguity, semantic confusion, and so on – it would remain the case that concepts and models of rationality would be invaluable tools for analyzing and explaining these types of irrationality. My basic claim is that non-agential and a-rational approaches to literature could never be satisfactory because actions and practical reasoning are central to many of the most important types of literary phenomena. This point is established by adducing uncontroversial examples of ways in which a moderate rationality heuristic is directly pertinent to the writing and reading of literary works.[7] Yet I also explore an even stronger claim, which is that there are *no* literary phenomena that can be adequately understood or explained without relying, at least implicitly, on a rationality heuristic. Although I consider this stronger claim to be correct and think that some of the arguments I give for it should be persuasive, my more general point about the pertinence of concepts of rationality in literary enquiry does not hinge on the correctness of the stronger thesis: it is sufficient that I establish that a large number of non-trivial claims about literature rest upon concepts of rationality. My examples and arguments indeed establish this point, which can only be questioned by making some rather extreme sceptical contentions about the entire framework of agency and rationality. No one has to date successfully presented a genuinely a-rational alternative to the assumptions I am defending, and although it is possible that someone may some day do so, there is no reason to be persuaded by the contemporary a-rationalists' programmatic proclamations. At the end of the chapter, I discuss some different ways in which theoretically oriented readings of literature can contribute to the elaboration of models of rationality, thereby identifying the nature and goals of the analyses that follow in part two of the present study.

A first point that needs to be made in support of my general claim about the relevance of concepts of rationality to literary enquiry is that a large number of the items falling under the fuzzy rubric of 'literature' are obviously instances of human action. Deciding to write a poem, uttering it before an audience, and arranging to have it published are some typical examples. Acquiring a copy of a book, attending to the words printed in it, and trying to understand and evaluate the claims that are made there – as my benevolent reader is presently doing – are others. It may be safe to assume that concepts of agency (and by extension, moderate rationality) are directly related to all such instances of literary action (writing, reading, performing, etc.) – unless, of course, one has more fundamental and general reservations about all categories of agency and rationality. When a critic argues that the author Holberg included certain features in his play *in order to* express certain ideas about freedom and *in order to* oppose a certain political policy, this is clearly a matter of an application of the kind of schemata of practical reasoning that I evoked in chapter 1. Many critical arguments in fact take this form and thus rely on assumptions about rationality. Some do so explicitly: my sample statements (2), (3), (4), (6), (9), and (10) are of this sort, for all of them refer directly to relations between the play and its maker, who is viewed as an intentional agent having beliefs, desires, and other attitudes. Holberg uses, writes, intends, conveys, imitates, etc., and aspects of the play are explained by referring to these actions. Here we see the basic schema of the rationality heuristic at work. Other critical statements implicitly rely on claims about the purposive activity and practical reasoning of agents: statement (1), with its claim about influence, could be of this sort, as could (7), which implicitly refers to the actions of individuals who have contributed in the relevant manner to the politics of Danish literary culture.

In the introduction to the present study, I evoked an aspect of the relation between concepts of rationality and literature by discussing a passage from *Egil's Saga*. The basic idea was that understanding narrative discourses invariably requires readers to apply background beliefs concerning not only intentional attitudes, but subjective schemata of practical reasoning: given the narrative description of an action, the reader understands it by linking it to background information about the depicted agent's possible beliefs, desires, and intentions, thereby applying a basic rationality heuristic. In order to understand discourses that depict the actions of agents, readers need to rely on moderate assumptions about the depicted agents' rationality. This does not mean that readers always find rational intentional reasons for what depicted characters do; even less does my statement imply that readers always explicitly describe and evaluate characters by using the particular vocabulary of rationality.[8] Sometimes applications of the rationality heuristic yield the conclusion that described actions are nonsensical; or again, the reader may feel that an action must make sense, but that he or she simply has not grasped it. The basic idea is not that readers apply the *theme* of rationality to the stories they read, but that their comprehension of characters and actions as such requires reliance on the rationality heuristic's various intentional notions. This means, for example, that given textual information about a character's desires and beliefs, readers form expectations about what the character is likely to do as the story unfolds; given descriptions of actions, readers make sense of them – in diverse and sometimes conflicting ways – by filling in intentions and motives, based on general background beliefs as well as on information already encountered in the text.

Descriptive enquiries into the processes of reading explore the complex ways in which the reader's background beliefs and attitudes interact with the features of the textual 'input'. My claim is that concepts of rational agency are directly pertinent to such descriptive models of reader's competence, and could help to identify some of the most salient features of narrative dynamics. For example, a question that has been debated at great length in the literature on discourse comprehension concerns the notions that allow readers to distinguish between discourses that tell a story and those that do not. Although many divergent answers to that question have been proposed, there is evidence suggesting that readers' judgements about the coherence of narrative discourses are correlated to their identification of textual elements' consistent co-reference to an agent or agents engaged in purposeful endeavour.[9] Narrative discourse is, then, a subset of all discourse depicting the action of agents. Stories are discourses in which the reader follows an agent or agents as they strive to achieve some goal, usually encountering some unusual – or otherwise pertinent – form of difficulty. As a minimal definition of narrative discourse, then, I would suggest that a narrative discourse is a discourse about action in which at least one agent has a goal and difficulty in realizing it, and in which attitudes about the story are expressed by at least one implicit teller (who may or may not be the same agent). It is clear that the agent or agents in question do not have to be presented literally as human beings; nor do they have to satisfy any of the more stringent philosophical criteria concerning personal identity. Discourses about such entities as balloons, cockroaches, and planet-sized agglomerations of self-organizing computers can be recognized as stories if goals and strivings are attributed to them.[10]

Sometimes readers' applications of the rationality heuristic to textual input may lead to explicit evaluations of the rationality or irrationality of the narrated actions and attitudes – and of the author who is thought to have conceived of them. In such special cases, a basic rationality heuristic (the assumption that behaviour is generated and explained by the agent's reasons) helps to make understanding possible, while the theme of rationality comes to the fore.[11] For example, judgements of the irrationality of the creatures depicted by Franz Kafka or Samuel Beckett often arise against a background of notions about rational belief and action. The hopeless strivings of the denizens of Beckett's worlds – for instance, the hapless prisoners in *Le Dépeupleur* (1970) – only make sense to us because we understand what instances of successful striving are like. We know what it means in some cases to find what we were looking for, or to escape from some unpleasant situation or place. The cylindrical abode that Beckett imagines is a place where successes of this sort are impossible, but none the less meaningful.

Another example is Beckett's comic description, in *Murphy* (1938) of a modern Irishman's attempt to organize his life following the wisdom of an astrological pundit. Although the pundit's prognostications are absurd, the erudite Murphy none the less seems to take them quite seriously, futilely trying to follow such directives as the following:

Mercury sesquiquadrate with the Anarete is most malefic and will greatly conduce to Success terminating in the height of Glory, which may injure Native's prospects. The Square of Moon and Solar Orb afflicts the Hyleg. Herschel in Aquarius stops the Water and he should guard against this. Neptune and Venus in the Bull denotes dealings with the Females only medium developed or of low organic quality. Companions or matrimonial Mate are recommended to be born under a fiery triplicity, when the Bowman should permit of a small family. (p. 33)

Readers are likely to find Murphy's reliance on Suk's script quite comic, and such a perception involves comparing Murphy's strategy to the reader's own sense of rational planning. In Beckett's caricature, the pundit's discourse is an awkward, contradictory, and totally implausible mixture of wild predictions and useless advice. Making important decisions in function of such dicta therefore constitutes a fundamental violation of a rather basic norm of practical rationality, for the agent has no reason whatsoever to think that his chances of realizing any of his goals are enhanced in this manner; indeed, he cannot even consistently believe it possible to follow this incoherent and rather opaque advice: how does one guard against Herschel (Uranus) in Aquarius stopping the Water? How can success terminating in the height of glory injure one's prospects?

Some readers may understand Beckett's passage as ridiculing a traditional practice, held up as 'absurd' or 'irrational'. Yet it is important to see that the *topos* of rationality does not entail any such particular reading.[12] Instead, the comic effect could in some cases arise from a reader's awareness of the difference between Murphy's relation to Suk and cases of astrological divination in genuinely traditional contexts. It is quite coherent to believe that it is rational for someone raised in a traditional Hindu society to consult a pundit and act on his directives, for only the most objectivist (and unrealistic) definitions of rationality yield the contrary judgement. Why? The individual in the traditional context knows that he lacks knowledge of the forces that will determine many important aspects of his personal history or destiny; he has been told that there are individuals who possess this kind of knowledge, and having no compelling reason to put these widespread beliefs in doubt, seeks and follows the advice of a pundit. In a truly traditional context, such an action may not stand in contradiction in any obvious way to any of the agent's other beliefs and actions; not to follow the custom could, on the other hand, be known to bring about unpleasant social consequences. Thus the action matches the agent's most reflective beliefs about ways and means, and promises to realize some of the agent's desires. Yet the conditions just outlined clearly do not hold in the case of Murphy, which is one reason why it is ridiculous for him to attempt to find the referents for Suk's outlandish terms in the streets of London.

As Henri Bergson and other theorists have suggested, many comic effects may be generated by perceived contrasts between norms of agency and those events and actions that transgress them. An example among thousands is the moment in Paul Scarron's *Le*

Roman comique (first published in 1651) when the members of a theatre audience are made to knock each other down like a row of skittles. The text reads:

He wanted to back up but fell over backwards onto a man behind him, knocking him, along with his chair, over onto the unfortunate Ragotin, who was knocked over onto another man, who was knocked over onto another one, who was also knocked over onto another one, and so on until the end of the chairs was reached, so that a whole line had been knocked down like skittles.[13]

Such comic antics are quite obviously contrasted in the reader's mind to instances where human volition wins a degree of control and success. Scarron's phrase underscores this, for it begins with reference to an agent's desire ('He wanted to back up') but ends by reducing the action to a chain reaction along a row of contiguous objects.

These examples are meant only to illustrate the pertinence of the line of enquiry in question, not to exhaust it. As a final instance of a narrative where the reader's background assumptions about rational agency are at once called into play, foregrounded, and partially challenged, we may refer to Stanislaw Lem's novel *Katar* (1976; published in English translation as *The Chain of Chance* in 1978). The text is structured like a typical detective story in which an investigator rationally seeks to discover the cause of a strange series of deaths. Various hypotheses are generated and tested, all of them involving the possible motives of the victims and suspected culprits. When the investigator happens to reproduce the rather unusual circumstances that were common to all of the deaths, he in turn experiences the suicidal frenzy that led the others to their deaths, but in a moment of foresight, he has chained himself to a radiator and cannot do himself any harm.[14] The cause of the suicidal states of mind turns out to have been a totally mindless and unintended by-product of a number of circumstances, culminating in an unusual chemical reaction in the brain caused by the conjunction of a particular antihistamine, after-shave lotion, and various other substances. In short, the answer to the riddle is neither rational nor irrational, but a-rational. Thus this unusual dénouement of a detective plot seems to overturn belief in the priority and autonomy of meaningful agency, diverting attention away from the usual motives (greed, jealousy, revenge, etc.) to a neurophysio-

logical process. Yet the story none the less draws its interest from
its focus, not on purely impersonal forces, chance, and causal conditions, but on the conflict between such forces and the actions and
attitudes of the protagonist. The investigator's experience, recounted in the first person, remains in the foreground, even as that
experience is shown to depend in crucial ways on sub-intentional
conditions and processes.

My goal in the present context is not to pursue this kind of
descriptive enquiry into the rôle of norms and heuristics of rationality in processes of reading – although such investigations are an
important avenue of literary research. Explanations of the conditions under which literary works are created need to be supplemented by investigations of the conditions under which they are
experienced and used, and an open-ended model of readerly competence (that is, one that is not guided by aesthetical norms of
'expert' reading) is a necessary means to that end. I think that I
have established my point that readers and critics in fact often rely
on a rationality heuristic and at times even think explicitly in terms
of a thematics of rationality and irrationality. A thematic approach,
however, is not enough, and in a moment, I show how the notion of
rationality can be applied in an analysis of a writer's strategic
relation to the public, a relation mediated by a particular pragmatic stance in regard to the concept of fiction. First, however, I
turn to the stronger claim that I mentioned above, namely, the idea
that *all* adequate enquiries concerning literary phenomena implicitly rely on a rationality heuristic.

This stronger claim may seem implausible to readers who are
inclined to believe that an important aspect of literary studies
involves the analysis and appreciation of the intrinsic literary
properties of texts, properties which, once created, do not depend
on any agents' actions. Sample statements (8) and (11) above could
reasonably be said to be of this sort, for they describe aspects of a
play without linking them to the doings of any human agents.
What, then, of critical statements about completed literary artefacts as opposed to actions? Is there any reason to think that they
also require reference to concepts of agency and rationality? A
fundamental issue in this regard concerns our ability to individuate
and identify literary works of art and their features without
reference to the purposive actions and/or identities of their
maker(s). For some, it goes without saying that the literary work

can be identified with a *type* of textual inscription. That works cannot be identified with any *particular* inscription – and not even with the original one written by the author's own hand – is shown by the fact that we invariably consider that we have access to a literary work of art whenever we possess at least one faithful transcription of the relevant semiotic features of the author's first inscription. Any token inscription of this type is generally deemed to make the literary work of art available to us. One hypothesis is that it follows from this fact that the intrinsic properties of works may be associated directly with individual types of inscriptions, and that we need not refer to any agent's actions in order to describe the semantic and aesthetic properties of works individuated in this manner. Yet this assumption about the identity of literary works of art is not, in fact, as unassailable as it may appear. There are good arguments for holding, on the contrary, that no semantic function, not even a partial function, maps all types of inscriptions on to works. Some types of textual inscriptions are not thought to constitute works at all, and some types of inscriptions may be correlated with more than one literary work. Nor can there be even a partial function that maps works on to types of inscriptions: some works may be correlated with more than one type of inscription (e.g. cases where there are different versions of the same work).[15] In other words, if we had a procedure that could compare particular textual inscriptions and unfailingly determine whether they were tokens of the same type, this procedure could not by the same stroke identify individual literary works of art. Types of information to which the procedure would be oblivious would need to be taken into account to perform the latter task. In actual critical practice, correspondences between works and types of inscriptions are established by pragmatic factors, and hence can only be described by making reference to the relevant actions and attitudes of agents who make and use the textual artefacts in question. For example, when a critic deems two significantly different types of textual inscriptions to be versions of the same work, this judgement is typically motivated by information about the writer's attitude towards the two symbolic artefacts, both of which are said to be the result of the artist's intentional effort to create a single work. When the spelling of a text has been corrected and modified, the revised version is often considered to constitute the 'same' work of art because it is assumed that all of 'the relevant' or 'aesthetically significant' features have been retained, and often this kind of decision is supported by the assumption that the artist would not have objected to such alterations. Perhaps more importantly, critical judgements about the very nature of the aesthetic qualities of a type of textual inscription are often inflected by information about the context in which the author initially created the work: if we know that a work having a certain archaic style and spelling was in fact penned in the twentieth century, our understanding of the significance of these properties is different from what it would have been had we believed, on the contrary, that we were reading a faithful transcription of a sixteenth-century manuscript. It could very well be that certain aesthetic properties of texts, such as newness and originality, cannot be described without reference to various contextual factors. The reference to the agent who created the document can make a very significant difference even in cases where it does not involve any detailed, accurate information about that agent's life and attitudes. Gregory Currie's argument along these lines is that the identification of works of art involves what he calls the 'heuristic path' that led to the creation of an aesthetic 'structure' (in the case of literature, a sequence of word types, or what I have referred to above as a type of textual inscription). In Currie's proposal, artworks are individuated in terms of action types involving a relation between the following items: a structure, the heuristic by means of which it is discovered, the agent(s) doing the discovering, and the time(s) or interval(s) of the discovery. According to Currie, the latter two items are variables, for the individuation of works requires only that the other elements remain constant. Reference to the action of discovering a structure by means of an heuristic, then, is held to be the essential manner of identifying works.[16]

More generally, it may be argued that complex background beliefs about agency must be in place for us to recognize anything as a text or work at all. Although we may recognize a curve in a river or a highway as an 's', we do not literally judge them to be texts; it is metaphorical – or theological – to speak of the 'prose of the world'. We should only call something a text if we believe that some sentient agent produced it, and we usually assume that this agent was acting on a certain sort of expressive, strategic, and/or communicative intention (except, perhaps, in instances of genuinely compulsive and unintentional scribbling).[17] Consider the case of a textual artefact that results from a surrealist exercise in 'automatic writing'.[18] We are right to think that such texts are not fully determined by the author's conscious intentions, but we none the less must assume that there was an agent acting on the intention to write (that the intention was to write in an uncontrolled and spontaneous manner does not alter this more basic fact). Moreover, the more general aims of the surrealists in acting on such intentions are not a total mystery to us, for the surrealist ascribes to a number of general beliefs, desires, and goals, presented in a series of manifestos. We know as well that the surrealist's decision to engage in automatic writing is followed by a second one: when the surrealist writing experiment is over, the writer must decide whether to publish the results (and in most cases, the surrealists decided to destroy their automatic writings). The example of the *cadavre exquis*, a text produced when different agents add lines to it without having seen those already written, merely shows that a particular kind of 'we-intention' can motivate the production of a textual artefact.[19]

It is safe to assume that all artefacts, including symbolic ones such as inscriptions, are produced by the efforts of an agent or agents. In other words, no artefacts are literally 'self-organizing', which implies that realistic causal explanations of the production of artefacts require true (or approximately true) descriptions of the pertinent doings of the agent or agents involved in making them. Now, although not all artefacts are texts (inscriptions or types of inscriptions), all texts are artefacts, and we may assume that they only come into existence as a result of some agent's behaviour. Agency, then, is a necessary ingredient in any explanation that describes the conditions of the production of a literary text, for such conditions always include as a proximate cause the behaviour of the writer(s) or speaker(s) responsible for the text or discourse. Thus statements that make claims about how the play *Mascarade* came into being make reference to Holberg, and to his conscious and unconscious aims and methods. In this broad class of literary explanations, the writer's beliefs, desires, and intentions are central – unless, of course, we can somehow reduce or eliminate any and all reference to intentionality in an explanation of the agent's behaviour.

The relationship between assumptions about agency and critical explorations of a literary artefact's intrinsic properties appears to be even more intimate when we reflect upon the kinds of causal powers that may reasonably be associated with symbolic artefacts. To make this point, we may develop a distinction between two types of intrinsic properties that an artefact can have: properties with significant autonomous causal powers, and properties having no such powers. It should be uncontroversial to note that as a result of its maker's activity, an artefact can have certain determinate physical properties. Once the artefact has been made, these properties are intrinsic and no longer depend on anyone having any particular attitudes towards the object. Once it has been made, the steel head of a hammer is, under normal temperatures on the surface of this planet, a solid (instead of a liquid or gas), and has a certain mass and density; that the object has these intrinsic properties is not the case because I or anyone else likes it that way: should everyone on earth suddenly conceive of a burning preference for liquid hammers, the objects that have already been fashioned after the old-fashioned taste in hammers would not suddenly become any softer as a result. Now, some artefacts, once they have been created by an agent, have causal powers of their own. Thus they can figure as proximate causes in the explanation of some subsequent event. One need only think of an engine which, once it has been constructed and set in operation, is able to continue producing various effects for some time, including effects that were never intended by the machine's creator. An explanation of the proximate causes of the latter effects need not refer to the agent who fabricated the machine. One can identify the effects and explain their presence by pointing to the machine and to its causal impact on the world, and it is only if we want an explanation for why the machine is there that we have to make reference to its maker.

Once these very trivial background observations are in place, it becomes possible to raise a question that has some implications for literary enquiry: what kinds of autonomous causal powers can symbolic artefacts (texts, types of inscriptions, literary works of art, etc.) have? In response to that question, the crucial observation to make is that the semantic and aesthetic properties of a symbolic artefact have no significant autonomous causal powers. Under certain conditions, a book (the physical object) could have some causal effect on the family pet, but *Hamlet* could never do so. Whatever effectiveness the work's semantic and aesthetic properties may have requires the contribution of rather complicated human cognitive and affective processes. A text cannot literally have an intentional attitude because the conditions that would make any such thing possible simply are not satisfied (to put this point bluntly, configurations of signifiers are incapable of thought, emotion, desire, and so on).[20] Instead, if a text seems to have intentional properties, they are in fact 'on loan' to it from some genuine intentional system or agent. It follows that genuine explanations of a work's semantic and aesthetic effects require descriptions of the pertinent doings of the agents in question. Explanations of a text's effects and consequences must be relational, for their goal is to say why a particular agent (or class of agents) attended to a particular text, to particular features of the text, and why they were affected by the latter in a particular way. The effect of the text is not inscribed within it and does not lie there waiting to be deciphered; nor does it have the causal power necessary for it to be able to 'force itself' on anyone. In short, if I want to know why a certain kind of novel has a certain kind of effect on people whose relation to literature resembles that of Madame Bovary, I need a psychological theory, not just a theory of texts.

There are implications here for the evaluation of literary works. When we say that an artefact, such as a hammer, has a goal, what we usually mean is that it has been fashioned by someone with this goal in mind: 'its' goal is its maker's goal. The fact that the object has certain intrinsic properties does not warrant us to conclude that the object literally 'has' a goal, even when the properties in question make the object particularly well-suited for a particular use. By virtue of its other properties, the object may be useful in a number of ways and it may not even be especially well-suited to the realization of the end that the maker had in view. Genuine questions about the rationality of an artefact may be raised, then, but not in regard to the object taken in perfect isolation from the agents who make and use it. Rather, the necessary starting point of such an evaluation is the fact that some agent has a particular goal and considers using the object in some way to achieve that end. Evaluations of this sort may be quite rigorous in so far as the objective features of objects either facilitate or prevent them from serving as a means to a particular end. It is sometimes the case that particular objects or types of objects are, by virtue of their objective qualities and in particular kinds of situations, intrinsically well-suited or ill-suited to the realization of the end in question.

Texts are artefacts, and as such, may be evaluated along similar lines. No text literally has a goal in and of itself: an entity must have intentional attitudes if it is to have a goal in any strict sense of the term. Thus questions about the effectiveness and rationality of a symbolic artefact – for example, a text or work of literary art – should be reframed as questions about the means–end schemata in which that object may actually figure for at least one genuinely intentional agent. Thus, if it should be determined that Theodore Dreiser had the aim, in writing *The Financier*, of publicly expressing his own naturalistic philosophy in narrative form (while at the same time he expressed these views in popular essays and by other means – which he in fact did), then the rationality 'of the text' (or more accurately, of Dreiser's action in writing and publishing it) could be measured in these terms. Although it is true that some readers have taken Dreiser's text to be a univocal expression of such a doctrine, others have not, for they find textual evidence that runs contrary to that end – in which case one may conclude that the novel was not a particularly successful means to the hypothetical end. If, on the other hand, one attributed different goals to Dreiser, and by extension, to the text, then the judgement of its supposed efficacity could be altered.

As was suggested above, it is sometimes highly rational to employ a particular tool in a way that was neither intended nor foreseen by its maker. Similarly, the evaluation of the rationality of a symbolic artefact need not be centred on the author's putative goals in making the artefact. Thus, one may meaningfully and usefully ask whether a particular reader is making a rational or irrational use of a particular symbolic artefact, without basing oneself on the author's putative purpose in creating the text. For example, if one's goal is to lash out at American forms of rank bourgeois ideology and thereby make an effective intervention in today's cultural sphere, one may ask whether discussing the ideologemes in *Sister Carrie* is reasonably thought to be the best, or even a slightly effective, means to that end. If it is not, then it is probably irrational to use the novel in that manner, but this judgement has nothing to do with any claims about the violation of Dreiser's intentions or the 'intrinsic powers' of his writings. Similarly, if what I want from a play is a high degree of innovativeness in relation to anterior plays, then it probably does follow that Holberg's *Mascarade* is not the one I am after, even though it may have served the author's purposes quite well.

Although literature is not a sharply defined concept, it seems reasonable to assume that at the heart of literary history are those activities that may be associated with the creation and use of a number of symbolic artefacts. Typically, literary enquiry embraces various attempts to explain, understand, and evaluate those activities and artefacts. My contention here is that if such efforts are to succeed, reference must be made to agents and to their intentional attitudes – and hence to such items as desires, actions, and beliefs, and to the different kinds of rational and irrational relations between them. This claim is not a matter of imposing a highly restrictive, normative model on the diversity of literary-critical enquiry, for my conviction is that a number of significantly different, complementary avenues of enquiry satisfy that broad condition. For example, literary-historical explanations can concern both the writing and reading of texts, and the conditions of the former do not magically govern the conditions of the latter. Analyses of the processes by means of which readers make sense (and nonsense) of texts today emphasize the reader's pragmatic and purposeful orientation towards the textual input, as well as the reader's application of extensive background beliefs and knowledge to this textual input. Critics should explore the possibility that the various actions that readers may perform in relation to a text are explicable in terms of beliefs, desires, and intentions, only some of which have the author's putative intentions as their object. Moreover, to suggest that the framework of intentional explanation should be taken as being basic to literary enquiry is not to argue that criticism should return to its former crippling reliance on a great man theory of history, with its idealization of the powers of singular masculine individuals. Instead, the goal should be to examine the psychological processes at work in the formation and transformation of literary artefacts and institutions. My point here is not the absurd one that for every property of a text, there must have been a corresponding instance of authorial intention. Nor am I arguing that the literary scholar's only task is to describe these hypothetical correspondences. A distinction between the intended results and unintended consequences of an action is basic to the framework of action theory, and focusing on the ways in which intentions generate actions does not entail an inability to recognize the many unintended consequences that actions have.[21] In recent work in action theory, emphasis has been placed precisely on the

ways in which agents intentionally produce certain consequences
without having acted with the specific intention of doing so; for
example, some unintended consequences are the expected by-product of an action aimed at a rather different goal.[22] My emphasis on
the rôle of concepts of agency and rationality is anything but an
instance of the 'intentional fallacy'. It is one thing to say that I
cannot individuate a literary work of art without reference to
aspects of the history of its production, but it does not follow from
this claim that I am committed to the erroneous view that the only
meaning a textual inscription has is the meaning the author consciously intended to convey.

In short, my point is not that authors, readers, texts, and works
should be thought of in relation to some substantive and highly
normative standard of rationality; rather, the point is that if we are
to produce genuine explanations of some (if not all) literary
phenomena, we must attend to the multiple forms that the practical
reason and unreason of agents may take. In the rest of this chapter
I shall go on to identify some of the different ways in which concepts of agency, rationality, and irrationality may be employed in
literary explanations, one of my goals being to isolate the specific
nature of the avenue to be explored in my subsequent chapters.

Although theories of rationality focus quite generally on agents'
practical reasoning in relation to any and all contexts, of special
interest are those cases where the consequences of the actions of
two or more agents depend on what the other agents do. In such
situations, rational actions are guided by reciprocal expectations of
the others' actions. Such situations are called 'strategic' ones, and
the body of research known as 'game theory' takes such situations
as its object. Strategic 'games' or situations, then, are distinguished
from those where the outcomes enjoyed by an agent are determined
primarily by skill or by chance. While many of the highly sophisti-
cated mathematical developments of game theory are not in any
direct way applicable to the domains typically associated with
literary history, some of the basic intuitions and distinctions most
certainly are.[23]

Game theorists describe a spectrum of situations in which the
interests and aims of the players involved coincide or diverge to
different degrees. At one extreme, then, are so-called 'co-ordination
problems' where the players' interests coincide perfectly and there

are several possible 'solutions' equally satisfactory to all players; at the other extreme are situations of pure conflict, where no interests are shared; and in between are the many mixed cases, such as bargaining and negotiation, where the players share some goals but compete over other interests. It should be clear that such distinctions are wholly pertinent to the various intersubjective relations that figure in literary activities. Some thinkers find it tempting to assume that literary situations are essentially examples of communicative interaction, where authors and readers share the common goal of arriving at mutual understanding. When this process breaks down, the critic-as-elucidator kindly offers to help the poets and 'common readers' come to an understanding, and as the happy hermeneuticists would have it, reciprocal comprehension is always possible. Other theorists are tempted by the opposite conclusion, which is that writers and readers share no goals, interests, or background beliefs. In that case, critics, like the other players in the game, are simply in it for themselves, and one can never know whether one has peeled beneath the layers of cunning and miscomprehension. A more interesting hypothesis is that the majority of literary situations belong somewhere between these two extremes, for even when conflict, competition, and misprision come to the fore, the players in the game often must share certain interests and expectations in order to be able to compete successfully.[24] The insight to be retained here is not in any case a general thesis about the nature of all literary interactions, but a methodological point, namely, that a pragmatic analysis of literature should attend to the specific manner in which agents' diverse goals do and do not coincide in particular situations. A hypothesis to be explored suggests that sometimes successfully achieving shared goals is a necessary means to the end of competing over other goals.

Another, related methodological insight can be derived from the basic intuitions of a game-theoretical perspective on strategic rationality. Strategic situations, I have said, are those characterized by an interdependence of decisions and outcomes. The game of chess is an example, for the moves made by both players combine to determine the course of the game. To play chess well is to think about the moves that the other party might make, which also means that one should assume that the adversary is engaged in similar thinking about one's own strategy. Although it is possible to play chess without thinking much about what the opponent is going to do next, people who play this way are quickly defeated by anyone who is even slightly competent. When I observe that someone plays well, I had better assume that this person's moves are chosen in function of anticipated responses. It follows that any adequate analysis of a game of this sort involves claims about the extent to which the parties involved form accurate expectations about the reasoning of the other party. An important part of such an analysis concerns the degree to which the players possess complete and accurate information about various aspects of the game. Along these lines, game theorists assume that players may have limited or extensive knowledge of the following sorts of factors: (1) the actual consequences that will result from any particular combination of decisions acted upon by the various agents involved in the situation; (2) the ways in which the other agents rank different possible consequences in terms of their relative preferences for them; (3) the other agents' attitudes towards risk and uncertainty; (4) the amount of reliable information other players have about any of the factors just listed. Game theorists refer to these factors in discussing the extent to which players have 'complete' information, but they also draw a distinction between perfect and imperfect information: situations where there is 'perfect information' are those where all players know the nature of the game as well as all of the moves that have previously been made within it. What is more, there are various possible assumptions that theorists may make about the nature of the players' rationality, for it is not always the case that we should expect players to make all and only optimal decisions given the information they possess. In mathematical models of game theory, concern for this issue motivates a distinction between pure and mixed strategies, the latter involving a random element. In an informal context, this same issue could be dealt with by weakening our assumptions about the rationality of the agents' deliberations and actions. These assumptions have to do with the accuracy, coherence, and completeness of the players' background beliefs and information about the situation; they concern the players' ability to draw the right inferences about which move is most optimal given their preferences and information; they also have to do with the ordering of the players' preferences. There is room here for many variations, a fact that is simply not taken into account by anyone who thinks that game theory is an overly 'rationalistic' construction having no relevance to the domain of literature. In fact, game theorists do not contend that we should always assume that players adopt optimal strategies based on perfect knowledge of the situation. In some models, a single 'player' is comprised of a number of 'agents' that are not even aware of each other's moves and strategic rationales.[25] Interpreted psychologically, such a model would amount to describing a single individual whose multiple personalities take turns deciding, each of them being totally oblivious to the existence of the other personalities that govern the player's behaviour. It should be clear that game theory contains no requirement that the players should be assumed to function as perfect philosophical subjects.

The kinds of interdependencies of deliberation, knowledge, and action that I have just evoked are directly pertinent to many literary situations. For example, it is clear that while writing, authors often make decisions in function of certain expectations about readers' future beliefs and preferences. Moreover, some of these authorial expectations may concern the readers' future expectations about what the author is most likely to have believed and intended. And indeed, many readers make decisions about the meaning of a text by thinking, at least in part, in terms of what the author may be expected to have meant, and some of these meanings are taken to have been intentionally communicated to the reader, who understands that he or she is supposed to understand them as such. Thus, genuinely reciprocal expectations – the very heart of strategic rationality – sometimes guide literary activities and shape the artefacts that mediate between the parties involved in them. In many other instances, unilateral expectations about another party's reactions play a crucial rôle.

In the rest of this section, I briefly present an example of an analysis of the strategic rationality of a literary author. I focus on the writer's complex expectations about his public's potential reactions to his text, expectations that were related in turn to his own short- and long-term plans for responding to, and profiting from, those very reactions. This sample analysis is meant to demonstrate something of the pertinence of a non-reductive, non-atomistic approach to the writer's rationality. It is not presented as an exclusive or exhaustive model of literary criticism in general. The analysis does not try to show that the value of an author's work is measurable in terms of judgements about its objective or substantive rationality. My remarks do demonstrate that the topic of agential rationality is pertinent to literary history and to a central critical concept, the notion of fiction. What is more, the results that I have developed by drawing on models of rationality are not reducible to the static and inadequate notions that have dominated pragmatic theories of literature. Yet I am not claiming that critics must focus exclusively on the practical reasoning of authors: in the next section, I turn to a discussion of a variety of readerly strategies towards authors, texts, and works.

Many literary theorists today take it for granted that speech act theories of fictional discourse are flawed by an emphasis on the speaker's intentions. This point was stressed by Jacques Derrida in his polemics with John Searle and may be amplified by saying that the entire conception involves an overly 'Cartesian' understanding of the human subject's internal mastery and control.[26] I think that this is an erroneous conclusion about what follows from the particular weaknesses of some versions of the speech act approach. That approach goes wrong not because it rests on 'too many' assumptions about the rôle of intentions in communicative action, but because it offers only a truncated version of the kind of intentional psychology upon which we necessarily rely the moment we identify something as a text, utterance, or literary work. The problem is not that it is incorrect to link any particular fictional discourse, or any other kind of behaviour, to any mental attitudes or states; as I have argued above, we successfully engage in such action explanations on a regular basis in our everyday lives. The problem, rather, is that many theories of the pragmatics of fiction work with an inadequate version of that kind of psychological explanation and hence make an easy target for a sceptical attack, for it is indeed hard to imagine how we could successfully explain a fictional utterance by pointing to a single, isolated mental state that is supposed to be responsible for its entire status and meaning. That some particular application of an action-theoretical approach to fiction is limited does not entail that no more robust version of the approach could be more successful. To develop these points, I turn now to my example.

In August 1844, Edgar Allan Poe published a piece entitled 'Mesmeric Revelation' in the *Columbian Lady's and Gentleman's Magazine*, a New York monthly.[27] This is a text that begins by evoking the existence of universally admitted facts about mesmerism and that ends by suggesting that a mesmerized person has gone on conversing after his death, a motif that Poe further exploited in his notorious 'The Facts in the Case of M. Valdemar', which first appeared four months later in a periodical called *American Review: A Whig Journal* (*Works*, pp. 1228–44). In both of these texts, Poe's style is that of a factual case history meant to document actual occurrences. Thus the narrator of 'Mesmeric Revelation' begins by castigating the 'unprofitable and disreputable tribe' of people who continue to doubt the facts about mesmerism; he describes his habit of mesmerizing a certain Mr Vankirk, who frequently calls him to his bedside, apparently for medical treatment. The largest part of the text consists of a transcription of the narrator's last conversation with Vankirk who, under mesmeric influence, details a metaphysical revelation in which the dualism of mind and matter is resolved. Similarly, the narrator of 'The Facts in the Case of M. Valdemar', a certain P—, purports to convey the factual record of his experiment in mesmerizing a man *in articulo mortis*, and claims to have thereby arrested 'the encroachments of Death' for a period of seven months.

The publication of Poe's mesmeric pieces gave rise to some interesting responses. There is ample evidence to suggest that for some readers they were fact, for others they were fiction, and for others still they were unsuccessful hoaxes. The texts were reprinted several times in the months immediately following their initial appearance and were discussed in various other periodicals; in several instances, editors went so far as to preface the texts with the claim that they were strictly factual accounts. Many were the believers. 'Mesmeric Revelation' was reprinted in at least six American periodicals, including *The Philadelphia Saturday Museum* and *The American Phrenological Journal*. In 1845 it was published in London in the *Popular Record of Modern Science*, which also reprinted 'The Facts in the Case of M. Valdemar', which it presented as 'a plain recital of facts' (*Works*, pp. 1231). It is perhaps significant that 'Mesmeric Revelation' was the first text by Poe that Charles Baudelaire selected for translation, and in his introduction to the French version that appeared in *La Liberté de Penser* in 1848, Baudelaire referred to the piece as *'une haute curiosité scientifique'*.[28] Although some editors and readers took the two mesmeric pieces to be non-fiction, others did not. In the editor's introduction to 'Mesmeric Revelation' in the *Universalist Watchman and Christian Repository* of Montpelier, Vermont, the reader was told that 'We do not take the following article as an historical account, nor, as a burlesque on mesmerism; but, as a presentation of the writer's philosophical theory which he wished to commend to the attention of his readers' (*Works*, pp. 1027).

What were Poe's attitudes towards his mesmeric texts? Was he guided by the aim of successfully communicating a fictional discourse, one firmly bracketed off from the world of sincere assertions, true and false claims, and successful and unsuccessful attempts to deceive? Is this simply a case of an author whose work was initially miscategorized by some gullible and naïve readers who were avid to believe in the mysterious powers of mesmerism? The facts in the case of M. Poe do not support any simple answers to those questions. To begin, we know that four months before the appearance of 'Mesmeric Revelation', Poe wrote a newspaper article now commonly referred to as 'The Balloon Hoax'. This was an article that purported to describe the first successful transatlantic balloon flight, and hundreds were taken in by the deception. Poe himself later commented that 'The more intelligent believed, while the rabble . . . rejected the whole with disdain' (*Works*, p. 1067). Why should the intelligent believe? Perhaps because, as the subsequent retraction stated, 'The description of the Balloon and the voyage was written with a minuteness and scientific ability calculated to obtain credit everywhere . . . We by no means think such a project impossible' (*Works*, pp. 1067–8).

Shortly after the publication of 'The Facts in the Case of M. Valdemar', Poe confided in at least two letters that the case was a hoax.[29] Does that mean that the mesmeric texts should be categorized as wilful attempts to deceive the public? Further insight into Poe's aims is provided by the manner in which he presented the next mesmeric story: at a time when he had already seen that many readers took his 'Mesmeric Revelation' as gospel, Poe did nothing to make certain that others would not similarly believe that the next piece was meant to be a factual account. On the contrary, when he reprinted the Valdemar story in the *Broadway Journal*, he prefaced it with the following introduction: 'An article of ours, thus entitled, was published in the last number of Mr. Colton's "American Review," and has given rise to some discussion – especially in regard to the truth or falsity of the statements made. It does not become *us*, of course, to offer one word on the point at issue. We have been requested to reprint the article, and do so with pleasure.

We leave it to speak for itself. We may observe, however, that there are a certain class of people who pride themselves upon Doubt, as a profession' (*Works*, p. 1230). Poe does not lie directly, but his last line was certainly designed to encourage belief in his tale, which may be one reason why Poe later referred to its publication as a 'hoax'.

Poe claimed in a letter to have found it 'unsurpassably funny' that some people were gullible enough to be taken in by his mesmeric narratives, but this fact should not lead us to conclude that he either wanted or intended his readers to see through his style of *vraisemblance*. Poe's reaction to those who were not duped is significant in this respect. In response to an editor who marvelled that anyone could have believed in the story of Valdemar, Poe wrote:

For our parts we find it difficult to understand how any dispassionate transcendentalist can doubt the facts as we state them; they are by no means so incredible as the marvels which are hourly narrated, and believed, on the topic of Mesmerism. *Why* cannot a man's death be postponed indefinitely by Mesmerism? *Why* cannot a man talk after he is dead? *Why?* – *why?* that is the question; and as soon as the Tribune has answered it to our satisfaction we will talk to it farther.[30]

Here Poe would seem to have been trying to sustain credence in his tale by claiming that the incredulous cannot prove the events recounted by his narrative to be impossible; he even refers explicitly to 'the facts as we state them', a rather deceptive phrase if the author's sole intent was to present his tale as a mere story. The hypothesis that Poe fully and genuinely intended his two mesmeric narratives to be taken as fiction is contradicted by such statements and by others like it, which suggest on the contrary that he would have been disappointed had none of his readers lent credence to the story. At the time of composing his mesmeric pieces, Poe was fully aware of the widespread interest in the topic and he could not have been oblivious to the fact that many of his readers were eager to believe in the kinds of fantastic effects he had set out to evoke. In his own words, the dispassionate transcendentalists would be in no position to doubt such a story; moreover, the accounts were published in periodicals that regularly carried non-fictional reports. If we were to assume that Poe sincerely desired to have these texts be recognized as fictional stories, then we should fault him with having been highly irrational, for he could easily have found ways to label his texts more clearly. That he chose, on the contrary, to adopt what he himself referred to as a style of *vraisemblance*, publishing his accounts without any of the typical framing devices, strongly weighs in favour of the supposition that Poe was not interested merely in engaging in a successful act of fiction; he was also interested in being believed by some of his readers. In short, some of the writerly and editorial choices he made in composing and publishing these texts are best explained by assuming that he did desire to be believed by at least some of his readers.

Yet Poe's intentions are not sufficiently described by saying that he wanted some of his readers to believe in his tales, for there is evidence that his thinking about his audience was more complex than that. Poe must have been fully aware that many readers could never be induced to believe these fantastic narratives, and he was not so foolish as to set out to try to deceive or convince such readers. With the experience of the balloon hoax fresh in mind, he probably knew that he could never provide the kind of factual support that a long-term deception would require, and he most likely had a future-directed intention not to engage in the hopeless task of trying to defend the literal veracity of his mesmeric narratives. If at the time of publishing his piece, Poe fully intended to arouse belief in as many readers as possible, he could also look forward to the moment when others would challenge the veracity of the narratives, and it seems safe to assume that he had every intention of abandoning any literal factual claims at that point. That is precisely what he did in his private correspondence.

The fact that Poe had the intention not to defend the factual accuracy of his narratives does not imply that he pledged his full and undying allegiance to the literalist's notion of truth. Instead, Poe publicly challenged the sceptics to prove that the events he recounted were not in some sense possible or true. We might interpret this move as a purely cynical attempt to sustain the controversy surrounding the author's publications. Such an interpretation may have an element of truth, but other evidence suggests that Poe's thinking was more complicated. In the case of 'Mesmeric Revelation', Poe's attitudes about the contents of his tale are not adequately characterized by saying that he resolutely believed them to be devoid of any and all truth value. The largest part of that tale is taken up by the metaphysical theses pronounced by Mr Vankirk, who is presumably held in a state of living death by the force of animal magnetism. These philosophical ruminations concern the nature of God, immateriality, and the soul, and defend a monism based on a distinction between particled and unparticled matter. These are the same ideas that Poe earnestly broached to his friends in private correspondence, and he presented them to the public in his mystical essay *Eureka*, published in 1848. There are critics who deny that Poe believed in any of his angelic and mystical writings, and these critics have devised an ironic Poe, 'a skeptical demystifier of origins'.[31] Such an interpretation of Poe is flatly contradicted, however, by the relevant evidence.[32] For example, in a letter written shortly after the publication of 'Mesmeric Revelation', Poe sent the story to a professor at New York University with the following remark: 'You will, of course, understand that the article is purely a fiction; but I have embodied in it some thoughts which are original with myself and I am exceedingly anxious to learn if they have claim to absolute originality, and also how far they will strike you as well based' (*Works*, p. 1025). Apparently the sceptical demystifier of origins wanted to know whether he could claim authentic authorship and originality for some metaphysical ideas, and thus asked for the professor's learned opinion. Poe's well-documented investment in his metaphysical speculations suggests that he should not be taken as an author who espoused only a common sense conception of reality – or no conception at all. It follows that his apparent belief in the literal falsehood of the events he recounted in his mesmeric pieces must be viewed alongside a long-term fascination with certain metaphysical views. It may simply be a mistake to assume, then, that Edgar Poe had no convictions, or that his convictions corresponded to the literalist's notion of truth and falsehood. Most importantly, there is evidence that in Poe's mind a story about what is non-factual but possible had a rather different status from a story about impossibilities. Who, he asks, is in a position to exclude his mesmeric revelations from the realm of possibility?

It is possible, of course, that we know nothing at all about Poe's motives and beliefs, just as it is possible that the universe was created five years ago, only with all of the traces arranged so that the universe would look much older. My claim is not that I have directly read the mind of Poe and have infallible knowledge of it. Rather, my contention is that the evidence that we have about Poe's authorship of the mesmeric texts supports some hypotheses about his motives and deliberations – but does not fit very well with other hypotheses. For example, the evidence I have just evoked does not support a story in which the author's decisive attitude towards his discourse was a univocal intent to see that discourse be bracketed off from any and all claims of truth and falsehood. Nor does the available evidence lend any support to the idea that Poe's writerly purposes and activities were part of a blind textual process in which a number of previously available 'codes' – including the 'symbolic' code of Lacanian psychoanalysis – somehow combined to spin out a bit of *écriture* that we now only arbitrarily associate with the proper name Poe. Such would seem to be the explicit pragmatic assumption in Barthes's analysis of the 'conditions of possibility' of the significance of Poe's 'The Facts in the Case of M. Valdemar'. Barthes proclaims that writing is totally divorced from all 'origins' and 'motives', which are replaced by various unspecified 'indeterminations and overdeterminations'. The proper name may be the 'prince of the signifiers', as Barthes puts it, but this prince wields no power and is devoid of authority: it is impossible to identify who is speaking in any instance of writing, Barthes comments, for writing begins quite precisely at the moment when we can only observe that '*ça commence à parler*' [it – the Id – begins to speak].[33] Here it would seem that the claims made in favour of an anti-agential, textualist theory of writing rest on a highly speculative strain of Freudianism in which communicative and symbolic action are held to be totally reducible to primary processes. At the same time, Barthes wisely takes several steps back from this textual and libidinal abyss. He suggests that he has elucidated some of the conditions that make the text's multiple meanings possible.[34] This is an interesting psycho-linguistic claim, but unfortunately, what Barthes presents as a descriptive model of readerly competence is just a particular performance in disguise. In this regard, some of Barthes's remarks about his use of the term 'code' are quite revealing: 'The word *code* itself must not be understood here in the rigorous and scientific sense of the term. Codes are simply associative fields, a supra-textual organization of notations that convey a certain idea of structure.'[35] The critic's descriptions of 'codes' in the non-rigorous sense should hardly be accepted as providing a model of the conditions that effectively make a text's various meanings possible for readers. What is more, if we look more closely, we see that Barthes does not really manage to divorce his critical practice from standard assumptions about the special relation between particular authors and writings, for he consistently refers to *Poe's* work and to *Poe's* context, even as he cites Baudelaire's French translation, which he generally presents as a reliable stand-in for the original work. How could such equations and references be pertinent or even possible in a domain of perfectly de-personalized textuality?

The hypothesis to be preferred to a metaphysics of purely textual processes is that the agent who intentionally composed and published these stories was a highly strategic writer whose plans and intentions were multiple, being oriented not only in relation to several different audiences, but to several different stages in the reception of his pieces.[36] Herein resides the complexity of Poe's authorial rationality. Poe's intentions were speculative in a dual sense: he speculated metaphysically, being interested in certain ideas and hopeful that he had something profound and original to say. At the same time, he speculated on the reception of his texts and was ready to respond to, and profit from, several distinct types of response. He had reason to expect that some would literally believe in his texts. This was something he desired, for belief would attract attention to the articles and to the more general metaphysical ideas in which he was strongly interested. Belief would also serve as a tangible sign of his writerly talent and persuasive force. He also had reason to believe that others would take his texts to be fiction; this too, he desired, for Poe was hopeful that his texts had literary value and was eager to have that value be acknowledged, particularly given his view that his metaphysical notions could be fully developed and appreciated in such a context. And so in the book review that he wrote of an edition of his own tales, Poe commented that the article was meant to be 'the vehicle of the author's views concerning the DEITY, immateriality, spirit, &c., which he apparently believes to be true, in which belief he is joined by Professor BUSH'.[37] Yet Poe also had reason to believe that some would perceive his texts as a hoax. This too was what he wanted, for then he could enjoy laughing along with those who approved of hoaxes. When necessary he would claim with impunity that he never meant his stories to be taken literally. In any case, the controversy that some readers' belief in the narratives was bound to stir up would place Poe in a privileged position, that of the person who witholds a secret sought by the others. His wit, talent, and distinction could thereby be valorized. I think we see Poe exploiting this position in a playful response to a query about the text's factual basis, for he answers as follows: 'the truth is, there was a very small modicum of truth in the case of M. Valdemar – which, in consequence, may be called a hard case – *very* hard for M. Valdemar, for Mr. Collyer, and ourselves. If the story was not true, however, it should have been – and perhaps "The Zoist" may discover that it *is* true after all' (*Works*, p. 1231).

I shall now survey the points about the pragmatics of fiction that are illustrated – but of course not proven – by the example of Poe. The case casts doubt on the wisdom of basing a pragmatic theory on an 'atomic' approach to purposeful behaviour, that is, an approach that seeks to identify an action in terms of a single intention that is extracted from the broader context of the agent's beliefs, desires, and plans. The atomic approach posits a 'time-slice' agent who performs an isolated action that can be identified and explained in terms of a single, global mental state, the present-directed intention that defines the state of affairs that the behaviour is meant to realize. Yet this atomic approach fails to explore the ways in which the purposeful behaviour of human beings involves complex temporal relations as well as cases where intentions and actions are linked in hierarchized, means–ends schemata, extending across time in structures of planning. The atomic approach leads to mistakes in those cases where the intention that it isolates only has its real explanatory significance when viewed in relation to some of the agent's other attitudes, including expectations about the future actions and reactions of other parties.

Thus, when it is bounded and oriented by various other goals and attitudes, an author's intention to bracket his or her discourse as fiction no longer has the meaning that many pragmatic theories would ascribe to it. I have in mind here the various versions of a speech act analysis of fictional discourse, which identify the action of doing fiction in terms of the special kind of intention that governs the communicative action and that distinguishes it from other types of purposeful behaviour.[38] According to such theories, types of communicative action are identified, if not 'explained', in terms of a single cognitive item, namely, the discrete moment of intention that specifies the state of affairs aimed at by the agent. Typically, this goal or end is the state of affairs where the speaker utters a discourse and makes manifest his or her intention that this discourse be taken as fiction, and not as a sincere assertion, as an attempt to deceive, or as any other sort of speech act. Whatever the speaker or writer does, this behaviour is supposed to be oriented by what Searle calls 'intention in action', and reference to the latter is taken to be adequate to identify the kind of action that has been performed.[39] This is an atomic approach because it does not attend to the complex relations between the different sorts of attitudes that generate action: what is lacking is a broader perspective on the subjective rationality of the agent.

Poe's intentions and desires were multiple, and it would be a mistake to ascribe to him a simple and definitive intention to classify his mesmeric texts as fiction, just as it would be a mistake to make the logically opposite ascription. Either of these two assumptions entails that the author of the mesmeric stories was inept and inconsistent. Yet Poe's craft becomes apparent once we assume, on the contrary, that the notion of fiction had a local, provisional, and strategic status within a complex network of attitudes. It may be that the intention to make fiction is sometimes a discrete end in relation to which an author's every effort is subordinated, but it seems more promising to assume that the rationality of fictional communication more often resides in its relations to the various practical ends that story-telling is meant to serve. If that is the case, then we can only provide adequate pragmatic explanations of such discourses by embracing a broader range of the author's motives and reasons, including the author's complex anticipations of the readers' various responses. This means that we should think in terms of deliberations that are situated in contexts where the agents' decisions are interdependent. Instead of an approach based on the model of a one-shot game based on skill and/or luck, then, we need approaches based on temporally dynamic, strategic models. The kind of approach that I am advocating need not be linked to any of the more idealized assumptions about the completeness and perfection of the individual agent's beliefs or knowledge: the rationality heuristic that I am recommending is meant to identify and explain all sorts of errors, oversights, and forms of motivated and unmotivated irrationality.[40] In other words, my emphasis on applying rationality heuristics in the analysis of the pragmatics of fiction does not mean that no place is left for what Poe called the imp of the perverse. Note as well that I have not claimed that Poe's speculative relation to mesmeric ideas satisfies any of the more robust and substantive criteria of rationality, for indeed I believe that it does not.

The pragmatic dimension of fiction is multi-faceted and unfolds in time, for it embraces the ongoing projects and deliberations of agents who commit themselves to various stances and tactics, but who are capable of adjusting or abandoning some of these stances as situations unfold. The speech act theory of the pragmatics of fiction is useful because it identifies some pertinent distinctions, but it remains a static and inadequate model of a communicator's practical reason and fails to emphasize the motivational dimensions that must figure in any genuine explanation of action. Thus the scope of the pragmatic explanatory models needs to be enlarged in two directions: first of all, in regard to particular actions, the model must embrace a wider range of attitudes, linking present-directed intentions to the motives and beliefs that necessarily figure in practical reasoning; secondly, the rationality of particular actions should be understood within the larger context of agential rationality, a context where particular moments of practical reasoning are linked to ongoing projects, plans, and long-term dispositions.

Although I quite obviously value the type of pragmatic analysis of literature that I sketched in the previous section, this is not the avenue of enquiry to be adopted in the rest of this book, and I shall now situate the assumptions and aims of the analyses that follow. Critics often set out to describe what happens in the plots of selected literary works, couching their interpretations in terms of some particular psychological doctrine (and most frequently, the doctrine is some version of psychoanalysis). Thus scores of critics have applied psychodynamic notions to texts in order to produce interpretations of the characters' actions. This method in turn leads to debates over the validity of this or that psychological doctrine, and to arguments over the correctness of different ways of applying them. But such debates will remain fruitless until a more basic question has been answered: what explanatory payoffs can be expected, in principle, from the application of a specialized psychological theory in the reading of a literary work?[41] Note that this is not a question about whether critics can produce diverse 'understandings' of texts in this manner; I have already suggested above that readers must work within the general framework of intentionalist psychology if they are to make sense of the actions depicted in literary narratives, and it is clear that any number of more specialized psychological thematics can be used to produce readings of texts. My question concerns, rather, what is explained when critics expressly apply some particular psychological theory to the agents and actions depicted in a work. My response to that question is that there is no good reason to be particularly sanguine about the explanatory merits of this kind of interpretive approach unless the critic adopts a very particular type of strategy, which I shall identify in what follows.

In some cases, interpreting the actions depicted in literary works in terms of a psychological theory does not genuinely explain anything and would not do so even if the theory were true, justified, and had any other epistemic virtues one might want a theory to have. Suppose that one granted that some version of psychoanalysis was the very best – or even the one correct – theory of the psyche. It would not follow that applying this theory to the action in *Hamlet* explains why *Hamlet* is a play in which the protagonist hesitates. After all, in some plays the characters' behaviour is not the least bit realistic, so even the one correct psychological theory could not successfully explain their antics. To explain a case where the characterizations do match the theory, we must go outside the fictional actions and look at the other factors that could have been responsible for bringing the characters into line with the correct psychological science. If an analysis of the psyche of the characters does not explain why the play was written one way instead of another, what does it explain? The only plausible response is that the psychological theory is being used to explain 'what goes on' in the fictional world of the drama: when we feign to look upon the characters as agents capable of irrational and rational action, a psychological theory can 'explain' the fictional behaviour in terms of the characters' mental states.

Perhaps other kinds of explanatory payoff could be had from applying psychological doctrines to the interpretation of the actions depicted in literary works. Critics need not seek to explain the action in terms of the theory; their goal could instead be to determine the 'validity' of the theory. But when the doctrine 'matches' the work's action, does the interpretive operation genuinely provide some measure of confirmation of the doctrine? Hardly, for even if we take it for granted that the argument for the fit between pertinent aspects of the fabula and the theory is not circular, the fact remains that many literary depictions of behaviour are distorted. That literary representations match a theory is not evidence for believing in the theory, otherwise, Matthew Lewis's novel *The Monk* (1796) provides evidence for demonology and allows us to 'explain' a person's debauchery in terms of the various metamorphoses of the devil's cunning minions.

The point to be underscored here is that critics need to be lucid about the directions in which their critical goals do and do not lie when they mobilize theories and hypotheses in readings of the actions portrayed in literary works. If a critic cannot really explain anything about *Hamlet* by means of an interpretation that shows how the actions in the work can be read as 'fitting' some psychological doctrine, what cognitive goal could a critic hope to achieve by means of such an operation? One proposal is that the critic could hope to 'illustrate' the doctrine, to make it more detailed and comprehensible by reference to the example. The idea that literary interpretations could have this kind of illustrative rôle has been defended by Simon, who stipulates, however, that literary critics should not waste their time illustrating theories that are dubious and out of date (and the example he has in view is psychoanalysis): 'the scientific content must be valid . . . If the humanities are to base their claims to a central place in the liberal curriculum on their special insights into the human condition, they must be able to show that their picture of that condition is biologically, sociologically, and psychologically defensible'.[42] Yet most critics will not be satisfied with this rather limited claim in favour of the cognitive value of literary elucidations. Literary interpretation figures here as a wholly dispensable and secondary means to a cognitive goal that could just as well be achieved by a number of other means; what is more, literary insights play absolutely no rôle in the selection of the goal.

There is, however, a more ambitious cognitive aim for literary readings, namely, the goal of complexifying and developing hypotheses about various aspects of human affairs.[43] Following this strategy, the critic is not simply looking for ways in which a particular social or psychological theory 'fits' or 'illustrates' aspects of a work. Obviously, there must be a relationship of congruence or relevance between the theory and the particular document – that is, the critic selects a work because it appears to have features that make it particularly significant in regard to some conceptual problematic, theory, or question. The critic then sets out to explore the relation between some of the work's features and the theory. But the critic's goal in exploring that relation is neither to confirm the hypothesis nor to explain the artefact, for it is understood that even a perfect and detailed fit between the two cannot achieve either of these two ends. As I have argued above, a superbly detailed and coherent psychoanalytical reading of Hamlet's actions and statements does not give us any additional reason to think that psychoanalysis is an accurate theory of the dynamics of human mental life, nor does it explain why a work was created in which the protagonist behaves in this particular way. The goal of the kind of interpretation I have in mind here is different. This goal must be a matter of an independent heuristic aim, that of clarifying and developing the theory, which is not the one correct psychological doctrine, but an imperfect explanatory model requiring improvement. The questions orienting such interpretive enquiries may be formulated as follows: what is the meaning of a text or work when analyzed in the context of a particular programme of research (typically, a particular body of hypotheses and evidence)? In what ways can the interpretation of the literary work contribute to the research programme through a refinement of its hypotheses? The assumption here is that contrasting the work and the theory's explanatory schemes and models can help us discover ways in which the latter may be inadequate, either because the actions and attitudes evoked by the work seem to challenge the theory in interesting ways, or because details and circumstances evoked by the work are simply not taken account of by the theory, which thus stands in need of elaboration and refinement.

In the chapters that follow, my primary goal is to pursue the type of heuristic readings just evoked. Thus it will not be a matter of analysing literary works with the goal of elucidating the author's strategies and intentions. Nor is it a matter of describing or prescribing the thoughts and emotions of the works' ideal or actual readers. It is not a question of pretending to assess the intrinsic aesthetic merit of this or that work or text. Instead, the aim is to explore and make manifest some of the cognitive value of theoretically oriented readings of particular writings. Drawing upon this cognitive value does not require that one seek to analyse every aspect of a work, or that one respect the kinds of features and topics that are typically pertinent to other modes of literary analysis. In my context, it is the research programme associated with rationality, and more specifically, with particular issues and problems related to that notion, that defines the principles of pertinence observed in a selective reading of the literary texts. The goal, then, is not an aesthetic appreciation, a recounting of the 'common reader's' experience, or even a depth-hermeneutical exegesis. The goal is to present the results of readings that were motivated by the heuristic value of a selective approach to some literary narratives. It should be obvious that I am not proposing that this is the only or the best avenue of critical enquiry. It is, however, a good, if not the best, manner of arguing for the cognitive value of literary interpretation.

Why would the analysis of literary works be a good means to improving hypotheses about human agency? Am I reviving the old claim about the propositional content of literature, following which literary works are direct expressions of the authors' genial insights into the eternal truths of human nature – insights that it is the job of the critic to rescue? Not at all. What I am proposing is not a matter of detecting and amplifying the correct arguments that authors have put in the mouths of their characters and narrators. In the case of Dreiser's writings, my analysis in fact brushes 'against the grain' of the author's project, for I am interested precisely in the ways in which the claims made by Dreiser's naturalist narrators are flatly contradicted by other aspects of the work. I deem this encounter with the contradictions of Dreiser's and Zola's naturalist fictions to be of special heuristic value. One reason why readings of literary narratives can have heuristic value in the context of hypotheses about rationality flows from what was proposed above about some of the most basic features of stories, namely, their invariant emphasis on purposeful activity and on the multiple ways in which such activity can go wrong. Literary narratives depict an extraordinary variety of situations where agents' practical deliberations and actions do not work smoothly to the attainment of the desired ends. These diverse literary depictions of the breakdowns and subversions of rationality are often particularly revealing because of their emphasis on the corresponding attitudes of the agents involved. By depicting ways in which our individual and collective schemes falter and fail, literary narratives help make it possible to articulate the intuitions and concepts that enable us to say more explicitly what precisely has gone wrong in such cases. Such, at least, is a hypothesis to be explored in what follows.

PART II

Textual models

CHAPTER 3

Naturalism and the question of agency

At the end of *The Financier*, the first novel in his *Trilogy of Desire*, Dreiser turns away from the story of his protagonist's life and appends a few paragraphs, which at first glance may seem quite unrelated to the rest of the novel. Dreiser's coda has two parts: 'Concerning Mycteroperca Bonaci' and 'The Magic Crystal'. The former begins like a lesson in natural history: 'There is a certain fish, the scientific name of which is Mycteroperca Bonaci, its common name Black Grouper, which is of considerable value as an afterthought in this connection, and which deserves to be better known.'[1] The black grouper, we are instructed, is a prosperous organism that enjoys a long and comfortable existence by virtue of its remarkable ability to imitate its environment. 'Lying at the bottom of a bay, it can simulate the mud by which it is surrounded. Hidden in the folds of glorious leaves, it is of the same markings. Lurking in a flaw of light, it is like the light itself shining dimly in water. Its power to elude or strike unseen is of the greatest.' The mimetic fish is said to be 'a living lie, a creature whose business it is to appear what it is not, to simulate that with which it has nothing in common, to gets its living by great subtlety, the power of its enemies to forefend against which is little'. Yet the lesson in natural history is at the same time an argument in moral philosophy: the duplicity of this predatory fish is explicitly set in opposition to man's moral illusions, which are supposedly belied by what Dreiser calls the remorseless 'secrecy' of nature. Called upon to testify in an 'indictment' of the 'beatitudes', the example of the black grouper fish shows that it is not the weak and honest who inherit the earth; rather, only those who employ force and cunning prevail in the incessant and immoral struggle that is life. Such is the condition of humans and animals alike, the only difference being that the former are prone to illusion: 'Man himself is busy digging the pit and

89

fashioning the snare, but he will not believe it. His feet are in the trap of circumstance; his eyes are on an illusion.' And thus Dreiser's novel concludes with the suggestion that referring to the behaviour of a species of fish is of considerable value in illuminating the nature of the novel's protagonist, a predatory financier, and with him, the human condition.

Dreiser's extended metaphor succinctly expresses the essential tenets of what may be referred to as a key naturalist dogma. This dogma is an instance of scientism, and a particularly bad one given the fact that biological knowledge does not really support its claims about the nature of human behaviour. A critical analysis of this dogma will be useful to us here for a number of reasons. First of all and most importantly in the present context, the dogma in question constitutes a typical manner of trying to answer some of the basic questions about agency and rationality introduced in chapter 1, and developing an alternative to this response is a way to make some progress in dealing with these questions. Secondly, this dogma should be criticized because of the importance of the rôle it continues to play in contemporary culture: the ideas I have in mind here are hardly limited to a certain corpus of nineteenth- and early twentieth-century fiction, nor are they primarily a literary matter. Rather, what is at stake here are attitudes that have adherents in various social domains and that are frequently expressed in popular and academic discourses alike.[2]

What are the tenets that we associate with this naturalist dogma? Four inter-related notions may be mentioned. The first and most general idea is suggested by Dreiser's very choice of a biological metaphor, for the use of such imagery implies the belief that it is possible and appropriate to understand human nature by referring to the traits of animals. In the case of Dreiser's text, this amounts to the implicit claim that the human condition is strictly equivalent, in certain key respects, to that of other species of life. Now, to disagree with this first thesis it is not necessary to ascribe to the rather untenable notion that human beings are not living organisms, or to claim they have absolutely nothing in common with any other species. The emphasis, then, is on the 'key respects' in terms of which the dogma tries to achieve its reduction of the human to the animal. The second tenet of the naturalist dogma flows from here, as it is a matter of specifying a particular sense in which the reductive identification of the human and the animal is supposed to be warranted. Basically, this is a thesis about the motivation and generation of behaviour, a thesis stating that animal and human doings alike are specified by an inherited natural mechanism. In one version of this story, instinct, or rather, the instinctual appetites, drives, or urges that emerge as a result of an instinctually governed process of ontogenesis, are the motivating forces of the doings of all individual organisms. The activities of the grouper fish, then, are motivated by biological impulses or appetites, not by reasons, and the fish itself is said to be but a living illustration of the constructive 'forces' of nature.

The next tenet of the naturalist dogma identifies these naturally determined appetites or impulses. Typically, there are but four: nourishment, reproduction, escape, and combat. Dreiser's metaphor of the black grouper fish exemplifies these assumptions, for the fish 'gets its living', 'prospers', 'eludes', and 'strikes unseen'. That the latter item is included in the list of primary and essential needs provides the motif for yet another major tenet of the naturalist dogma: rivalry with one's natural enemies is an essential part of the 'struggle called life'. That, presumably, is what it means to 'adapt to conditions', for evolution, in both nature and culture, is a picture of rivalry bearing a single caption: 'the survival of the fittest'. Finally, we come to the theme at the centre of Dreiser's naturalist metaphor, the conflict between nature and morality, a conflict resolved when the former gives the lie to the latter. Driven to engage in a ceaseless struggle without even knowing it, man's eyes are on an illusion.

Proponents of this kind of naturalist dogma typically lay claim to being informed by the latest scientific findings and theories, so that unless we want to be guilty of the absurdity of doubting such authorities, we should lend credence to their various reductions. The authorities, however, diverge. One source informs us that the human animal is governed entirely by drives, which are generated by instinct, itself genetically overdetermined, while the genes that do this determining are themselves fashioned in a process of evolutionary selection. Change the authority, however, and the terms of the dogma shift: human doings are then completely determined by katastates, chemisms, brain states, the influence of the milieu, unconscious representations, tropisms, or what have you. Thus in the case of naturalist literature we witness a curious turn of events. The naturalist author is someone who verses himself in the science

of the day and returns to the writing table to copy over these truths
in literary form, thereby hoping to assure the veracity of an art
work that is thereby elevated about the status of mere fiction. Yet
when we retrace the lines of influence, we discover that the 'nature'
of naturalism is inscribed within a network of texts, and often, those
of pseudo-scientists and vulgarizers who are anything but reliable
authorities. Thus Dreiser can be caught at paraphrases of such
dubious authorities as Elmer Gates, Jacques Loeb, and Ernst
Haeckel, the result being that the references that were supposed to
give this kind of literature the aura of science now have quite the
opposite effect.[3]

At first glance, the second half of Dreiser's coda to *The Financier*,
'The Magic Crystal', is strikingly different from the first, for it
proposes a mystical viewpoint on the fate of the novel's protagonists: 'If you had been a mystic or a soothsayer or a member of that
mysterious world which divines by incantations, dreams, the mystical bowl, or the crystal sphere, you might have looked into their
mysterious depths at this time and foreseen a world of happenings
which concerned these two, who were now apparently so
fortunately placed.' Science, then, is suddenly replaced by magic.
And what is the content of this witches' vision that takes the place
of the naturalist image? Dreiser's seer intones that his characters
dwell in illusion: ' "Hail to you, Frank Cowperwood, master and no
master, prince of a world of dreams whose reality was disillusion!"
So might the witches have called, the bowl have danced with
figures, the fumes with vision, and it would have been true.'

Is there a link between the two halves of Dreiser's coda, between
the naturalist and supernaturalist perspectives which they voice?
In spite of the fact that there are many ways in which these two
perspectives are strictly incompatible, there is none the less a
strong, unspoken link between them, a link having the form of a
common thesis on the nature of human agency. We may begin to
understand this thesis by turning to a theatrical metaphor proposed by one of the most influential nineteenth-century naturalist
critics, Hippolyte Taine. The metaphor figures in a passage from
the preface to *De l'Intelligence*, which runs as follows:

The more bizarre the fact, the more it is instructive. In this regard, even
spiritualist phenomena point the way to discoveries by showing us the
coexistence of two distinct thoughts, wills, and actions, at the same time
and in the same individual. The individual is conscious of only one,

attributing the other to invisible beings. The human mind is, then, a theatre where several different plays are being performed all at once on different levels, only one of which is illuminated. Nothing is more worthy of study than this fundamental plurality of the self; it goes much further than we imagine.[4]

Although the lanterns of consciousness illuminate only one scene, there are others where the action of the individual is being determined, unbeknownst to the self, which remains ignorant of its 'fundamental plurality'. Here we indeed have a basic formula which has been developed in divergent ways in countless doctrines, all of which propose to shed light on the unknown determinations of individual action.

Although naturalist and supernaturalist discourses disagree violently about what kind of drama is being enacted in the unillumined theatres of the mind, they share at least one thesis about the overdetermination of human agency by other factors. This central clause holds that the individual agent inherits some set of drives or forces, and it is the latter that cause or otherwise direct behaviour. This central clause can also be characterized in terms of the view that it adamantly denies, namely, the idea that human behaviour is to any significant extent caused or oriented by conscious belief or intentional attitudes not overdetermined by an inherited motivational mechanism.

In the present context, the salient feature of these naturalist and supernaturalist discourses on agency is their reductive stance on human motivation. In a nutshell, this stance amounts to the idea that human doings are never effectively motivated by reasons, for the agent's attitudes are wholly epiphenomenal. Behaviour, then, is neither rational nor irrational, being governed by a-rational forces. Clearly, one need not be a naturalist to hold such a position, and it is indeed the case that a variety of discourses assert that our deliberations and intentional control never really guide our doings. The reductive thesis need not be anchored in a reference to the central scientific metaphor of natural law, and may move instead in the direction of the 'cosmic order', in which case the term or terms serving to designate the extra-human source of determinations cease to be drawn from any identifiable scientific authority or pseudo-authority. The unreasonable, uncontrollable inner mainspring of our doings ceases to be a matter of genetically determined instincts or drives, and is presented instead as an inscrutable 'force' or 'energy', at once nervous, power-seeking and libidinal. Sometimes the source of it all is a mysteriously potent, yet essentially blind, fragment of some great symbolic system, composed of unconscious archetypes or drifting signifiers. Behaviour is said to be generated by 'desiring machines' and their nomadic connective syntheses; it is the result of systems, structures, diagrams, and various discursive continents that emerge from the seas of history, only to return there after two or three centuries. Or perhaps it is all really a matter of events in the history of *Sein*, and no one is in any way responsible.

Obviously, in regard to some of the discourses I have just evoked, it is quite inappropriate to speak of naturalism, for the overarching determinations of human life to which they point are not supposed to be natural and scientific, but supernatural and occult, historical and psychodynamical. Even so, these different discourses share some basic theses about the nature of human agency, and we are justified in pointing to an affinity between them, the central point being their common defence of a-rational models of agency. It is a curious and perhaps revealing feature of intellectual and literary history that naturalist and supernaturalist versions of the reductive thesis were often penned by one and the same writer. A striking example is August Strindberg, who was at one point in his career totally enthralled by the reductionist mechanistic discourse of Max Nordau, according to which phenomena of interpersonal influence were to be explained in terms of the movements of the molecules of the brain. Thus, when one person follows another person's lead or is swayed by their statements and opinions, the influence is understood as having been caused by the impact of the more forceful brain molecules on the weaker brain, and psychology is reduced to a billiard-ball model of causality. Strindberg eventually abandoned Nordau's tenets in favour of the 'invisible forces' postulated by Emanuel Swedenborg, and so the naturalist author's 'vivisections' were replaced by his diary of the occult.[5]

Dreiser is an example of a writer who, like a narrator or character in a nineteenth-century fantastic tale, hesitates between the two possibilities evoked by Taine's theatrical metaphor. On the one hand, the basic intuition that there is another, unillumined space where the individual's behaviour is determined, translates into a number of properly supernatural beliefs having to do with invisible agents; on the other hand, the same intuition is supposed to lead to naturalistic 'discoveries', as the truly material mechanisms governing nature are uncovered. Dreiser oscillates constantly between naturalism and superstition, the particular ideas defining both poles of this oscillation themselves being anything but stable, for Dreiser could never make up his mind about where the truly determining forces were to be sought.

A few examples may be evoked in support of the last point. In *The Genius* (1915), Dreiser allows a fortune-teller to give detailed and accurate predictions of the hero's life course, suggesting that there is a properly supernatural destiny or cosmic order defying naturalistic explanation, yet knowable to someone having certain occult 'powers'. The same author, however, regularly has his narrators present reductive naturalistic explanations of the characters' behaviour. For example, in *An American Tragedy* (1925) we are told that the morality and immorality of the world are based on 'rearranging chemisms', and when a young woman's demeanour leads a doctor to change his opinion of her motives for coming to see him, the narrator explains that the cause of this event is her 'thought waves attacking his cerebral receptive centers'.[6] In *Sister Carrie* (1900), one of the narrator's intrusions tells us that the heroine is subject to 'super-intelligible forces', including 'the city's hypnotic influence', the sway of the moon, and 'things which neither resound nor speak': 'We are', the narrator sums up, 'more passive than active, more mirrors than engines, and the origin of human action has neither yet been measured nor calculated' (p. 78). Yet, later in the book these maxims no longer seem to be observed, for the narrator presents one of his characters not only as an engine, but as an engine the malfunctioning of which can be scientifically explained:

Now it has been shown experimentally that a constantly subdued frame of mind produces certain poisons in the blood, called katastates, just as virtuous feelings of pleasure and delight produce helpful chemicals, called anastates. The poisons, generated by remorse, inveigh against the system and eventually produce marked physical deterioration. To this Hurstwood was subject. (p. 339)

Nor were Dreiser's hesitations and oscillations limited to his fictional writings, for in various essays, he manifests the same indecision as to the source of the overarching determinants that shape human life. That there were such determinants, however, was indubitable. An essay entitled 'Suggesting the Possible Substructure of Ethics', written sometime around 1919, contends that 'the human mind with its very limited equipment of sense, suited only to minute measurements in connection with itself, is not and cannot be a fit implement for the detection and measurement of forces and matters which create and limit it and which lie outside the range of its various organs of perception'.[7] A few pages later, Dreiser arrives at the following stunning definition of 'man':

[Man] is a chemical compound, bottled and sealed in realms outside his ken and placed here willy-nilly but subject to the laws of his own substances and such others as govern them ... as all chemists and physicists now know, he is stimulated to and chemically moved or drawn to certain actions and forms; in short, compelled by the forces which have produced him to respond as he does and be as he is. Not he, but they, are responsible ... Only seemingly are we free to make those choices which our emotions compel us to make – not all of them without pleasure, to be sure. Pleasure is the great bait or result, and when achieved allays most ethical uncertainties. (p. 209)

Is the level of description at which the essential determinations may be situated physical, chemical, biological, psychological, or cosmic? Dreiser slips and slides between them, suggesting for a moment that he believes in fundamental chemico-physical laws, yet then allowing psychological constructs – the experience of emotion and pleasure – to have a decisive part. Thus, although we are said to be 'chemically moved', it would seem that this operation somehow requires our assent, for 'pleasure' is 'the great bait'. Surely it is not molecules and chemical compounds that experience pleasure. These incoherent slippages are apparent in the string of 'ors' and 'ands' in the following passage from an essay appropriately entitled 'Some Additional Comments on the Life Force, or God': 'the thing which is creating and supplying these instincts and impulses to man is none other than Nature Herself, or God, or the chemical and physical forces which underlie life, or whatever it is that makes life' (p. 212). In another essay, the 'whatever' becomes the 'It': 'Whatever It is, life-spark or ego, that sits at the centre and does the deciding (self-interestedly and selfishly always), there is no least evidence that we control It, Its wishes and instincts, but that It controls us.' It is a matter of wishes and instincts, but It can also be characterized as an 'internal spirit', as the unconscious, as a 'chemic compound', and once more, as 'the real representative of biologos' (p. 221).

In the light of such oscillations, it is no surprise when Dreiser moves without transition from his lesson in natural history at the end of *The Financier* to a prophetic bit of mystical nonsense entitled 'The Magic Crystal', in which we are invited to peer into the witches' pot to foresee the preordained destiny of the characters. The link between the natural and supernatural metaphors is their common denial of the rationality of the human agent, who is reduced – by the fiat of bald assertion – to the status of a marionette.

In its stance on the question of human agency, the constellation of positions that I have in view adopts a very general thesis about the motivation of behaviour. For shorthand we may refer to this thesis as the doctrine of motivational mechanism, thereby embracing many disparate variations on the same theme. What remains constant across these variations is the idea that the strivings of the individual agent are essentially a matter of the playing out of a pre-established set of impulses or wants, and not intentionally directed action, be it rational or irrational. In general, then, it is a matter of a model of agency in which mental states and intentional attitudes, when they are thought to be present, are purely epiphenomenal. However, a closer look reveals important differences, and the solidity and coherence of the deterministic thesis is called into question. The basic idea turns out on closer examination not to be so very basic, nor is it such a good idea, and the very writers who advocate it are not consistently able to respect its rather drastic implications.

A crucial problem for the dogma of motivational mechanism concerns the status to be given to intentionality in the putative apparatus. To what extent do people's motives for behaving involve genuine intentionality? There are, in fact, various significantly different stances that one may take on this matter, and a careful examination of them is needed. Different models of agency may be mapped in relation to the different possible answers to a few basic questions: How are a living organism's wants or desires generated? What are they? Is there a limited set of them, generalizable across species, or across the members of species or families of them? To what extent do attitudes of belief and intention play a rôle in the generation of these motivational states? What is the rôle

of belief and intention in attempts to satisfy those desires? To what
extent can belief and intention generate effective motivational
states, or overrule those generated by non-conscious processes? To
what extent do belief and intention merely act out rôles assigned by
a more basic, limited, and non-conscious system of motivation? To
what extent can the agent have any accurate, conscious beliefs
about the nature of its own motivational processes? Can having
such an awareness, when it is possible, make any difference in the
control of action? Are there no effective links between the different
'scenes' on which the plurality of the self is played out?

The answers one gives to such questions specify what may be
called a basic 'model of agency', and it is not the least bit clear that
the solutions proposed in reductive and mechanistic discourses – or
in their symbolical brethren – are adequate. What, exactly, are the
answers proposed by these discourses? Some clarification is
required if the discussion is to have any rigour. In what follows I
shall delineate some of the characteristic features of some discourses making programmatic claims about the validity of an a-rational
model of agency while effectively proposing – and presupposing –
descriptions of behaviour of a qualitatively different nature. Briefly,
what is in an assertive tone banished by the theories of agency
proposed by any number of naturalistic, supernaturalist, and
semio-historicist dogmas is in fact not eliminated, removed, or
reduced at all, the result being the flagrant inconsistency and
implausibility of these doctrines. I shall now begin to illustrate this
point by reference to the writings of Theodore Dreiser, an example
that is of particular value for at least two reasons: first of all,
because in Dreiser the inconsistency I have just delineated is particularly accentuated, and as a result, all the more instructive ('*plus
un texte est bizarre, plus il est instructif*'); secondly, because the latter
pole of Dreiser's contradiction – his non-reductive description of
agents – is in fact quite insightful in relation to a number of important issues. In terms of the survey of issues presented in chapter 1,
my goal in the present chapter is to use Dreiser's texts as a means of
clarifying intuitions about the basic question of agency, and more
particularly, the question of the plausibility of a-rational models of
the human agent's motivation.

Dreiser concludes his historical novel based on the life of the
American financier, Charles Tyson Yerkes, with a naturalist lesson

about a fish. The intellectual background that went into the writing of the book combined extensive study of the historical record of Yerkes's life with a number of semi-philosophical and pseudo-scientific ideas that the autodidact Dreiser had gleaned from his disparate readings.[8] We know that Dreiser knew quite a lot about the life of Yerkes and about the kind of personalities and attitudes that he wanted to depict in his novel.[9] We have good reason to think that Dreiser had a lot of confused and undeveloped notions about the 'chemic' and 'instinctual' determination of people's thoughts and actions. These ingredients went into the writing of a heterogeneous artefact expressive of divergent attitudes and intuitions, a testimony to 'the fundamental plurality of the self', perhaps, but not to any consistent theory of a-rational agency. As Dreiser puts it in *The Financier*, 'All individuals are a bundle of contradictions – none more so than the most capable' (p. 90).

Let us try to unravel some of the tangled threads in Dreiser's text, then, with an eye to singling out the explicit claims, and implicit assumptions, about the nature of human agency and motivation. The novel ends with the metaphor of the grouper fish. Early on, we are given another aquatic image that is supposed to inform us about the hero's earliest philosophical musings. The passage is famous: the young Frank Cowperwood sees a lobster and a squid trapped together in a tank at the fishmonger's outdoor stand, and observes as the 'stronger' kills the 'weaker'. From this natural event – an event framed by the artificial tank in which the two organisms are rather unnaturally enclosed – the boy is supposed to learn the immorality of nature. '"How is life organized?" Things lived on each other – that was it' (p. 5). In the young man's mind, slavery and the disputes surrounding it are but another example of this universal principle, and it would seem that Dreiser, his narrator – or both – endorse the lesson, fully identifying with a hero whose sole motto is 'I satisfy myself.' I shall follow this standard reading of the novel for a moment, but we will soon see that things are not so simple.[10]

A few pages later, Dreiser's narrator informs us that nature pushes the young Cowperwood in the direction of finance. 'He was a financier by instinct, and all the knowledge that pertained to that great art was as natural to him as the emotions and subtleties of life are to a poet' (p. 8). To Cowperwood's instinctual financial proclivity there corresponds an essential object of desire: the 'medium

of exchange, *gold*, interested him intensely' (p. 5). Even the young
man's very physical being is marked by his naturally given com-
merical leanings: 'Nature had destined him to be about five feet ten
inches tall. His head was large, shapely, notably commercial in
aspect, thickly covered with crisp, dark-brown hair and fixed on a
pair of square shoulders and a stocky body' (p. 25). Such are the
naturalistic proclamations and commentaries of Dreiser's narrator,
who in telling the stories of his characters' lives, purports to explain
them in precisely the same terms that he would use to explain the
curious doings of this or that specimen in an aquarium.[11] Cowperwood's eyes are inscrutable and deceitful? So are the lobster's.
Cowperwood is cunning and treacherous in dealing with his adver-
saries? So are all animals capable of mimicry. Cowperwood is
ruthless? So is the 'lovely Drosera (Sundew) using its crimson calyx
for a smothering-pit in which to seal and devour the victim of its
beauty' (p. 501). Does the creature strive consistently after some
type of object? Then it must be a matter of instinct, an innate
yearning, the compulsion of natural appetite or inborn desire.

Financial success is not the only object of Cowperwood's 'instinctual' drives, for the novel in fact plots the course of his acquisitive
strivings across three different domains: commerce, eros, and art.
As the theme of the 'financier as artist' is central to the book, it is
particularly worthy of attention, and I will begin the analysis with
it. We are told early in the book that Frank 'had come instinctively
into sound notions of what was artistic and refined' (p. 59). Does
the human organism come equipped, then, with a set of aesthetic
criteria, or an inbuilt need to satisfy some artistic instinct? It would
seem so, and the narrator comments at one point that 'One of his
earliest and most genuine leanings was toward paintings' (p. 64).

Let us examine the case of the text's depiction of Cowperwood's
instinctual artistic tastes more carefully. At one point in the narrative, we learn that Cowperwood, who has begun 'to take a keen
interest in objects of art' purchases a sculpture by the Danish
sculptor Albert Thorvaldsen depicting the head of David (p. 107).
How is it, then, that he chooses this particular object? Following
the naturalistic model of agency advocated by many of the narrator's explicit comments, Cowperwood would have an instinctual
desire, not for Thorvaldsen's sculptures, which is clearly impossible, but for aesthetically pleasing objects, or that subset of them
capable of satisfying his innate 'notions of what was artistic and

refined'. But this is not what happens in the story at all, and the narrative's presentation of the events leading up to the purchase of the sculpture by Thorvaldsen flatly contradicts the narrator's theoretical proclamations. I shall document this point in some detail, not only because it is interesting to contradict Dreiser's own reductive statements about his characters, but because a reading of the passage may yield some important insights about models of motivation.

How does Cowperwood come to choose a Thorvaldsen? Cowperwood, we are told, has early on in life 'come instinctively into sound notions of what was artistic and refined'. Yet the rest of the paragraph in which this phrase figures tells us something quite significant about the process of young Frank's aesthetic education:

He had seen so many homes that were more distinguished and harmonious than his own. One could not walk or drive about Philadelphia without seeing and being impressed with the general tendency toward a more cultivated and selective social life . . . In the homes of the Tighes, the Leighs, Arthur Rivers, and others, he had noticed art objects of some distinction – bronzes, marbles, hangings, pictures, clocks, rugs. (p. 59)

Here we have encountered a characteristic moment in Dreiser's fictions, a moment which, oddly enough, is as typical of him as are his spurious references to chemisms and tropisms. The moment in question here is an essential social and developmental scenario in which an impressionable individual contemplates a scene in which the symbols of social distinction and value are on display, thereby learning what the society's most successful and prestigious individuals deem to be worthy of pursuit. Thus the young and impressionable Caroline Meeber observes the spectacle of wealth and distinction in Chicago, first while wandering through its department stores, then on buggy rides through the wealthy districts in the company of Mrs Hale, whose 'extended harangues upon the subjects of wealth and position taught her to distinguish between degrees of wealth' (p. 115). Similarly, the young Clyde Griffiths's self-concept and ambitions are fashioned by his envious vision of the wealthy dandies of Kansas City, whose costumes represent to him 'the last word in all true distinction, beauty, gallantry, and bliss' (pp. 19, 29).

The same emphasis on social learning is prevalent throughout Dreiser's depiction of Frank Cowperwood's artistic development in the business novel. Cowperwood, we learn as we move forward in the narrative of his aesthetic development, happens to have met a young architect named Ellsworth, with whom he discusses art. When Cowperwood decides to have his home redecorated, it is Ellsworth who is commissioned to do the job (p. 60). Five chapters later, Cowperwood has made quite a lot of money and has a new home and office constructed, on which occasion he again calls on Ellsworth's services:

It was an enlightening and agreeable experience – one which made for artistic and intellectual growth – to hear Ellsworth explain at length the styles and types of architecture and furniture, the nature of woods and ornaments employed, the qualities and peculiarities of hangings, draperies, furniture panels, and floor coverings. Ellsworth was a student of decoration as well as of architecture, and interested in the artistic taste of the American people, which he fancied would some day have a splendid outcome. He was wearied to death of the prevalent Romanesque composite combinations of country and suburban villa. The time was ripe for something new . . .
Ellsworth showed Cowperwood books of designs containing furniture, hangings, étagères, cabinets, pedestals, and some exquisite piano forms. He discussed woods with him – rosewood, mahogany, walnut English oak, bird's-eye maple . . . Ellsworth advised a triangular piano – the square shapes were so inexpressibly wearisome to the initiated. (pp. 106–7)

Lacking knowledge in the business of decorating his home, and in fact lacking any innate or acquired set of criteria or inclinations to follow in making the multiple choices involved in furnishing a sufficiently distinguished mansion, the financier evidently requires the services of an aesthetic model. That model is Ellsworth, a figure whose guiding motif is the importance of asserting one's difference and distinction in matters of taste. Thus he proclaims the current stylistic tendencies to be sadly lacking, at times even 'atrocious'. In his snobbery, he elevates European standards of taste above the local customs: although American art may one day have a splendid outcome, he thinks, it must be recognized as being presently inferior to European trends. The Americans no doubt believe that their square-shaped pianos are pleasing to the eye, but the truth of the matter is that such things are wearisome to the initiated, inexpressibly so. How can people bear to go on living in these Romanesque composite combinations? The impact of these words on Cowperwood? The narrator who has informed us, a few pages earlier, that this man has a sense of good taste – an inbred taste grounded in nothing less than his instinctual nature – makes the following succinct comment: 'Cowperwood listened fascinated' (p. 107). Swayed by his aesthetic adviser's words, Cowperwood begins to imagine his distinguished new home and is filled with joy. The narrator pursues: 'It was now that he began to take a keen interest in objects of art, pictures, bronzes, little carvings and figurines, for his cabinets, pedestals, tables, and étagères' – a repetition of the very liturgy of desirable decorative objects which two paragraphs earlier figured in the books that Ellsworth showed to Cowperwood. (We are reminded of another list of commodities of distinction, the enumeration of Clyde Griffiths's objects of desire: 'a better collar, a nicer shirt, finer shoes, a good suit, a swell overcoat like some boys had! Oh, the fine clothes, the handsome homes, the watches, rings, pins that some boys sported' (p. 19).)

The point – not the naturalistic point proclaimed by the theoretical asides of the narrator, but the point implicit in this narrative's juxtaposition of the events in the character's life – is that the objects of Cowperwood's desires, the goals of his 'instinctual' strivings, are not part of his inherited nature, but are read out of a book that is held up to him by someone else, the man who serves as his artistic adviser and model. Cowperwood's aesthetic judgements, then, are the product of social learning, a learning that occurs in the context of a relationship of 'fascination'. Nor is the lesson learned in one reading, for Cowperwood's aesthetic education is a process of trial and error in which the student's errors must be corrected. Cowperwood's 'keen interest' in art leads him to acquire works by two American sculptors, Powers and Hosmer, whose works, we are told, were then famous (Cowperwood has in this instance been following not the model of Ellsworth, but a more diffuse model, namely, what Cowperwood has gleaned about the general public's designation of what is 'famous'). Yet here Ellsworth, who understands the importance of distinction and difference in these affairs, intervenes: 'Ellsworth told him that they were not the last word in sculpture and that he should look into the merits of the ancients. He finally secured a head of David, by Thorvaldsen, which delighted him, and some landscapes by Hunt, Sully, and Hart, which seemed somewhat in the spirit of his new world' (p. 107).

Now we are in a position to propose an answer to the question of the nature of Cowperwood's motivation in choosing the marble by Thorvaldsen: the selection is guided by a very general desire, acquired early in youth, to have those objects and dwellings generally perceived as symbolizing social distinction – the 'cultivated and selective' social sphere. The choice of purchase is guided, moreover, by Cowperwood's belief that Ellsworth possesses the knowledge and ability that he personally lacks, namely, the capacity for judging which styles and objects presently embody this distinction – which ones, for example, are neither wearisome nor ordinary to 'the initiated'. And finally, because he has not yet become a good enough pupil to be able to extrapolate on the basis of the teacher's model, Cowperwood is in this instance following his model's explicit advice: 'look into the merits of the ancients' (for the ancients are, quite paradoxically, said to be the 'last word' on sculpture). The text does not tell us whether Ellsworth approves of the disciple's manner of carrying out the exhortation, but Cowperwood is satisfied that Thorvaldsen's imitation of an imitation of an imitation is quite ancient enough to satisfy his teacher's strictures. In any case, this is the best the financier can do along these lines, given the market conditions in the Philadelphia of the time – 'Philadelphia did not offer much that was distinguished in this realm – certainly not in the open market' (p. 107). Cowperwood is in any case delighted, and even the narrator seems convinced that a good choice has been made.

Dreiser's contradictory narration adjoins to this rather lucid lesson in social learning a totally incompatible passage about how a person's possessions reflect inner character. Suddenly the statue by Thorvaldsen and the rest of the financier's new acquisitions are presented as the expression of his authentic being, an equation (for Dreiser, an 'inevitable equation', it would seem) conveyed by yet another reductive naturalistic image: 'Cut the thread, separate a man from that which is rightfully his own, characteristic of him, and you have a peculiar figure, half success, half failure, much as a spider without its web . . .' (p. 108). A few lines earlier, Cowperwood was a bumbling novice whose art purchases had to be guided closely by an adviser, yet the result of the operation is now presented to us with a spurious natural analogy: Thorvaldsen's sculpture is to Cowperwood what the web is to the spider, an image that is only accurate if we focus on the predatory aspects of the situation. There is, however, nothing specifically natural about Cowperwood's acquisitive desires, nor is there anything natural in his relations to the art objects he purchases following Ellsworth's coun-

sel. The narrator tells us that Cowperwood prefers paintings to
nature, for he 'fancied he could best grasp it [nature] through the
personality of some interpreter' (p. 64); the rest of the story shows
us that Cowperwood's relation to the paintings he purchases is
itself mediated by another personality, or rather, by a string of
them, for as the narrative proceeds, Cowperwood follows the advice
of other aesthetic models.[12]

It may be useful to repeat the foregoing demonstration in relation
to the central domain of Cowperwood's pursuits so as to have a
more complete view of the contrasting models of agency implicit in
Dreiser's *Trilogy of Desire*. I have already cited various passages in
which the narrator tells us that the young Frank was a 'born leader'
and an instinctual financier. Yet the very paragraphs where these
remarks figure go on to compile overwhelming evidence for a rather
different conclusion. More specifically, the narrative documents the
many influences that shape the young Frank's inclinations, thereby
establishing a context that makes his 'instincts' appear in a different light. Frank, we are told, is raised by a father who speaks to
him incessantly about money, the glories of finance, and the
importance of moving upwards in society. A bank clerk, Cowperwood senior is 'neither anti- nor pro-slavery', but he does believe
quite sincerely that 'vast fortunes were to be made out of railroads
if one only had the capital and that curious thing – a magnetic
personality – the ability to win the confidence of others' (p. 2).
Although the naturalist narrative emphasizes the impact of the
spectacle of the lobster and the squid on the young Cowperwood's
thinking, the first chapter concludes with the following words,
suggestive of a more ordinary social process, the kind of intensive
interpersonal modelling involved in the relation between parents
and children: 'From seeing his father count money, he was sure he
would like banking; and Third Street, where his father's office was,
seemed to him the cleanest, most fascinating street in the world' (p.
6). Pleased by his son's interest, the father explains various technical aspects of finance to him, and describes the operations of the
most famous and successful financiers. The young Frank thus
learns how inside information and governmental influence can be
used to manipulate prices and turn a rate of profit that would be
impossible on an open market; he hears of the financial prowess of a
certain Steemberger, whose cleverly conceived plan to acquire a

monopoly on the beef market has enabled him to extract exorbitant prices from buyers throughout the entire Eastern seaboard. As the story unfolds, we see that Cowperwood does not fail to put these childhood lessons into practice.

A visiting uncle is another important model for the budding financier. Uncle Seneca Davis arrives from his plantation in Cuba in the company of his slaves, bearing a collection of Indian curios that cannot fail to fascinate the young boy. The prosperous uncle takes an interest in Frank, and gives him advice about how to be successful in business. Curiously, the text recounts an exchange between them in which it is the uncle, not the narrator, who speaks the language of naturalism. Uncle Seneca: 'Well, what are you interested in?' Frank: 'Money!' Seneca: 'Aha! What's bred in the bone, eh? Get something of that from your father, eh? Well, that's a good trait. And spoken like a man, too! We'll hear more about that later. Nancy, you're breeding a financier here, I think. He talks like one' (p. 12). Uncle Seneca, the slave owner, certainly seems to believe that an interest in money is an inherited trait, bred in the bone. Yet more significant to the progress of Cowperwood's career in the story is a rather different form of inheritance, for Frank's first breakthrough comes when he inherits his uncle's fortune and is in a position to put the advice he has received from him into practice. Later in the work when the mature Frank has to make a crucial business decision, the image of the uncle returns in his mind, suggesting that the uncle's model, as well as his capital, are still factors in this 'born financier's' actions. Whatever Seneca and the novel's narrator may say at times, it is the social transmission of practices, attitudes, and capital, not some form of unspecified genetic influence, that orients Frank's desires as well as the advancement of his career.

For this to be the case, he must be an organism capable of learning, not a mechanism having motivational states that are quite limited in number and fixed in advance by means of some non-intentional and mechanical process of transmission. Cowperwood learns, for example, that railroads and street railways are a highly promising domain for investment and development: this is his overly cautious father's longstanding financial phantasy, and the idea is brought up once more when Cowperwood meets Mr Semple. Frank certainly emulates these models, becoming a financial pioneer in this domain and developing vast holdings in

Philadelphia, Chicago, and finally, London. Along the way to these goals he must acquire a great deal of knowledge about the practices and institutions of the financial world, beginning with his learning of the speculative logic of the stock market, and moving on to his initiation into the corrupt profit-seeking methods employed in what the narrator rather uncharacteristically refers to as 'as evil' a financial system as a city ever endured (p. 94).

For example, Cowperwood engages in an elaborate scheme whereby he makes a small fortune by means of the fictitious buying and selling of city loan certificates, placed at his disposal by a corrupt city treasurer. These operations require that he mobilize his knowledge of a papery world of financial conventions, a world where the apparently autonomous laws of the market are in fact manipulated to the ends of a handful of financial and political insiders. If Cowperwood becomes involved in the scheme proposed to him by the city treasurer Stener, it is not because he is drawn to him by some 'chemisms'. Cowperwood decides to engage in these corrupt practices because he prizes certain values, and not others. And what makes it possible for Cowperwood to begin to realize his financial ambitions by means of this illegal scheme is not his animal mimicry, but the complex knowledge he has learned about the organization of the financial world. The narrator emphasizes this fact in evoking Cowperwood's first meeting with the city treasurer, for while the latter feels overwhelmed by the complexity of the situation his political superiors have placed him in, Cowperwood instantly sees an opportunity:

The abstrusities of the stock exchange were as his A B C's to him. He knew if he could have this loan put in his hands – all of it, if he could have the fact kept dark that he was acting for the city, and that if Stener would allow him to buy as a 'bull' for the sinking-fund while selling judiciously for a rise, he could do wonders even with a big issue . . . Looming up in his mind was a scheme whereby he could make a lot of the unwary specu-lators about 'change go short of this stock or loan under the impression, of course, that it was scattered freely in various persons' hands, and that they could buy as much of it as they wanted. Then they would wake to find that they could not get it; that he had it all. Only he would not risk his secret that far. Not he, oh, no. But he would drive the city loan to par and then sell . . . Wisely enough he sensed that there was politics in all this – shrewder and bigger men above and behind Stener. (pp. 101–2)

The basic idea behind the scheme that Cowperwood engages in is quite simple, and involves a flagrant violation of the neo-classical economic principle of the autonomy of the market. Conducting the 'invisible hand' of the marketplace will be another invisible hand – Cowperwood's – manipulating the prices by means of fictitious buying and selling of the loan certificates. Yet this basic idea is not so simple that it could be successfully implemented by a non-rational agent, and Cowperwood is only able to succeed at it for a while by virtue of a series of remarkable manoeuvres and calculations, a feat of long-term planning that organizes particular actions in an extensive structure of means and ends.

As the previous citation from the novel suggests, the ways of finance are Frank's A B C's, a language, or better, a complex network of practices, that he has learned at an early age. Is this instinct, inheritance? Normally, children's ability to learn the language or languages spoken by the adults around them is a matter of biological inheritance, yet an infant does not inherit in this manner any particular alphabet or phonetic system, which is why the offspring of Swedes could, if raised by people with perfect English, normally learn to speak English like natives. At one point in *Sister Carrie*, Dreiser writes of a man born in America of a Swedish father that 'there was a certain Swedish accent, noticeable in his voice, which he must have inherited' (p. 13), suggesting that either Dreiser had absurd ideas about the transmission of language, or that he sometimes used the word 'inherit' in a non-biological sense.

Yet how are the ways and means of financial manipulation learned? The narrative, we have seen, emphasizes the rôle of social influence and learning. But does this fact entail the inaccuracy of the kind of reductive stance on agency and motivation with which we began our discussion? The naturalist might respond that Cowperwood continues to resemble the grouper fish in all of his dealings, for like the mimetic organism, he merely takes on the colourings of his surroundings so as to suit his own ends. Cowperwood's mimicry is, of course, much more complex and 'plastic' than that of the fish, which presumably has a limited repertory of possible colours, yet it plays essentially the same purely instrumental rôle, and the agent's apparent rationality is but the product of a blind mechanism.

Perhaps this kind of argument is indeed the way to rescue the coherence of Dreiser's naturalist view of social influence. Dreiser was no stranger to the ancient idea that human beings are imitative by nature.[13] His narrators often refer explicitly to the imitative propensities of the characters. For example, imitation is frequently underscored in *An American Tragedy*. Clyde Griffiths is a young man who at an early age senses that the parental model is at odds with the standards of behaviour that he sees all about him in the world, and who sides with the latter. Thus when he gets his first job as a bell boy in a hotel, it is the bell hops and the other people around him – and not his parental models – from whom he gleans his ideas about the 'chief business of life'. Clyde is utterly 'fascinated' by one of his camarades – Doyle – and engages in a jealous and slavish imitation of his dress and manners (p. 50). The bell hops educate him in their pleasures, an influence that is decisive later in Clyde's career, for although he later temporarily manages to imitate some 'soberer people' (p. 169), it is the callous bell hop's attitude towards women that resurfaces at a crucial point. Thus when Clyde is trying to decide what to do about Rita's unwillingness to be seduced, the narrator has him rehearse in his mind the lessons he had received years earlier from another of the bell hops. The basic thrust of these lessons was that he should be less honest, harder, and more selfish in his sexual demands ('And had not Ratterer always told him that in so far as girls were concerned he was more or less of a fool – too easy', p. 295). When Rita has become pregnant and Clyde is desperately looking for a way out, he writes to this same Ratterer, pathetically expecting that his former mentor will have some ready solution to the problem. Yet there is none, and Clyde's subsequent course of action involves yet another form of mimetism: a newspaper article about a boating accident provides the scenario for the murder plot at the centre of the novel.

Perhaps the single most stunning example of Dreiser's emphasis on imitation is a full paragraph in *Sister Carrie* that expounds on the theme. Drouet surprises Carrie engaging in imitative antics before her mirror, and the narrator instructs us that 'She possessed an innate taste for imitation and no small ability' (p. 157). Carrie imitates the gestures, tone of voice, clothing, and manner of walking of the women who in one way or another carry, in her mind, the 'halo' of glamour, the 'ineffable charm [of] the world of material display' (pp. 104–5). She imitates Mrs Hale, who is for a while her mentor in the ways of feminine charm; she imitates the young music student who lives in the same building; later, in New York, she imitates Mrs Vance, whose clothes she envies; and she imitates the characters in the novels she reads and the plays she sees (p. 324).

Is an imitative instinct the key, then, to a viable naturalist model of agency that might be rescued from Dreiser's texts? Yet one must ask to what extent the varieties of imitation evoked by these stories really correspond to a mechanical and a-rational model of mimetism. Do the analogies evoked by Dreiser's naturalistic imagery really hold? Are the human forms of imitation that he describes significantly similar to those of the black grouper fish?

Our response should be obvious, but the reasons supporting it are not. The varieties of imitation in which Dreiser's creatures engage are by no means reducible to animal mimicry – although it would be realistic to assume that they do have some natural basis in an inherited propensity or disposition. The fundamental difference is quite simple: although in the case of the grouper fish and other instances of insect and animal mimicry, an organism does display behaviour resembling features of the environment (including other organisms), and although in some of the more complex cases of this sort of thing, the behaviour may be punctually triggered by a change in the environment – which suggests that there is a fairly complex and effective perceptual linkage of behaviour to the latter – these varieties of 'mimesis' involve no learning, and this in several senses. I shall develop this point a bit, because it is a way to articulate our conception of the ways in which an adequate model of agency diverges from a-rational perspectives on human motivation.

Animal mimicry does not approximate the more developed forms of imitation, first of all, because there is in most cases no learning of new behaviour once the creature's limited behavioural repertory has been developed.[14] Changing its colourings to match certain conditions in the environment is part of the black grouper's basic equipment; it is not learned behaviour. Moreover, this behaviour is not engaged in by the individual grouper fish for any 'reason' or with any goal in view, i.e. it is not caused by the presence of any intentional attitude towards some 'adaptive' or other goal. The fish does not change its colours because it wants to hide, and whatever its motivational states may be, they are not intentionally related to specific goals. Whatever 'goals' we see the organism realizing are implicit in its mechanical motivational structure, one where intentional attitudes play no rôle. As a result, such an organism is two steps removed from complex forms of imitation or 'modelling'. For the first step to be made, motivational states would have to be able to generate instrumental actions requiring the operation of effective intentional attitudes. In this form of imitation, a creature or agent already has some motivational state specifying a goal, and imitation is a matter of copying a behavioural sequence that may serve as a means to that end. For example, an animal wants something to eat and sees another animal successfully engage in some behaviour that gets it food; the first animal, although it has never performed this particular stunt, applies the lesson and engages in the same type of behaviour, winning the reward. Now, this kind of 'instrumental imitation' can go quite far and may lead agents to engage in a wide range of new behaviour, a limit being the complexity of the organism's intentional states and motor skills, which set constraints on its ability to understand, memorize, recall, and re-enact the new types of behaviour it observes. At some point, the chain of means to ends becomes so complex that we may speak of a qualitative break. The second step to a truly complex form of imitation involves precisely this transition from a purely instrumental imitation of means to an imitation of qualitatively different ends, or desires: the imitation of behaviour is no longer simply a way of adding to the repertory of means, and instead leads to the generation of qualitatively different goals, and with them, the search for ways to realize them. In cases of imitation of this variety, there may be no simple resemblance between the behaviour of the model and that of the imitator, for the simple reason that what the latter has really gleaned from the model is not a type of physical gesture or even an abstract schema of ways and means; rather, what the imitator derives from the model is the desire to realize a certain goal, which may be a state of affairs that could be brought about or maintained by various means, including sequences of behaviour that the imitator does not need to copy from the model.[15]

With these points in mind, let us turn now to an example of an imitative sequence in Dreiser's first novel. Drouet points out to Carrie a particularly attractive woman who passes them by in the street:

Fine stepper, wasn't she?'
Carrie looked again and observed the grace commended.

'Yes she is,' she returned cheerfully, a little suggestion of possible defect
in herself awakening in her mind. If that was so fine she must look at it
more closely. Instinctively she felt a desire to imitate it. Surely she could
do that too. (p. 99)

This text explicitly evokes Carrie Meeber's instinctive desire to
imitate. Yet even this schematic and apparently simple description
carries features that simply cannot be accomodated by any reductive, a-rational model of agency. Carrie is walking with her lover,
Drouet, who calls her attention to the passer-by; observing the
woman, Carrie has an 'instinctive' desire to imitate her manner of
walking. What are the essential ingredients in this imitative episode? We may note first of all that although Carrie seems to be a
passive figure in this sequence of events (a 'mirror' and not an
'engine', as Dreiser puts it elsewhere), the narrative in fact implicitly points to the rôle of her attitudes in determining what happens. This point is already suggested by the fact that Carrie does
not have any 'instinctive' desire to imitate anything and everything
around her. Not only are her attention and receptivity necessarily
selective, but her inclination to act in function of what she observes
is also selective.

This point is crucial to the analysis of imitative phenomena:
observation of something does not entail imitation of it, for it is
clear that no conceivable organism could imitate every feature of
the environment that it happened to observe, or even all of the
behaviour that it happened to perceive its fellow creatures engaging
in. Note that in the episode at hand, the narrator has told us that
Carrie had already 'spied' the woman before Drouet spoke, 'though
with scarce so single an eye'. Carrie had observed the woman, but
the observation had had no great implications for her, and certainly
no automatic and 'instinctive' impulse to imitate had been set in
motion. In short, for a basic sequence of imitation to be engaged,
observation of some other being's actions must be followed by a
certain kind of motivational process (and unless the imitation is
instantaneous, the observation of the behaviour must in some way
be remembered by the potential imitator). In other words, we must
ask why Carrie does not observe the graceful walk of this other
woman in the manner that she might observe thousands of other
things in the world, that is, without the observation having any
practical consequences for her.

The crucial factor is Carrie's reaction, not to the woman taken

separately, but to Drouet's comment about her, and to the woman
as the object of Drouet's comment. The narrative expresses this in
the remark that Carrie's attention is drawn to 'the grace commended' and not simply to the 'grace' on its own. Yet what is the
significance for Carrie of this grace commended? A sketch of an
answer to this question is implicit in the narrative, for although
Carrie maintains an external show of cheerfulness, she thinks that
Drouet's recommendation of the other woman may imply a possible 'defect' in herself, and the narrator's claim about her 'instinctive desire to imitate' is in fact immediately preceded and followed
by clauses that attribute bits of reasoning to Carrie: 'if that was so
fine she must look at it more closely . . . Surely she could do that
too. When one of her mind sees many things emphasized and re-
emphasized and admired, she gathers the logic of it and applies it
accordingly.' These phrases destroy any possibility that this narrative could consistently advocate a purely mechanical model of
imitation, for it is clear that Carrie's intentional attitudes and
reasoning are indispensable parts of the episode: having been confronted with the proposition that a particular bit of behaviour is to
be valued, she concludes that it must be observed more carefully;
she asks herself whether it figures among the realm of her possible
actions, determines that this is indeed the case, and moreover,
manages to extract the very 'logic' of the evaluative statements,
extracting from the various particular instances those kinds of traits
to which Drouet's recommendations invariably refer. No passive
'mirror' could ever achieve such a feat. Rather, only complex intentional attitudes of perception, belief, and inferential reasoning
could make such a process of learning possible, for we must recognize that it is a matter of learning here, even if we go on to add that
what is being learned are stereotypical and reprehensible forms of
gender-specific behaviour, and more precisely, a certain masculine
image of the erotic feminine ideal. (The narrative has already
informed us what lurks in Drouet's conception of the 'fine stepper':
the 'grace and sinuosity' with which women swayed their bodies.
'A dainty, self-conscious swaying of the hips by a woman', everything that is 'alluring' to the eye of the male (p. 99). Such is what
the *ingénue* from the country has not yet learned.)

Yet what motivates Carrie's apprenticeship of these things? That
she has the intelligence and skill necessary to the learning of such
behaviour is not sufficient to explain why she should engage in it,

and the motivational dimensions of her imitation must be filled in. Once more the idea of an instinctive and a-rational desire is totally misleading, not only in regard to the way human action may plausibly be assumed to work, but also in relation to the contrary tendencies that are implicit in Dreiser's narrative. There is no imitative behaviour without a desire (or other motivational state or 'pro attitude') to imitate. Yet what gives rise to such a desire? Is it an inexplicable and mechanical event that occurs in the agent, without itself bearing any of the features that may be associated with intentional action or agency proper? Is Carrie's desire to learn to sway her hips like the other woman supposed to be an event on the order of our suddenly experiencing hunger when breakfast is long overdue?[16]

In relation to these questions, we see once more how the story that is told by Dreiser's text is far more informative than the brief intrusions of the narrator. The latter tells us that some form of blind, feminine instinct is what generates Carrie's urges, whereas the former evokes a complex tissue of experiences of personal and social relations that shape and orient Carrie's condition. Her motivations can only be understood properly in the latter context. We must recall, then, that Carrie has left her familial home to venture a life in Chicago, her long-term intention being to exchange the life and manners of the country for those of the city. Once there, she is confronted by the dreary and suffocating world of her sister's home, and by the even more dreary and exhausting world of the factory where she finally manages to secure her first job. The text insists repeatedly on this fact. Nowhere here does she find examples of the kind of experience she hoped to encounter in the city. When she falls ill and loses her factory job, she is confronted with the prospect of returning home as a failure. Such is the context in which she allows Drouet, whose manner is sympathetic and supportive, to give her money and set her up in a flat of her own. In Carrie's perspective at the time, Drouet's seductive manner contrasts quite favourably to the brutal sexual aggressivity that Carrie has encountered everywhere during her search for employment and on the job. At the moment when the imitative episode occurs, being kept by Drouet is, in Carrie's mind, her sole alternative to returning to the harassments and exhaustion of factory work at subsistence pay. It is in such a context that on their first walk together, Drouet's praise of the other woman's manner of walking is of direct pertinence to Carrie's most basic interests and long-term projects. Yet the remark is also of pertinence to a less immediate interest of Carrie's, which the narrative has also stressed: Carrie has a strong interest in all matters connected to feminine models of grace and beauty, for her self-evaluation is at present conducted largely in such terms, and it is in such terms that Drouet's remark points to what she herself would consider to be a real 'defect', quite independently of Drouet's opinion. Thus her motivation in attending carefully to Drouet's recommendation is dual. On the one hand she has reasons for desiring to please him, hence a reason for taking note of whatever it is that he praises in other women; Carrie can very well anticipate that if she does not fashion herself in the image that Drouet recommends, she risks being compared unfavourably by him with other women. And so she takes an interest in the *commended* grace of the other woman. On the other hand, she has an interest in her own self-image, a reflexive image that is formed in part by her conception of how she stands in relation to other women, a standing that is conceived of by her in the limited terms of dress, demeanour, beauty, and everything that goes into the making of what the text refers to as 'glamour'. Thus she takes an interest in the commended *grace* of the other woman, which she takes to be real, and which she would like to acquire, not because of any immediate or long-term goal involving her relation to Drouet, but as a positive feature to be added to her own self-concept.

Thus the recipe for even this simple episode of imitation is quite complex, for if it involves a measure of basic necessity, it also requires an elaborate preparation of beliefs, desires, beliefs about beliefs and desires, long-term aims, and so on. The latter ingredients are anything but natural and basic, for they concern abstract inter-personal relations and social comparisons as well as the dynamics of a reflexive self-image that is formed in terms of others' potential evaluation of self. Drouet, then, serves as a personal mediator for Carrie, for her understanding of his values and desires plays an active rôle in the generation of those wants and ends that are most central to her self-image. Carrie, it is true, wants very much to avoid returning to her former poverty, and these wants are grounded in the most basic and natural appetites (as these emerge within a particular social setting). But she wants even more powerfully to become the kind of woman that Drouet most admires, and that is in no way the product of any basic natural appetite. Rather, these desires involve an ideal, one that is explicitly identified only a page later in the narrative. Drouet takes Carrie for a drive past the mansions of millionaires, and they glimpse a girl of her age:

Drouet was all eyes. There was the woman for him. What a thing to sit up with such a girl as that . . . Carrie felt this, though he said very little. She envied the stiff, dressy slip of a girl. She even saw what was uncomplimentary to Drouet, the distinction of the youth who went along with her. So that was what it was to be rich . . . Carrie looked and well remembered. She owed her keen impression as much to Drouet's unspoken feelings as to the appearance of the objects themselves. She was being branded like wax by a scene which only made poor clothes, worn shoes, shop application and poverty in general seem more dire, more degraded, more and more impossible. How would she not like to have something like this – what would she not do to avoid the other. (p. 101)

We have returned to the recurrent scene that, in Dreiser's fictions, has the status of a kind of generative matrix of his protagonists' desires. Its elements are simple, if the implications are not: the hero contemplates a display of material wealth and then desires to have these things and live in such surroundings. Yet why are these the objects coveted by Dreiser's desirers? Surprisingly, Dreiser answers this question in no uncertain terms: these objects are not desired for themselves, for the material comfort they might offer or for whatever other basic, instrumental function these artefacts could have. Some people may desire such objects this way, but Dreiser's exemplary desirers do not. Instead, they desire these objects not for themselves, but for what they represent, for their status as the symbols of wealth. And why do they desire this thing, or rather, this non-thing, which is wealth? In *The Financier*, Dreiser answers this question in terms that are totally at odds with the text's naturalistic moments: the true financier, he asserts, wants wealth because of his knowledge that wealth is what 'releases the sources of social action'. He wants it, not 'for what it will buy in the way of simple comforts', but for what 'it will control – for what it will represent in the way of dignity, force, power' (p. 205). Such are the 'ultimate' objects of the financier's desires as Dreiser portrays him, and we must conclude that in making a certain position within a type of social relation the agent's ultimate goal, as well as the matrix in which these desires are generated, this text takes us far from the small and murky pond where naturalism finds its exemplary specimens.

What does our reading of Dreiser's narratives tell us about models of human agency and motivation? Although Dreiser's narrators at times explictly espouse models of agency in which human behaviour is supposedly explained in terms of simple, a-rational motivational processes, many other highly plausible details in the stories imply the validity of quite a different model, namely, one in which intentional action, motivated by complex relations between attitudes of desire and belief, plays a determinant rôle in the generation of effective motivational states.

A figure such as Cowperwood genuinely desires the expensive art objects that he selects and purchases. Yet the processes by means of which such desires are generated have little to do with a mechanical or semi-mechanical model of motivation. Beliefs − not only about the intrinsic properties of the object and its general cultural significance, but also about what others are likely to believe about it − play a determinant rôle in the story. Cowperwood desires these art objects as a means to other ends − social prestige, distinction, recognition − yet the choice of which means will effectively serve these ends requires him to engage in a complex form of practical reasoning, for he must decide which means is in fact likely to realize the desired goal. He makes his decision by weighing the information that is available to him. Thus, when he decides that he wants to furnish his new home in a distinguished and lavish manner, he must inform himself as to which purchases should be made, and relies on Ellsworth to that end. When he gathers from Ellsworth that the 'ancients' are 'the last word' in sculpture, Cowperwood carries this rough heuristic to the market and applies it in choosing the sculpture by Thorvaldsen. Thus we have returned full circle to the basic schema of practical rationality: given a desire for q (distinctive and pleasing decorations of the home), and a belief that p (the purchase of Thorvaldsen) is a good means to q, it is rational to decide to do p. Rationality, then, at least in this rather minimal and schematic sense, plays a rôle in the formation of Cowperwood's desire.

Dreiser's novels about Cowperwood form what he called *The Trilogy of Desire*, and in spite of the text's reductive moments and rather irrational contradictions, what they have to say about desire is quite instructive. Our reading of aspects of Dreiser's texts suggest the hypothesis that in an adequate model of human agency, emphasis must be laid on the rôle of belief and other attitudes in the generation, not only of effective intentions to act, but of desires themselves. Desire may be the necessary 'starter', but it is not itself a primitive or given fact: it is not to be conceived of as a limited set of irresistible primitive states or urges that are the output of some opaque internal system, isolated from cognition. Instead, desires may be learned, and need not have any direct association with some more primitive or natural need or want. Cowperwood's desire for the kind of symbols of social distinction he had observed in his youth is not presented as the means to some basic instinctual need or end.

In describing objects of desire, it is important to be aware that they are only 'objects' in the most abstract philosophical sense; no one simply 'desires a physical object', rather, one desires to have this object stand in a certain relation to oneself. For example, even when the object of desire really does centre upon a physical object, what is desired is more accurately described as a situation or a course of events, such as the following: 'Here and now, I possess this sculpture by Thorvaldsen, which means that no one else stands in this same exclusive relation to it.' Or again, agents desire to realize some course of events in which the physical object figures as an essential prop (for example, 'I enjoy the pleasure of eating this apple'). When other agents are what figure at the centre of someone's desire, the 'object' of desire is most typically a situation or course of events involving attitudes and sequences of action. Not: 'I desire Albertine.' Instead: 'I desire that Albertine have such and such attitude towards me, and I desire that she cease having such and such other attitudes; I desire that she engage in certain actions, and cease engaging in others – and this of her own accord.'

How are the objects of desire to be described? As a very general strategy, we may assume that what desire 'intends' or 'aims at' may be defined as a 'situation' or 'type of situation', individuated from the agent's perspective and in that agent's context. This 'object' of desire is not to be confused with whatever may happen to satisfy or otherwise extinguish the desire; rather, it is defined in terms of the agent's perspective on what would realize the desire as it is desired by her. In this respect, desire shares the 'opacity' characteristic of attitudes of belief, so that in defining its object, we cannot simply substitute in any logically equivalent expression.[17] Oedipus desires Jocasta, and Jocasta is his mother, but it is illegitimate to conclude on this basis that Oedipus desires his mother, at least as long as he does not know that Jocasta is his mother. Yet this point about the opacity of desire does not warrant us to conclude that objects of desire are all purely imaginary and phantasmatic, and that an adequate description of them may be had by ignoring their possible relations to real states of affairs. In fact, an adequate general theory of the individuation of the contents of states of desire and belief remains to be formulated.

The foregoing analyses have put us in the position to delineate some significantly different models of agency, listed in order of an increasing emphasis on the rôle of complex intentional attitudes in motivational processes. These descriptions are meant to evoke types of positions; important variations could be developed by filling in the details, such as the list of basic needs:

(a) Purely mechanical, unconscious motivation. The motivational mechanism involves no intentional attitudes and is unknowable to the agent. The mechanism generates a basic repertory of behaviour having the implicit goal of satisfying a limited set of inherited needs. States of awareness or belief, if they exist, are epiphenomenal. For example, the depletion of some substance within the organism's body triggers a drive for its repletion, and the corresponding behaviour is automatically engaged, without conscious intention or volition.

(b) Semi-mechanical, unconscious motivation. The motivational mechanism involves intentional attitudes, such as a fairly complex perceptual registering of selected features of the environment, but the motivational process remains largely unconscious and unknowable to the agent. The mechanism generates unconscious intentional states of need or desire, capable of being satisfied only by a limited set of courses of events that it is the implicit goal of a basic behavioural repertory to realize. These desires unconsciously motivate instances of behaviour drawn from a limited repertory, itself defined by the goal of realizing these courses of events. Attitudes of belief and awareness, if there are any, remain epiphenomenal.

(c) Semi-mechanical, partly conscious motivation of unintentional behaviour. The motivational system involves intentional attitudes, all of which may in principle be known to (or consciously experienced by) the agent. This motivational system generates conscious and unconscious intentional states of need or desire, capable of being satisfied only by a limited set of courses of events. These desires consciously or unconsciously motivate instances of unintentional behaviour drawn from a limited repertory, itself defined by the goal of realizing these courses of events. Conscious attitudes are still epiphenomenal.

(d) Semi-mechanical, partly conscious motivation of unintentional behaviour as well as of instances of intentional action. The motivational system involves intentional attitudes, all of which may in principle be known to the agent. The system generates conscious and unconscious intentional states of need or desire, capable of being satisfied by only a limited set of courses of events. These desires consciously or unconsciously motivate instances of intentional action or unintentional behaviour drawn from a limited repertory, itself defined by the goal of realizing these courses of events. In other words, the determination of behaviour by desire sometimes is mediated through conscious attitudes of belief and present-directed intention, but the latter do not effectively change the behavioural repertory, and are essentially overdetermined and subjected to the basic motivational system. Thus conscious attitudes are not strictly speaking epiphenomenal, but they are causally overdetermined by another system.

(e) Motivational system with partial intentional generation of behaviour. The same as (d), except that the repertory of intentional behaviour that sometimes serves as means to the realization of the desires is less limited, and admits of learning of new means to the same inherited set of ends. Intentional attitudes, then, have a more extensive causal rôle in directing behaviour, but its ends are still determined by the basic motivational system. In so far as there are instances of an intentional choice from a set of means to a given basic end, there is a minimal sort of rationality in this model of agency, and conscious, present-directed intention does have the rôle of controlling action.

(f) Intentionality conflictually subordinated to the semi-intentional motivational system. The same as (e), except that the agent's intentional attitudes of belief and intention can generate new motivational states defined by qualitatively different ends (that is, desires the realization of which would require different courses of events from those specified previously). However, the previous, basic motivational mechanism with its limited set of ends has a great deal of priority within the organism's overall control structure, so the agent experiences tension and conflict between incompatible ends. Yet in such cases of conflict between basic needs and other ends, the former almost always (or usually) prevail. Sometimes they do so by virtue of the direct influence that basic motivational states can have on cognition, generating or distorting belief (and with it intention).

(g) Intentional agency with significant autonomy of intentional generation of desire. Similar to (f), yet the basic motivational states and its limited needs have no absolute priority; other intentional states, such as belief, allow for learning and the generation of new motivational states having qualitatively different ends. In cases of conflict between basic needs and these new ends, the former need not prevail in the emergent choice, providing that a basic level of satisfaction of primary needs is maintained. Moreover, the agent's intentions to act are not all rigidly present-directed, and the agent becomes capable of long-term planning based on future-directed intention and extended deliberation (with reflective as well as non-reflective reconsideration and non-reconsideration of previously formed intentions).

By referring to this spectrum of models, we may identify and evaluate some of the assertions that naturalist and other discourses make about the status of human agency. As the preceding discussion has shown in some detail, Dreiser's narrators frequently claim to describe a world where human agents are creatures whose essential features are captured by models situated near the beginning of our spectrum. Yet the narratives themselves, even when they explicitly speak of the characters as beings guided by an 'instinct' for imitation, in fact ascribe to them capacities for rational choice and planning that correspond to the features of models situated at the end of our spectrum.[18] In so far as Cowperwood engages in a choice between different actions that he considers to be candidates for satisfying one of his desires, it must at the very least be a matter of model (f). Yet the long-term planning that he undertakes in relation to his financial speculations requires him to exercize the kinds of capacities associated with (g). Although this finding in relation to Dreiser's narratives certainly does not warrant us to draw any direct conclusions about the nature of human agency in the real world, I think it does have the value of suggesting that it is highly unlikely that any mechanical model of agency, which cannot even be consistently adopted in the stories of naturalist fiction, could stand as a promising hypothesis for the human sciences. Stated more positively, our conclusion is that the hypothesis to be preferred is one which assumes the correctness of some basic schemata of practical rationality and intentional explanation. Moreover, the intuitions yielded by my reading of the narratives suggest that in building hypotheses about intentional explanations, we should eschew mechanical and naturalistic theories of motivation, granting instead a large rôle to the learning of ever more complex attitudes and structures of desire.

CHAPTER 4

Agent's rationality

Theodore Dreiser's novel, *Sister Carrie* (first published in 1900), offers a valuable occasion for reflecting on models of rationality and irrationality, particularly by virtue of its complex depiction of a character named Hurstwood.[1] Of particular interest is the narration of the episode relating this figure's robbery and flight to Montreal, and it is aspects of this episode that figure at the centre of my selective analysis of the text in this chapter. As I have stated above, my aim in turning to this and other literary texts in the present study is to explore issues in the theory of rationality, not to contribute to a hermeneutic understanding of an artist's life and works, or to an aesthetical evaluation of literary documents. My oriented and selective discussion of aspects of the text, then, will be followed by an assessment of some of its implications for contemporary hypotheses about rationality.

I shall begin with a discussion of a passage that is justly famous for its enigmatic and thought-provoking depiction of the breakdown of intentional control. Hurstwood, it may be recalled, is the middle-aged manager of a bar catering to a middle- and upper-middle-class clientele. The narrator has introduced him to us as 'an interesting character after his kind', adding that Hurstwood is 'shrewd and clever in many little things'. He has risen to his managerial position 'by perseverance and industry, through long years of service' (p. 43). Always fastidious in his dress, Hurstwood enjoys extending affable greetings to the establishment's distinguished customers. His home life is a stale and conventional arrangement, and at the moment in the narrative when the episode to be discussed takes place, he has become enamoured of Carrie, the mistress of an acquaintance. He has declared his love to Carrie, omitting to tell her about his marriage, and she has agreed to run away with him on the condition that he marry her. Having learned

about the affair, Mrs Hurstwood has become furious and has
locked him out of his own house; moreover, Hurstwood has
received threatening notes from his wife, followed by two letters
from her lawyers, demanding that he pay his angry spouse quite a
lot of money. He reckons that he stands to lose all of their $40,000
worth of savings to her. This crisis is aggravated by the fact that
Carrie has meanwhile learned of Hurstwood's marriage, and does
not come to the rendezvous they had agreed on. Hurstwood guesses
that she has found out and is made even more desperate by this
realization. Alone in a hotel room and at the bar, Hurstwood
cannot decide what to do. As the narrator comments, Hurstwood is
at this point 'altogether a fine example of great mental perturba-
tion' (p. 238). He sends his wife the first sum of money she has
demanded, but cannot make up his mind to meet with her lawyers.

Such is the general context when we find Hurstwood in his office,
about to close up for the evening (p. 266). Routinely checking the
safe, he is surprised to discover that his subaltern, Mayhew, has left
it unlocked. Suddenly Hurstwood has an unexpected problem to
solve, for he must now contemplate a course of action that was
previously never available to him. He examines the safe's contents
and discovers that it contains over $10,000. Tempted, he hovers
before the open safe, and a singular process of deliberation begins:
'The manager flounder[s] among a jumble of thoughts' (p. 268), as
the 'clock of thought ticks out its wish and its denial' (p. 269).

Hurstwood, we are told, would normally have known better:
'The manager was no fool, to be led blindly away by such an errant
proposition as this, but his situation was peculiar' (p. 268). The
narrator emphasizes the fact that Hurstwood has been drinking:
'Wine was in his veins. It had crept up into his head and given him
a warm view of the situation. It also colored the possibilities of the
ten thousand for him' (p. 268). Moreover, the opportunity to steal
the money arrives at a seemingly propitious moment, for he has
already been nourishing the plan of running away with Carrie and
has to face the unpleasant prospect of a costly divorce: 'He was
drawn by such a keen desire for Carrie, driven by such a state of
turmoil in his own affairs, that he thought constantly that it would
be best, and yet he wavered' (p. 270). He oscillates constantly; he
nervously takes the money out of the safe for a while, and then puts
it back in: 'He could not bring himself to act definitely' (p. 279). As
he puts the money in and out of the safe, his feelings shift between

fear and desire. He is fascinated by the sight of the money, by its ready availability, and physical presence: 'There was something fascinating about the soft green stack – the loose silver and gold. He felt sure now that he could not leave that' (p. 271). Here Hurstwood's calculations are vitiated by what cognitive psychologists have referred to as the 'availability heuristic'.[2] The agent's evaluation of the respective utilities of a number of options is coloured by the phenomenological proximity of one of them. Hurstwood seems at this point to have reached a decision: 'He would do it. He would lock the safe before he had time to change his mind.' Yet he hestitates still. 'He pushed the door to for somewhere near the sixth time. He wavered, thinking, putting his hand to his brow.' At this point the narrative reads:

While the money was in his hand, the lock clicked. It had sprung. Did he do it? He grabbed at the knob and pulled vigorously. It had closed. Heavens! He was in for it now, sure enough.

The moment he realized that the safe was locked for a surety, the sweat burst out upon his brow and he trembled. He looked about him and decided instantly. There was no delaying now.

'Supposing I do lay it on the top,' he said, 'and go away. They'll know who took it. I'm the last to close up. Besides, other things will happen.'

At once he became the man of action. (p. 271)

This text's description of Hurstwood's behaviour is a complex combination of intentional and non-intentional elements.[3] External circumstances have conspired in an unusual manner to place Hurstwood in an unfamiliar and tempting situation. The safe has been left unlocked, the narrator explains, because the employee Mayhew was distracted by other thoughts; that certain 'notabilities' had visited the establishment has led to Hurstwood's drinking with them and becoming intoxicated; that his wife has learned of Hurstwood's interest in Carrie, and has been threatening him with a lawsuit enhances his desire to escape. Hurstwood, then, has been cast into a situation which is not the product of any single, explicit choice on his part, and its unusual nature helps to make it a terrible challenge.

The deliberative process is quite long and involves a basic conflict between several factors. Among these are a desire for the money and Carrie; a fear of the consequences of theft – 'the scandal ... the terror of being a fugitive from justice' (p. 270); and a desire to avoid the conflict with his wife. Hurstwood is not restrained by

any belief that the theft would be wrong or evil: 'The true ethics of
the situation never once occurred to him', comments the narrator
(p. 270). Yet this inconclusive deliberative process comes to an
abrupt conclusion when the lock clicks. 'Did he do it?' At this
crucial point, the text gives us a question, not a description: Hurstwood himself does not seem to know whether he was the author of
an intentional action, or whether the gesture was automatic, an
'accident'. Yet in the context in which it occurs, even this automatic or accidental motion of the hand is somehow coloured in
Hurstwood's mind with the intention to steal. He had formulated
this intention, and had even acted in relation to it in so far as he
had taken the money out of the safe and begun to plan his flight; yet
he had also continued to deliberate over the wisdom of the entire
scheme and was thinking of putting the money back. Moreover, he
has even formulated an intention about acting so as to prevent
himself from going back on this momentary intention: 'He would
do it. He would lock the safe before he had time to change his
mind.' Once the door of the safe is locked, the fact that the money is
in Hurstwood's hand, not in the closed safe where it belongs, seems
to stand as tangible proof of his criminal intent. Oddly, Hurstwood
'becomes' the man of action after the deed is done, and this in spite
of the fact that 'he could not bring himself to act definitely'.
Immediately afterwards, he breathes to himself, as if in response to
the question of whether he had done it: 'I wish I hadn't done that.
By the Lord, that was a mistake' (p. 271).

In the passage in question, Hurstwood's desires, beliefs, and
intentions are crucial elements in shaping what happens. Yet they
are not presented as the necessary and sufficient terms of a practical syllogism. Hurstwood's deliberation does not lead to the formation of an intention that then becomes effective when it is executed
in the form of an intentional action. At every point when Hurstwood's deliberation seems to move in the direction of a conclusive
decision, contrasting inclinations go to work to upset his resolve.
Momentarily, Hurstwood does effectively decide to take the money
out of the safe and put it in his bag; but momentarily he also
decides to put the money back. He is comfortable with these decisions only as long as he does not believe them irrevocable. A final,
definitive choice is absent in the text, having been replaced by a
passive construction describing the operations of an impersonal
mechanism: 'It had sprung.' Unintentional behaviour, influenced

by intoxication and excitement, has vitiated conscious intention. The conflict between the desire to be rid of his wife, have the money and Carrie, on the one hand, and the desire not to live in terror, a fugitive from justice, on the other, is not resolved by an effective intention, and hence it is inappropriate to speak of an intentional action in this instance. Hurstwood locks the safe unwittingly, for at the moment when the lock clicks, he was only aware of 'pushing the door to', and is still 'wavering' and 'thinking'.

Here we have an example of an agent's doing something that is situated at the very borderline between behaviour and action. In other words, it is a matter of a doing which, although undeniably human, resists intentional characterization, while also failing to belong entirely to the level of purely physical causation and organic processes devoid of intentional meaning. This is the intriguing boundary where our basic rationality heuristic falters, but does not fully give way. Although non-intentional behaviour vitiates the practical syllogism of deliberate intentional action, the accidental gesture's meaning is inflected by the reasons and conflicts that surround it.

In the case at hand, the result merits, I believe, the term 'irrational' (and not simply a-rational or non-rational), and the judgement of irrationality is one that may be formulated in terms of a highly subjective understanding of the rationality of action. Are all non-intentional behaviours irrational in this way? Obviously not, for it would be preposterous to impose such a requirement on human agents. Many of the successful performances that we associate with practical rationality, including some of our most complex and highly valued skills, typically involve non-reflexive behaviour. In some instances it is very irrational to reconsider or to go back on an intention that has already been formed: if our previous intention was rational and the right conditions hold, rationality requires that we simply act on our intention at a later point in time, without subjecting it to a whole new process of deliberation. This general consideration could also cover examples of spontaneous, unreflective behaviour, where the absence of a present-directed intention to act does not entail irrationality in so far as the behaviour is oriented by the long-standing intention.[4] But in the example at hand, the spontaneous gesture abruptly supplants an important deliberative process that had reached no conclusion, and although the gesture seems purposive, it is not clear that it is voluntary: the passive construction suggests that Hurstwood is not trying to lock the door when it clicks shut, and he is surprised to find the safe definitely closed. One may readily contrast such a case to one in which a routinized sequence of behaviour follows from a conscious decision. On the one hand, the pianist makes a conscious decision to perform, and then lets the years of practice take over. On the other hand, the pianist is trying to decide whether to play when her hands suddenly begin to move across the keyboard! And Hurstwood's performance is one that he himself instantly hears as a false note. He pulls hard on the handle of the safe, futilely trying to undo what his hand has just done.

The implications of this detail for the theory of rationality are far from simple. Under what conditions do we extend considerations about rationality and irrationality to instances of spontaneous, unreflective behaviour? It would seem that taken separately, such doings fail to satisfy the basic criteria of intentional action, and therefore fail to respond to our basic rationality heuristic. Hurstwood's gesture of the hand in locking the safe, for example, may have been partially generated by some of his desires, but there was no overarching belief that this was what he wanted to do – no belief that the action is an effective means to an end to which the agent is committed. Nor was there a present-directed intention to perform the action. Thus elements required by every theory of atomic practical rationality and irrationality are simply missing. Yet in the context of a discussion of agent's rationality, we no longer shelve the matter by classifying this isolated gesture as a-rational or non-rational behaviour. In such a context, its relation to the same agent's other long-term desires and beliefs provides a framework for understanding the gesture and for evaluating its rationality or irrationality in the context of the agent's situation. Thus we may judge whether it is rational or not for this agent to have engaged in a particular bit of a-rational or non-rational behaviour in a particular situation. As a provisional and incomplete guideline, we may propose that spontaneous gestures not covered by some standing intention may be irrational for the agent to perform, even if they do tend to satisfy one of the agent's desires. Let us note, before we move on, that Hurstwood obviously believes that locking the safe and stealing the money will satisfy some of his desires: 'He could get Carrie – oh, yes he could. He could get rid of his wife' (p. 268). Yet this fact does not entail the rationality of the gesture of locking the safe, because Hurstwood has formed no decisive intention to the effect that these are the desires he wants to act on: he also desires to avoid living the life of a fugitive from the law, and he himself judges the spontaneous gesture to be inappropriate. Had it been a conscious intention, he would have had good reason to reconsider and overrule it, for in relation to the goal of satisfying his long-standing desires, it would have been irrational.

A second kind of irrationality follows immediately on the one that we have just explored. Closing the safe, Hurstwood tells himself, was a mistake, *his* mistake. Somehow, after the fact, an unintentional and accidental gesture is taken by him as his own mistaken action, an action for which he must take full responsibility. The narrator informs us that Hurstwood 'becomes the man of action' and decides that he has to flee with the money, and indeed he instantly leaves, spiriting Carrie away on a pretext, taking the night train to Montreal. Why does Hurstwood mistake his own action? The safe is locked, and Hurstwood tells himself that the money on top of it stands as proof that he is guilty of having wanted to steal it; nothing he can do will remove this evidence, and he reckons that the others will consider this to be ample proof that he closed the safe on purpose. He imagines that in the eyes of the world he is already committed to the theft. Because people will think that he wanted to run away with the money, he has to run away with the money.

Yet this is a mistake. The error here is an inability to think of the difference between being publicly shown guilty of having pondered the possibility of a theft, on the one hand, and actually committing it, on the other. Legally, these are not the same things at all, and Hurstwood has no good reason to deem the consequences equally bad in both cases. Nor has he any good reason to confound his entertaining an intention to steal with intentionally committing a felony. What, then, leads him to think this way? One phrase in the passage cited above is crucial in this regard: 'Besides, other things will happen.' This is what the narrator reports as Hurstwood's thought just after he has told himself he will be blamed even if he leaves the money locked up in the office. What are these other things? Here we can only conjecture, but the evidence points in the direction of the manager's earlier thoughts: he will have to face the painful and humiliating conflict with his wife; he will lose his savings to her; he will not be able to run away with Carrie; he will not be able to keep the money. These considerations still carry a lot of weight with him, which suggests that Hurstwood had not really made up his mind and is still torn by conflicting desires. Even as he tugs on the handle of the door of the safe, hoping to put the money back, he is excited by the prospect of being obliged to run away with Carrie.

Hurstwood may not have 'decided' to close the safe, but once his unthinking gesture has closed it, he does decide to steal the money, and this decision is irrational. This decision involves a highly tangled relation between the agent's own beliefs, desires, and intentions. One of its bases is a patently false belief, one that the agent himself would have rejected as absurd on a moment of sober reflection. This belief is Hurstwood's feeble idea that he has no choice but to flee with the money: 'I must get out of this', he thinks. But he badly misunderstands the options in ways that just do not fit well with the rest of his beliefs. He thinks that he has no choice, yet this belief in fact misconstrues what is in reality a situation of choice. Although the safe is locked and the money is in his hand, Hurstwood still has several possibilities before him. If he takes the money, he runs the same risks and enjoys the same prospects that he has been pondering all along. But if he leaves the money there, he will not necessarily be accused of theft. He may be able to provide an explanation and emerge from the situation without there being any serious legal or professional consequences for him. For example, he could say that he found the safe unlocked, got the contents out to check what was there, and accidentally shut the door. Returning the money the next day, he would remain the dutiful manager. In no case would the consequences of making such a statement to the owners of the bar be as bad as those he risks as a felon. So why does he ignore this option? Why is he incapable of making such an obvious conjecture? The answer seems to be that his thinking is vitiated by his desires. What seems to tip the scales, without him being fully aware of it, is not so much his desire for the money and Carrie, but his desire to flee from the prospect of a painful conflict with his wife; he is motivated by this desire, but this motivation is irrational in so far as he is oblivious to it and thinks that his real reasons lie elsewhere.

Hurstwood surely already knows the legal difference between an actual felony and accidentally closing a safe, yet he somehow fails to bring this knowledge of his to bear on his situation, and this in regard to a case of great importance to him. Instead, he settles on a faulty piece of reasoning that tells him that the circumstances require him to steal the money. A purely atomic approach to rationality would tell us that this is rational: if at the moment when he decides to flee the office with the money Hurstwood genuinely believes that this is his best course of action, then Hurstwood is subjectively rational in so acting. Similarly, if we recall the kind of minimal rationality conditions that Cherniak proposed in relation to the evaluation of an agent's beliefs, we may note that according to its strictures, it would be overly severe to require an agent to make any particular correct inference: it is too much to ask of Hurstwood that he contrast his thought about having to steal the money to everything else he knows about legal process (and we may note that later in the episode, he does reason accurately about the legal implications of his situation). And since Hurstwood thinks he is going to satisfy some of his desires by running away with the money, his action is subjectively rational following the minimal rationality condition.

Yet the conclusion to be drawn, I think, is that our reading of Dreiser's narrative suggests that the hypotheses of atomic and minimal rationality conditions do not correspond to our more robust intuitions about rationality. According to these intuitions, we are right to call Hurstwood's failure to think more accurately and consistently irrational, given the special nature of the piece of reasoning in question. Nor does this judgement of irrationality require us to adopt any of the more substantive and objective criteria of rationality and morality. It is not necessary to join the narrator in pointing out that Hurstwood does not grasp 'the true ethics' of the situation. Instead, we may understand and evaluate Hurstwood's decision in terms of a subjective approach to his agential rationality. It is in these terms that one may see what goes wrong in the deliberative process. Namely, Hurstwood fails to base his judgement on a belief that he could and should have held. The belief in question is an inference that is (a) subjectively highly appropriate, given its relation to a course of action that has tremendous consequences for a broad range of the agent's long-term goals and values; (b) subjectively quite feasible – on further reflection and under different conditions, Hurstwood would not find this inference particularly difficult; (c) subjectively of extreme importance to the agent; and (d) replaced by patently false thinking, which somehow takes precedence because of its covert relation to one of the agent's desires. These would seem to be conditions under which an adequate (and still quite subjective and moderate) theory of agent's rationality would require the agent to hit upon the bit of knowledge in question. In this regard, the narrative clearly illustrates the superiority of the agential perspective over atomic and minimalist approaches.

The question of the rationality of Hurstwood's behaviour is even more complex in regard to the rest of the episode. Once he has decided that he has to steal the money, Hurstwood really does become the man of action, and a very efficient one at that: he decides to try to spirit Carrie away to Montreal that very night, without telling her about the theft. He plans and executes all of this quite effectively, making sure to catch a train that will get him across the Canadian border before the police have time to pursue him. He lies quite skilfully to Carrie, tricking her into coming with him by claiming that her lover Drouet has had an accident, and by pretending to accompany her to the hospital. All of this involves a great deal of clever matching up of means and ends. One might well question the ultimate rationality of this way of treating Carrie, particularly in so far as 'making baggage of her' in this manner contradicts and may even subvert the real goal of his dealings with her, which is supposedly a relationship of love fundamentally different from his stale marriage.[5] Yet to the extent that his more pressing and immediate goal is simply to get her on the train with him and to avoid the clutches of the police, Hurstwood is quite successful, and manages to persuade Carrie to forgive him for the trickery and to agree to come along with him. From a purely atomic perspective, Hurstwood is behaving quite rationally here.

At the same time, however, once Hurstwood has realized this much of his plan, he is tortured by fear, regret, and confusion, and spends the night doubting the wisdom of the very scheme he is actively engaged in carrying out: '"What a fool I was to do that," he said over and over. "By the Lord, what a mistake!"' (p. 274). He views his present situation from a perspective that is completely different from the one that he had had only a few hours earlier: 'He could have gotten out all right. He could have acceded to his wife's demands . . . Why had he not done so? . . . He must have been mad, drunk, demoniac. He could not explain it upon any grounds whatever' (p. 283). He broods over everything that he has lost: 'He would not have his friends . . . He longed for Chicago, for his old ways and pleasant places. He wanted to go back and remain there, let the cost be what it would' (p. 288). Now his attitudes are the logical opposite of his former ones, for what he previously wanted is no longer desirable, and what he previously despised is now desirable: 'His condition was bitter in the extreme, for he did not want the miserable sum he had stolen. He did not want to be a thief. That sum, or any other, could never compensate for the state which he had thus foolishly doffed. It could not give him back his host of friends, his name, his house and family, nor Carrie as he had meant to have her' (p. 287). The objects of Hurstwood's desires seem to have undergone a curious revolution, and it is clear that it would be impossible for all of these different longings of his to be realized at once, for they are quite incompatible.

After he has taken a room in a hotel in Montreal, Hurstwood is accosted by a hotel detective who recognizes him as the thief. He ends up acting out the option that would have been most rational in the first place – giving back the largest part of the money and explaining the accidental closing of the safe – but at a point where it can no longer have the same benefits as before. Thus the plan that has brought him to Montreal with Carrie is aborted within a few days after his arrival. Yet a fragment of it survives: marrying Carrie under a false name, Hurstwood takes her to New York, but without the capital that was to have allowed him to live 'quietly' with her for years (p. 268).

How might we evaluate Hurstwood's rationality in deciding to send the money back? Although Hurstwood may seem to be contradicting himself at this point, one could very plausibly argue that this is the best choice: going through with a plan that was a mistake from the start, in the name of 'consistency' alone, is not necessarily rational, since the initial decision has no real rationality to transmit to any later actions.[6] It is the decision to send the money back that fits consistently with the rest of Hurstwood's views and aims. One may also note that now that Hurstwood has Carrie and has broken with his wife, he can abandon the theft, which no longer seems necessary to those two objectives. Retrospectively, it appears that the theft merely served as a catalyst to provoke a decision on Hurstwood's part, for he had been incapable of finding a way to resolve the conflict between his desire for Carrie and his desire to avoid the scandal and loss of money that his wife was surely going to inflict on him.

In spite of his possible rationality in giving the money back,

Hurstwood's actions are wildly incoherent if we look at the episode as a whole. Although many of his individual doings are, taken separately, quite good examples of atomic instrumental rationality, these actions are in contradiction with each other, just as his different beliefs and preferences are anything but compatible. Moreover, one may raise issues about the very rationality of his desires taken individually. In short, plotting the different ways in which Hurstwood is an incoherent agent is a task of no small dimensions. In every direction there is more work to be done: individual moments which at first glance seem coherent enough turn out to be much more problematic than expected, while the long-term and large-scale comparisons between Hurstwood's various attitudes and actions reveal, as we have already begun to see, even greater contradictions.

Hurstwood's irrationality has both cognitive and motivational dimensions. Hurstwood is impulsive when he should deliberate, and deliberates when it is too late, thereby spoiling whatever fruits his impulsive behaviour may have produced. When he most needs them, he fails to arrive at conclusions that should flow rather easily from his other beliefs; but as soon as these thoughts are no longer useful to him – indeed, as soon as they can be a source of pain, he cannot help but linger over them, brooding disastrously. It is ironic that he should be a 'manager', for after he runs away with Carrie, Hurstwood will never really be able to manage his life, and is drawn into the long process of his self-destruction. A crucial element in this process is Hurstwood's habit of constantly drawing painful comparisons between his present condition in New York, and the pleasures and satisfactions of his former life in Chicago (p. 311). Great emphasis is placed on Hurstwood's inability to learn to content himself with more modest means, and as his financial resources dwindle – a disastrous business venture robbing him of his capital – he fails to adapt, instead clinging, to the point of delusion, to his former identity as the manager. As the narrator suggests, 'A splendid paper might be prepared on the operation of certain preconceived notions which he had concerning dignity in the matter of his downfall' (p. 407). Hurstwood constantly distracts himself by reading the papers, lounges idly about in hotel lobbies when he should be actively seeking employment, and plays the gentleman with his last dollars, trying to shut depressing thoughts about his economic plight out of his mind. Although he has recently lost a badly needed sum playing poker, he fails to draw the obvious lesson, and embroils himself in another game on a subsequent evening, losing another significant percentage of his savings. His cognitive disorder climaxes in hallucinations, and ceases, at the end of a period of abject poverty, when 'one distinguished mental decision' is reached. 'People had turned on the gas before and died. Why shouldn't he?' With the end of Hurstwood's strivings come his final words: 'What's the use' – not a question, but a weary statement that there is no more use for Hurstwood, none in other people's eyes – which has been the case for some time already – and none, any longer, in his own. The pain and effort of plodding about in search of alms is too high a price to pay for the meagre ends to be achieved in this manner, and so Hurstwood has determined that rather than seek to offer himself one more temporary satisfaction of his basic need for food and shelter, he will terminate the entire endeavour. With his last purposeful action, Hurstwood satisfies his desire to have done with desire.[7]

The narrative of Hurstwood's romantic adventure and abject decline fairly bristles with examples of what our most basic intuitions would have to label as cases of 'irrationality'. By the same stroke, Dreiser's characterization of Hurstwood stands as a theoretical opportunity, for it provides an occasion for clarifying our intuitions about different standards of rationality. Hurstwood's behaviour clearly fails to correspond to the idealized rationality assumptions that are made in classical economics; nor does it square with atomic and minimal theories of rationality. The conclusion to be drawn, I think, is that the example suggests the need for a theory of 'moderate' rationality, more capable of expressing our intuitions about Hurstwood's irrationality.[8]

Cherniak's analyses usefully put us on guard against criteria of rationality that oblige an agent to make any one inference among the teeming possibilities, for the very good reason that any such requirement tends to conflict with the basic motivations of a theory of moderate rationality, namely, the recognition of our cognitive limits: finite agents cannot think through all of the valid inferences that follow from their beliefs, and they have no 'God's eye' perspective from which to judge the objective correctness or appropriateness of their assumptions and reasoning about means–end relations. Yet in pointing to Hurstwood's mistaken reasoning, I have none the less identified some of Hurstwood's specific inferences and intentions as incorrect, and I think our comprehension of the narrative requires this move and thereby points the way towards a modification of the theory of minimal rationality.

In what ways do our intuitions about the example call for a correction of the minimal theory of human rationality? First of all, as was suggested above, it would appear that a more adequate constraint on the rationality of an agent's behaviour must embrace not only genuine intentional action, but also the fit between intentional and unintentional action. Rational agency certainly does not require that everything the agent does be fully lucid and intentional, which would be absurd. But it does require that there be some kind of overall harmony between an agent's intentional actions and spontaneous and habitual doings: Hurstwood's accidental closing of the safe is an excellent example of the violation of this principle, for although the gesture is his own doing, he does not intentionally close the safe and is not sure that he would want to do so if he had the choice.

At the same time, the example reveals some of the problems that surround any radically subjective perspective on rationality: stiffer standards of appropriateness must be applied if we are to judge certain cases as being irrational, cases that our intuitions would hardly label as rational: Hurstwood may very well earnestly believe for a few hours that his theft and flight to Montreal are appropriate to the realization of his ends, but to call these actions 'rational' as a consequence is to violate our intuitions about the concept and to empty it of all interest. Yet what is the nature of the stiffer standards required? Psychological realism contradicts the idea that these standards should require the agent to find what is objectively *the* absolutely best means to his or her ends. Moreover, we grant along with Cherniak that rational agents cannot be expected to choose their actions by taking account of all valid and true beliefs that could be derived from their background beliefs – beliefs that may themselves be limited and may involve any number of falsehoods. Cherniak's alternative is merely to stipulate that agents have to think of some of the valid consequences and appropriate actions entailed by their own beliefs and desires. But the example suggests that we must work with a somewhat stiffer notion in so far as there must be certain classes of inferences that agential rationality will require and exclude in particular situations.

This stiffer notion could be couched in terms of privileged categories of correct inferences that a moderately rational agent may be expected to make, given his or her own assumptions. A first example is provided by Hurstwood's reaction to his accidental closing of the safe: although the gesture was not fully intentional – he is surprised and shocked when the safe clicks shut – he right away assumes that the closing of the safe must be understood – by himself and by others – as the result of his own intentional action. But this conclusion involves two mistakes: one pertaining to his own self-evaluation, and another having to do with the way he is likely to be judged by others. The former is a very basic misunderstanding of his own behaviour, for Hurstwood fails to know whether one of his own doings is accidental, intentional, or some complex mixture of the two. Although it would be unrealistic to require the agent to have some kind of unfailing or perfect knowledge on this score, it does seem correct to think that in this case Hurstwood fails to exhibit a moderate form of rationality. Obviously it would be excessive to expect agents to have to form explicit, second-order beliefs about the status of all of their own doings, determining whether they believe them to be 'intentional' or not, and formulating an evaluation of them. Even more exaggerated would be the idea that all of these beliefs and judgements would have to be true. Yet it is hardly extreme to expect that in an instance of tremendous personal significance to the agent's subjectively defined long-term interests, it would be rational for him or her to be able to reflect carefully about whether a particular gesture was intended or not, and to arrive at some reflexive decision about whether it is the kind of behaviour that corresponds to the agent's self-concept.[9] After all, Hurstwood is fully aware of his own oscillations and indecision, just as he knows that he has been drinking, and even a lenient and subjective standard of rationality requires that he bring this knowledge to bear on his crucial judgement concerning the status of the gesture. Hurstwood, however, does not do this, and what little thinking he does on the topic is vitiated by a logically distinct issue, that of what others may think: instead of consulting his own most immediate and recent knowledge of his behaviour, he trusts a tenuous inference about what others will think. It is possible, of course, that the others could all think that he fully intended to close the safe and steal the money, but his own mental states were anything but decisive, and the latter fact has

more weight if the issue is that of determining the extent to which
the gesture was actually intentional and 'internal' to his person.
Hurstwood might rightly decide that his gesture was not purely
accidental, but was an irrational action, unconsciously motivated
by a desire to force himself to make a 'decision'. But the fact of this
irrationality would not compel him to go on with the theft or to
assume any responsibility for it at that point in time, for only a
renewed, second-order acceptance of the scheme as his own will
suffice to do that.

That Hurstwood makes this latter mistake is no accident, but a
piece of motivated irrationality: Hurstwood knows he had been
pondering the possibility of stealing the money and so has some
reason to ascribe to himself the intent to close the safe; but more
importantly, Hurstwood now finds reasons why he is required to
take a step for which he could not find the resolve a moment before.
As I have argued above, this happens when some of Hurstwood's
desires vitiate an important decision by promoting a piece of faulty
reasoning over an accurate belief that is well within his reach. In
short, Hurstwood is guilty of a piece of wishful thinking, and
moreover, one that has very destructive consequences for his long-
term interests, as he himself defines them.[10]

The basic norm violated here is difficult to formulate, but runs
roughly as follows: although desires may rightly have a lot to do
with determining what one wants to know, the desire that something be the case is rarely, if ever, on its own a good reason for
believing that it is indeed the case; even less is it a good reason for
thinking that one knows something to be the case, or has some
strong warrant or justification for the belief. Are there exceptions to
this rule? The norm just stated would be contradicted by cases
having the following form: one desires that p be the case, but one
does not have adequate epistemic reasons for believing p; yet it is
none the less rational, for practical rather than for epistemic
reasons, to believe p, because one rationally believes that the belief
itself will help make p true. Yet are there any good examples of this?
Do people really believe that they are successful because they have
been convinced that having such a belief can make them successful?
It is not obvious that there are cases like this, especially ones not
involving some significant variety of self-deception or some other
irrationality. It seems rather that people have trouble really believing a proposition when they do not believe that they have adequate

evidence supporting it, or when they believe there is important evidence against it; consequently, they have to engage in various actions designed to change their situation so that the evidence will look different to them (such as seeing only sectarians so as to be able to believe in the sect), but then they have to conceal the traces of this operation from themselves so as to become unaware of the wilful manipulation of the evidence; and these concealings must in turn be concealed. Perhaps the result of such an operation could be a genuine belief, but it seems more likely to me that this kind of episode will be irrational.[11] Dreiser's depiction of Hurstwood provides a poignant illustration of the irrational cases, for the latter's decline involves the man's frequent attempts to persuade himself that his situation is not as bad as it really is, attempts having only the immediate goal of relieving his discomfort. Although these attempts effectively prevent Hurstwood from being lucid enough about his situation to act constructively, they even fail to bring about the hoped-for delusion. Although he dines at one of New York's finest hotels on his last dollars, this indulgence in comfort and extravagance does not really work: 'Anything to relieve his mental distress, to satisfy his craving for comfort. He must do it. No thoughts for the morrow – he could not stand to think of it, any more than he could of any other calamity. Like the certainty of death, he tried to shut the certainty of soon being without a dollar completely out of his mind, and he came very near to doing it' (p. 373). Hurstwood tries to get himself to believe what he knows to be a falsehood, with the goal of experiencing a moment of relief from his distress, but the operation fails.

My remarks on the various forms of irrationality that may be associated with Hurstwood's doings have been quite sketchy, and have hardly exhausted the implications of the text's characterization of him. Even so, certain provisional conclusions have been reached, and the importance of pursuing certain lines of enquiry has been stressed. It should be quite clear from what has been said that it is a theory of agent's rationality, and not a theory of atomic rationality, that is most likely to correspond to our more robust intuitions about rationality and irrationality. The very different understandings and evaluations of an unreflective gesture arrived at in the two different kinds of contexts is a telling example, for from one perspective it is simply non-rational or a-rational, whereas from the other it is an important instance of irrationality.

The important difference between the two perspectives holds in relation to many other features of the example. Viewed as isolated or atomic instances of practical behaviour, Hurstwood's actions in spiriting Carrie away with him to Montreal satisfy moderate, atomic conceptions of rationality simply because they manifest subjective, and even locally successful, beliefs about effective means–ends relations. An example is the sequence of planning and successful execution that gets Hurstwood from his office in Chicago to a hotel room in Montreal with Carrie, where he satisfies at least one of his burning desires. Yet within the larger context of Hurstwood's long-term goals and beliefs as an agent, these same items leap forth as instances of blatant irrationality, and this still from within a subjective and moderate conception of rationality (it is not, for example, a matter of saying that it is wrong of Hurstwood to ignore the objective morality of the situation, or of saying that he has failed to come up with what would objectively have been the most effective way of realizing his goals). Our reading of the example, then, raises the issue of the relation of atomic judgements of rationality to judgements of agent's rationality, suggesting that the latter are far more likely to express significant intuitions about people's activities.

I shall now develop the latter point in regard to the question of evaluations of the rationality of isolated instances of desire. Is it possible to articulate a meaningful theory of the rationality of particular desires? Atomic rationality, we have seen, is typically discussed in terms of a single constraint: logical consistency. What does it mean to require that a particular desire be consistent? Perhaps the nature of this norm can be made clear if we can find obvious examples of its transgression. For example, one may believe the norm to be violated when an agent desires that a certain situation be the case, but also desires that it not be the case. Yet what does this mean, exactly? Does the agent both have the desire and not have the desire, or is it rather a matter of a contradiction within the object or situation that is effectively desired by the agent? In fact, there are various possibilities to be considered when we take up the apparently simple and obvious idea of there being an inconsistency in a single instance of desire. These possibilities should be clarified. A first option would be spelled out as follows:

In spatio-temporal location l, agent A stands in an attitude of desire towards the situation S, and the same agent A does not stand in an attitude of desire for S.[12]

I think we want to say that this kind of situation is an impossibility, for it is a matter of there being an objective contradiction in the real world (A is and is not in a certain mental state, at the same time and in the same sense). It is like saying that a particular apple is and is not on the table at a particular spot right now. I think that we want contradictory desire to characterize not the real world, but the intentional object of an agent's desire. Perhaps, then, an elementary irrationality of desire should be described as follows:

In spatio-temporal location l, agent A stands in an attitude of desire towards the situation S, where the situation S is described as follows: at location l', *particular entity* x both has and does not have a particular property r.[13]

What would be an example that satisfies this basic schema? Hurstwood wants to be seated comfortably in a hotel lobby, but wants not to be seated there (at the same time and in the same place). Note that it is not a matter of saying that there is a sense in which the agent desires one situation, but another sense in which aspects of that situation are not desired by that agent at the same time (for example, Hurstwood desires the physical comfort of sitting in the lobby, but should this desire be realized he would regret the fact that he would be achieving nothing in regard to his other problems, and might be seen by former acquaintances). For there to be a pure contradiction, the agent must desire a contradictory situation, at the same time and in the same sense. Are such desires possible? Clearly, their realization is impossible, for Hurstwood could never get what he really wanted if this were the content of his attitude of desire. The desire itself, however, might still be possible, for people may very well desire impossible things, just as they can have desires without acting on them. In Marcel Proust's *A la Recherche du temps perdu*, Marcel is quite eloquent about why it is impossible for him ever to realize his dream of possessing Albertine in all of her states and conditions, yet the desire persists, and he seems to act on it.

Is a contradictory desire irrational? Before taking up that question, let us contrast it to a slightly different example. Suppose someone desires to realize a situation that is objectively impossible, but does not know that the object of this desire cannot be realized. Is such a desire irrational? The answer seems to depend in part on our evaluation of the relevant beliefs of the agent, which suggests that there is an important sense in which the evaluation of a desire's rationality necessarily involves reference to cognitive factors. A desire for the impossible may not seem irrational to us if we assume that the agent has no good reason to believe that the elements he wants to combine in a desired situation are mutually exclusive, and this might not be an unreasonable assumption for him to make, given his situation. In the absence of a perfect knowledge of all of the constraints of reality, it is impossible to judge in advance what features can be compatibly included in the situations we strive to bring into existence. In some cases, it is not irrational to desire an objectively impossible situation, because, for all one knows, the object of the desire could be possible, and there may be all kinds of excellent reasons for wanting to bring it into existence. Only from some omniscient perspective could we look down and judge it irrational to desire something that simply cannot be.

As may have been expected, we have been led to shift from the topic of the rationality of an isolated state of desire to that of the rationality of diverse relations between beliefs, desires, intentions, and actions. The reason is not that it is simply impossible to engage in an evaluation of the rationality of a particular desire, but that the results do not seem particularly valuable in that they do not express our more robust intuitions about rationality. One could very well stipulate that a particular desire is irrational simply because it aims at a contradictory state of affairs, but it is not the least bit clear what is achieved by such a judgement. Why should the person not have such a desire? The answer, we have suggested, cannot be simply that its realization is impossible and that the agent must know it.

Here we encounter a point that is frequently made in the literature on rationality, where it is stated that the rationality of a desire or a goal can only be discussed in terms of its relations to other goals: 'oughts' can be rationally disputed only in terms of their relations to other 'oughts'.[14] Why? Briefly, the assumption is that goals, ends, values, and the like have no ontological autonomy, and that there is no 'fact of the matter' to be contested when it is a question of evaluating the rationality of a particular goal taken in isolation. In isolation from agents and organisms, goals do not exist, for goals are reducible to the organism's preference for one internal state over another.[15] Thus, whether it is the case that some organism or agent has a particular preference is a topic subject to rational-empirical consideration, but whether any organism ought to have such a preference is not, for such a matter can only be rationally discussed relative to this or that organism's other preferences and attitudes. Thus the typical suggestion is that although it is impossible to make rational evaluations of a particular desire or end taken in isolation, it is possible to evaluate the rationality of some collection of desires by asking whether they are combined in coherent, instrumental, means–end relations, and whether their joint realization is compatible. In this direction, then, lie the more robust intuitions about the rationality of desire.

Yet such an approach does not exhaust the ways in which the rationality of desire may be discussed. Comparing reductionist theories of human motivation to literary narratives often supports the conclusion that we must abandon the idea that the desires of human agents are reducible to the outputs of some kind of blind mechanism within the organism; instead, we have seen how the agent's various beliefs play a crucial rôle in the generation of desires, which themselves have certain of the features that we associate with intentionality: Carrie's desire to imitate the other woman's manner of walking has a basis in her attitudes towards Drouet and herself. Cowperwood's imitation of Ellsworth's desire for certain types of sculpture depends on his beliefs about the latter's personal refinement and knowledge of the world of art. In short, people often have desires for reasons, and these reasons are not exhausted by the idea that this agent judges this state of affairs as a means to some other end. Other kinds of beliefs about the state of affairs, as well as beliefs about other agents and other states of affairs, may have an operative rôle in the generation of the agent's desire, and the rationality of these beliefs may be pertinent to the rationality of this desire. Elster makes a similar point, I believe, when he advocates evaluating the rationality of beliefs and desires in terms of their causal origins; his analysis of the phenomenon known as 'sour grapes' is an excellent example: the fox's lack of desire for the grapes, his judgement that they are sour, has as its distorting causal basis the fox's knowledge that they are out of reach: if he did not think they were out of reach, he would still desire them.[16] So that if it is not unusual to observe that desires may distort and shape our beliefs (a point that is constantly emphasized, as we have seen, by Dreiser's narrators), it is equally important to note that beliefs often have a large rôle in the formation of desires (a point that Dreiser's narratives, if not his meta-commentaries, also emphasize).

This very general intuition about the rôle of belief in the generation of desires suggests that we may explore the rationality of an agent's desires by referring to the rationality of those beliefs that contribute to their emergence and orientation. This approach, I think, complements the other manner of evaluating the rationality of desire, which focuses on the question of the coherence of means– end relations between desires. As an illustration of the type of analysis in question, we may take up the issue of the rationality of the bases of Hurstwood's desires in regard to Carrie. There is a sense in which he consistently desires his romance with Carrie, and thus the desire could seem to be invulnerable to criticism based on any moderate standards of rationality. Yet it is probably more important to observe that the character's very passion for Carrie is ill-founded and in a way incoherent.

The narrative permits us to observe the genesis and death of this passion, and singles out several different elements for our attention. Emphasis is laid on Hurstwood's boredom with his wife and children, which makes his home life no source of pleasure or interest for him: it is, on the contrary dessicated to the point of being 'tinder, easily lighted and destroyed' (p. 87). In Hurstwood's mind Carrie is a figure that stands forth against this dismal ground, an important feature of the *Gestalt* being Hurstwood's age: the young girl represents his own youthful experience of love, and reminds him that he may never again have the chance of enjoying such a passion (p. 203). Hurstwood's interest in Carrie is shown to be heightened by three other factors. First of all, as an 'innocent' young girl who has just recently arrived in Chicago from the country, she seems to him to be different from the other women with whom he has had the opportunity to engage in extra-marital affairs – women about whom he has become totally 'cynical' (pp. 121-3). Secondly, Hurstwood's interest in Carrie is stimulated by his rivalry with Drouet, who proudly presents her to him as his most recent conquest. Thus the narrative speaks of the man's 'envy' for his 'rival' (p. 108), insisting on this point in the following phrase: 'He envied the drummer his conquest as he had never envied any man in all the course of his experience' (p. 122). From envy, it is a small step to jealousy, and Hurstwood takes it: 'Never was man more harassed by the thoughts of his love being held by the elated, flush-mannered drummer. He would have given anything, it seemed to him, to have the complication ended – to have Carrie acquiesce to an arrangement which would dispose of Drouet effectually and forever' (p. 194). Thirdly, the narrative repeatedly shows how Hurstwood's desire is exacerbated by the other obstacles placed in the way of its satisfaction, first of all by Carrie's resistance, then by Hurstwood's marital crisis: 'She increased in value in his eyes because of her objection. She was something to struggle for, and that was everything. How different from the women who yielded willingly' (p. 149). The 'crystallization' – as Henri Beyle would have put it – occurs on the occasion of Carrie's first amateur theatrical performance, before the watchful eyes of the two rivals. In her rôle, Carrie seems to them to embody the very treasure of love – a treasure, which in the text of the melodrama in which she performs, is supposed to be 'without money and without price' (p. 192). To underscore the pseudo-transcendence of this theatrical scene, the narrator comments: 'They only saw their idol, moving about with appealing grace, continuing a power which to them was a revelation' (p. 193).

Such are the factors that the narrative presents as fueling Hurstwood's passion for Carrie, and what is striking is the extent to which they involve illusions and increase the likelihood of disappointment. Hurstwood misperceives Carrie and is deluded about her, as the conflation of the theatrical rôle and the performer's real qualities – a mistake likened to nothing less than idolatry – clearly suggests. Moreover, a desire to engage in a long-term amorous relationship with someone, where this desire is incited by envy of a rival, jealousy, and the loved one's resistance, is incoherent and inherently self-defeating: although Hurstwood's thoughts about Drouet, Carrie's resistance, and his own entrapment do strengthen his desire for Carrie, they are not themselves internally related to the desire's object, and once these obstacles are removed, Hurstwood's desire suffers as a result. The narrator's comment? 'His passion had gotten to that stage now where it was no longer colored with reason' (p. 209), a remark which we would amend as follows: where it was entirely coloured by bad reasons. The rest of the narrative bears this out: once Hurstwood has possession of Carrie and they have set up house together, his passion is quickly extinguished.

Is the fact that Hurstwood's desire for Carrie does not persist evidence of its irrationality? It is if there is also evidence that Hurstwood desires otherwise, and indeed what the narrative reveals about his thinking along these lines suggests that he hopes to 'build a life' with Carrie. Moreover, in acting on the desire for Carrie, Hurstwood has sacrificed the possibility of satisfying all of his other habitual wants. Thus no emphasis is laid on any experience of passion between Hurstwood and Carrie once they are together, and she soon returns to the background of his mind, an event marked by the return of his former practice of failing to return home for dinner. Running away with Carrie, Hurstwood does not experience the benefits he had hoped for, and his disappointment signals the delusory nature of his previous longing.

The foregoing remarks should have convinced the reader that Hurstwood's passion for Carrie is unlikely to satisfy even the most lenient and subjective norms that one might develop for evaluating the rationality of desire. Even should one somehow concoct an argument capable of saving Hurstwood's desire for Carrie from incoherence and delusion, this would still not rescue his motivational system as a whole from the judgement of irrationality. And that is so because whatever the precise nature of his longing for Carrie is, it is itself in contradiction with any number of Hurstwood's other desires and preferences, such as his deep-seated desires for his social standing, comfort, wealth, and security. The latter third of the book, which plots the disintegration of the couple, Hurstwood's descent into poverty, and his suicide, amply supports this statement. The contradiction is clearly expressed in the narrative by means of various juxtapositions. For example, we are explicitly told, long before the affair with Carrie develops, that Hurstwood is someone who has no sympathy for a man who lets his extra-marital adventures get him into trouble: 'A man can't be too careful. He lost sympathy for the man that made a mistake and was found out' (p. 85). As we move forward in the story, we encounter a Hurstwood who by his own standards would no longer qualify for sympathy. Far from being careful, he is so overrun with jealous passion for Carrie that he 'could have sold his soul to be with her alone' (p. 194). The manager cannot harmonize his own contradictory wants, and so, in acting on one of them, he cannot fail to compromise the others (as the narrator puts it, he had 'too many ends to consider' (p. 243)). The result is flagrant contradiction: although he does not desire to be a thief, he none the less engages in a theft that cannot possibly go undetected, thereby intentionally making himself a thief in the eyes of everyone he knows.

One last point may be explored in relation to the literary examples evoked in this chapter, a point concerning the explanatory limits of the type of analysis of agent's rationality under consideration here. A moderate theory of rationality, I have said, acknowledges the basic cognitive limitations of human agents and does not try to impose upon them a normative concept of rationality that could only be satisfied by some kind of Laplacean demon or other omniscient entity. Instead, the agent's own assumptions and inferential possibilities provide the measure in terms of which that agent's failures in reasoning are discussed. For example, it is not particularly interesting to argue that Hurstwood was irrational in taking a room in the particular hotel in Montreal that he chose because there was a detective there who would accost him, whereas there was another hotel where there was no such detective. An omniscient being could have known this, but then an omniscient being would not have been in Hurstwood's situation in the first place, so such considerations are not particularly pertinent to the question of Hurstwood's rationality. This means that an important part of the intentional explanations based on the approach we are advocating is the analysis of the agent's situation in terms of the agent's own perspective of that situation (which should not be taken to imply that a radically solipsistic theory of rationality is what is being developed here). Yet this point suggests that there will be explanatory limits to the situational analysis conducted from the agent's perspective, for there are aspects of the agent's real situation of which the agent is unaware, and which play a determinant rôle in what happens to the agent. In other words, although the intentional analysis, couched in terms of the reconstructed subjective perspective of the agent, may be a successful way to explain that agent's actions, it does not make possible an exhaustive explanation of the agent's personal history, or more simply, of everything that happens to the agent. Two basic reasons may be given in support of this point. First of all, there are other agents, whose individual actions, which may themselves be explained in intentional terms, will alter the situations in which a given agent will find herself. Secondly, there will be chance connexions between causally independent situations and courses of events (what Proust's Baron de Charlus calls *les enchaînements de circonstances*), which will be of great subjective significance to the agents involved, without having been the intended result of any of the agents' actions.

An excellent illustration is provided by Dreiser's depiction of the conditions leading up to Hurstwood's robbery and flight to Montreal with Carrie. What are these conditions? The intentional analysis focuses on the deliberative process that leads to Hurstwood's decision, yet this process would not have had an object had the employee Mayhew not left the safe unlocked, which is something he has never done before. Is there a reason why he does so? The narrator tells us that Mayhew inadvertently failed that night to turn the knob on the door so as to spring the lock. He thought he had, but 'had had other thoughts. He had been revolving the problem of a business of his own' (p. 267). Another condition, this time at the border of happenstance and intentional analysis, is the fact that on this particular evening Hurstwood becomes quite heavily intoxicated before going up to close his office, and we know that his drunkenness colours the deliberative process. Why does Hurstwood happen to drink that night? Again the answer resides partly in the 'chance' conjunction of Hurstwood's situation and the actions of other agents. 'It so happened', the narrator informs us, that that night a group of 'notabilities', including some of the city's most reknowned actors, arrive at the establishment around eleven, and draw Hurstwood into their festivities. Hurstwood, we are informed, has a 'leaning' towards notabilities, and was generally delighted by such situations in which he 'could shine as a gentleman and be received without equivocation as a friend and equal among men of known ability' (p. 266). 'It was on such occasions, if ever, that he would "take something". When the social flavor was strong enough, he would even unbend to the extent of drinking glass for glass with his associates, punctiliously observing his turn to pay as if he were an outsider like the others' (p. 266). The result is that, in this instance, he is soon intoxicated, and his mind is 'warm in its fancies'. We see here that it is not simply the raw fact of the chance arrival of the notabilities that contributes to Hurstwood's drama, but his manner of reacting to them: 'Tonight, disturbed as was his state, he was rather relieved to find company' (p. 266). Yet had they not come, the conditions required for Hurstwood's drinking would not have been satisfied, and thus the chance encounter, which is in no way intended by Hurstwood, is a crucial factor in the latter's history. The chain of circumstances that constitutes the latter is long, and it would also be necessary to trace it back to the conditions that have produced a climax in Hurstwood's conflict with his wife, conditions that include, among others, her chance meeting with an acquaintance who happened to be at the theatre the night when Hurstwood went there with Drouet to see Carrie on stage (while neglecting to inform his wife about it); the same chain, which when traced forward will make it possible for Carrie to be convinced to accompany Hurstwood to Montreal, leads back to the moment when Drouet and Carrie quarrel, and includes the fact that unbeknownst to her, when Drouet returned to make peace, she happened to be out. Assuming that the bridge called Drouet has been burnt behind her, Carrie is all the more prepared to forgive Hurstwood for his lies, and does not leave the train when she has the chance. It should be clear, then, even on the basis of this schematic illustration, that an intentional explanation of an individual agent's action is not equivalent to an explanation of the conditions of that agent's history or life course – which is not the same as saying that the intentional explanation has, as a result of its limits, no explanatory value.

CHAPTER 5

Plans and irrationality

Emile Zola's characterization of Lazare Chanteau in *La Joie de vivre* (1883–4) provides an excellent context for a discussion of the rôle of plans in the constitution of an agent's rationality. Quite simply, Lazare is someone who cannot 'make up his mind', and this incapacity has many undesirable consequences for him. Taking up and abandoning a number of different large-scale career projects, Lazare fails to carry any one of them to completion and ends up an abject failure. At first glance, then, the story of this character's failures would appear to stand as a simple and straight-forward illustration of an equally simple and uncomplicated norm: given certain types of goals – such as Lazare's desire to be a great composer – the ability to organize one's actions in function of complex, temporally extended planning is a necessary condition of rational agency. This first appraisal of the story's significance in relation to the theory of agent's rationality is certainly not wholly incorrect, but once we have explored it in more detail, it will become apparent that Lazare's transgression of norms of rational planning and deliberation is much more complex than this first impression allows.

At the centre of the story of Lazare's inconstancy is his inability to devote himself to a single career (and in this respect, Lazare has a direct literary antecedent in Richard Carstone of Charles Dickens's *Bleak House* (1852–3)). It is crucial to note from the outset that this inability is not simply a matter of an absence of ambition or long-term thinking on Lazare's part. He is not like those characters in a picaresque novel who pass from one episode to the next, never asking how these moments stand in relation to an image they have of what their desired life-time trajectory would be. Rather, Lazare is both strongly oriented towards the future and extremely ambitious, so that our only chance of understanding his reasons is to pay attention to the place of particular moments within long-term structures.

Let me begin the analysis with a brief survey of some of the most salient events in Lazare's career. At the time when he leaves the Lycée, Lazare has a 'passion for music' and seems to be entirely dedicated to this one pursuit, so much so that his entire self-conception is based upon the aim of being a famous composer. When his mother and cousin urge him to replace this goal with a more realistic and financially secure one, he threatens to commit suicide.[1] Lazare eagerly throws himself into the composition of a symphony that is supposed to evoke the earthly paradise, and he successfully invents the theme for a march meant to illustrate the expulsion of Adam and Eve from the garden. Yet after a few weeks of work, he runs into difficulties and begins to have doubts about his musical talent. One afternoon, he thinks he has solved his problem when he hits upon a new idea for the overall plan of his work: instead of writing the symphony of paradise, he will write the symphony of pain. The theme he has already written is incorporated into the new plan, where it serves as a death march. For eight days his enthusiasm for this project continues to build, but then he suddenly announces that he wants to go to Paris and study medicine. Lazare's doubts about his musical talent do not, however, lead to a clear-headed and resolute decision to give up on this ambition; instead, he tells himself that agreeing to study medicine in Paris is only a strategic manoeuvre, one that will in fact get him closer to the Conservatory. Once in Paris, he will see about pursuing his musical career (pp. 842–3).

Yet this manoeuvre is in fact but the first step in a long series of career reversals. During his first year in Paris, Lazare becomes caught up in his medical studies and decides that his earlier interest in music was foolish: now his sole ambition is to become a brilliant doctor. For a while he works assiduously towards that goal. Two years later, however, he has become totally cynical about medical science, and turns to chemistry. He becomes obsessed with a scheme to make his fortune by developing a new method for extracting valuable chemicals from seaweed, and managing to finance the project, he returns to his familial home to undertake the construction of a factory. When this project encounters difficulties, Lazare abandons it, selling out to his partner. His next idea is to design and construct a wooden barrier that will protect the local village

from the waves that are progressively eroding the small strip of
beach where it is located. Yet having undertaken this project, he
soon loses interest in it and decides that he wants to write literature
– only to return shortly thereafter to the construction of the barrier.
Lazare flirts for a while with the idea of founding a local
newspaper, but abandons this notion to return to his literary ambitions. Caught up momentarily in the latter, he refuses his father-in-
law's offer of a position in his insurance company, but subsequently
changes his mind. Yet Lazare soon tires of business, fails to apply
himself, and as always, manages these affairs quite poorly.

   This cursory description of Lazare's unhappy career should suffice to establish a first basic point. Lazare is an agent who has
certain kinds of desires falling into the very general category of 'life-
time career ambitions', and these desires are anything but modest:
born into a middle-class family, he wants to move upwards on the
social ladder and achieve a kind of personal recognition and success
that would place him at a great remove from his initial social
position. And this facet of Lazare's desires remains constant across
his various pursuits, for it is in each case a matter of his wanting to
distinguish himself and be recognized as an extraordinary
individual. Thus even when he gives up his goal of being hailed as a
great composer and turns to medicine, he never sets his sights on
being a typical doctor; instead, he wants to be a doctor of such
extraordinary genius that the whole world will be set astir.[2]
Moreover, these extremely ambitious life-time desires are not a
matter of some isolated episodes of phantasizing; it is not a matter
of some wholly private longings that never give rise to action.
Rather, the ambitions in question are the basis of the largest part of
Lazare's planning and activity. It is with the goal of realizing these
desires that Lazare forms various intentions about what to do in the
present and in the future, and he acts on any number of these
intentions. A first and quite basic point, then, may be couched as
follows: Lazare is, in many ways, a creature of long-term ambition
and planning, and to evaluate his rationality in these terms is not to
impose on him a set of external and inappropriate criteria.[3]

   A second basic point that must be made explicit here is that
Lazare's frequent altering of his initial deliberations and career
choices quite obviously has the effect of making it impossible for
him to realize his one fundamental goal, which is to win 'fame and
fortune'. This point, like the former, is obvious: Lazare may or may

not have the talent necessary to be recognized one day as a great composer, but he will certainly never achieve the latter goal by studying medicine, just as he will never be a doctor once he has invested all of his time and money in the building of a factory. He cannot enjoy the glory of defying the ocean waves with his plan for a sea-wall if he turns to literature instead of completing the project, just as he can hardly be acclaimed for his great novel if he turns instead to journalism, and then to a position in an insurance company.

Conjoined, the two basic points just set forth lead to the conclusion that Lazare is a highly irrational agent. Such an evaluation is not made by imposing some standard of objective rationality on the agent: in this instance, we do not even have to address ourselves to the question of the rationality of the agent's most basic desires in order to determine whether he is rational or not. Rather, our judgement of Lazare's irrationality is based on the major contradictions between Lazare's own most basic and long-standing desires and his own practical reasoning and action, contradictions that have the effect of preventing him from realizing his own long-standing and most basic aims. Thus he is irrational in terms of moderate and highly subjective criteria of agent's rationality, which specify that whatever an agent's major desires are, the rationality of that agent's reasoning and action may be evaluated in terms of their contribution to the realization of these desires. Yet this global judgement of Zola's literary figure is in itself of little theoretical interest, for it is hardly necessary to evoke such an extreme case to formulate this basic intuition about the criteria of agent's rationality. Rather, the interest of the characterization of Lazare resides in the additional implications of its detailed depiction of certain varieties of irrationality, as well as in what it suggests about their possible sources.

When we look Lazare's unhappy career taken as a whole, we observe a first, global type of irrationality, namely, Lazare's inability to remain committed to any of the long-term schemes in which he engages. Shifting from one long-term scheme to another, incompatible one is surely to fail to succeed with any one of them, and as was just observed, the overall outcome is that the agent fails to realize his most basic goals. Yet when we look at the episodes taken individually, the situation is not quite so simple: would it really be rational for Lazare to remain committed to any one scheme, just for the sake of avoiding the global type of irrationality just evoked? The answer to this question clearly must be negative, for there are obviously cases where it would be highly irrational for an agent to remain wedded to a long-term project when it is no longer reasonable for that agent to think that the project has a good chance of working. It is possible to imagine, for example, that Lazare's decision to replace music with medicine could have been quite rational under certain circumstances; for example, we need only suppose that it was quite coherent of him, given his own beliefs, to decide that he had better give up on his earlier ambition and replace it with one that it is more within his power to realize. This possibility suggests another one: could it be that the global irrationality emerges from a series of major decisions which, when viewed locally, are all subjectively rational? It could be that each time the agent decides to abandon a major project, there are good reasons for his doing so, just as there may have been good reasons for him to have engaged in the project in the first place. Although the result is a kind of global irrationality in so far as no major project ever gets realized, unpropitious circumstances and a lack of talent and resources, and not the agent's bad practical reasoning, are responsible for the overall failure. Nor should we fault the agent's initial ambition: at the outset, Lazare has no overwhelming reasons for concluding that he can never have a highly successful career.

These considerations suggest that in the evaluation of the agent's rationality, a global perspective will not suffice. Instead, we must investigate the rationale behind each local change of long-term plans and look at their specific interrelations. In the case of Lazare, we need not look far to determine that it is not a matter of a hapless creature who, innocent of local irrationalities, succumbs to a global incoherence and failure. Lazare's very first decision to change careers is presented as rather hasty and ill-founded, for it appears to be a manifestation of a momentary loss of confidence rather than the result of any careful deliberation. Although the young man's only passion is music, he lets his mother and cousin convince him not to pursue this ambition, apparently because he experiences some difficulty in writing his first symphony. Lazare's decision is irrational, then, because it is not the fruit of reflective deliberation, and is motivated instead by a lack of confidence.

One could also argue that when Lazare announces that he will study medicine, there is an element of confusion – perhaps even a significant form of self-deception – in his thinking. He states his intention to replace one long-term goal with another, yet he may be motivated in part by the thought that the first steps taken towards the new goal are in fact but a means to the realization of the former goal: taking up residence in Paris and beginning to study medicine will bring him closer to the Conservatory, he thinks, and he can see about pursuing his musical career later. Although Lazare effectively engages himself in a new project that will have irreversible effects on him (and he makes a significant promise to his family as well as an important investment of time and money), he has not entirely made up his mind, in the sense that his actual thinking about his long-term intentions remains tangled. Perhaps he believes that his immediate course of action really does serve both ambitions equally well, which would be patently false and an instance of wishful thinking. More likely, the tangle involves the idea that his decision is not irreversible: he agrees to try a year of medical studies, but enjoys thinking that he can go back on his decision if he does not like medicine.

Lazare's first major decision seems irrational because based on incomplete deliberation and the wrong motives. Are all of Lazare's changes in basic career plans irrational in the same manner? To respond to this question, we must take a closer look at the novel's episodes with the goal of determining the specific nature of Lazare's local irrationalities in abandoning his various plans. The result, I shall contend, is that although the details of Lazare's faulty reasoning vary from case to case, there is a single pattern that emerges.

Let us begin, not with the young man's shift from medicine to chemistry, but with the outcome of the ensuing episode, for the narrative tells us very little about how Lazare becomes disgusted with his professors during his second year of medical studies. During his third year in Paris, Lazare by chance meets a famous chemist, Herbelin, and becomes his assistant. He becomes wildly enthusiastic about the great chemist's discovery of a manner of extracting chemicals from seaweed, and reckons that he can make a fortune by building a factory that would put the new method into practice. The scheme, he argues in letters to his mother, has several factors in its favour: he has the help of a great chemist; the raw materials to be treated by the factory are abundant; the initial costs of setting up the factory are low (his original estimate is 60,000

francs, half of which is to be invested by a friend named Boutigny);
the chemicals to be extracted from the seaweed have a high market
value; and finally, the enterprise can be established near his family
home by the sea.

After a series of laboratory experiments that seem to prove the
efficacy of the method of extracting chemicals from the ashes of seaweed, the plan is set in motion. Lazare and his associate Boutigny
purchase a plot of land by the sea and begin construction of their
factory, following Lazare's plans. Yet as construction costs rise, the
two partners disagree, Boutigny arguing that they should begin on
a modest scale with the intention of expanding later, while Lazare,
certain that the scheme is going to make them a fortune, wants to
start with a battery of large machines housed in an immense
hangar. Boutigny reluctantly agrees that construction should pro-
ceed following Lazare's grandiose plans. When everything is in
place, a first trial of the machines is made, and ends in failure.
Lazare returns to Paris to consult Herbelin, who corrects his disciple's design of the system. Yet more money is needed to rebuild
the apparatuses, and Lazare already feels like abandoning the
entire project. Yet he reasons that he must find more money, for it
would be a mistake to give up on a scheme that will make millions
later. Lazare invests another large sum, the money being taken this
time from his cousin Pauline. The new machines are set up and the
work begins, but once more the yield is meagre. Clinging stubbornly to the hope of making a fortune, Lazare and his cousin
continue to invest more and more of the money from her trust fund,
hoping that the machines can be adjusted so as to perform as
expected. The narrator comments: 'They felt certain they would
make a fortune. And once this idea had made them stubborn, they
reacted against the signs of disaster, the factory becoming an abyss
into which they were throwing money by the handful, remaining
convinced that they would find it later in the form of a gold ingot,
lying at the bottom' (p. 876). Finally, when another 100,000 francs
have been spent, Lazare is overwhelmed by fear. He puts the entire
project in doubt and loses faith in his scientific master who, visiting
the factory, reflects that the procedure may only work efficiently on
the small scale of the laboratory tests. The problem, it seems, is
that of bringing about a controlled drop in the temperature of large
bodies of liquid.

At this point in the venture, the enterprise has an outstanding debt of 20,000 francs. Tricked by Boutigny's lies, Lazare signs over the entire property to his partner in exchange for a payment of 5,000 francs (Lazare's overall loss, then, being some 125,000 francs). Boutigny then sells the expensive materials that had been used in Lazare's system and sets the factory up so as to employ the traditional method of making fertilizer out of seaweed, but on a large scale. He makes quite a bit of money this way, and a few years later, with the help of a young chemist, successfully makes a fortune using Herbelin's basic idea (p. 1065).

What is the nature of Lazare's practical reasoning in this episode? Let us start with the initial decision to engage in the project. Boutigny's eventual success with the factory suggests that there was no initial error in Lazare's decision to engage in the project, for not only did Lazare have ample reason for believing in the possibility of its success, but the project indeed proves to be objectively lucrative when managed well. One might argue that Lazare's initial decision was a mistake given his lack of practical business skills and technical knowledge, yet there was in fact no reason for him to have made any such assumption at the time, and indeed his failure does not seem inevitable. What, then, is his mistake? Clearly a first error – if not a first instance of irrationality – rests upon a combination of haste and overconfidence. Instead of investing carefully, realizing an initial profit, and then reinvesting, Lazare boldly assumes that what has worked in the laboratory must work on a large scale, and designs the factory with this premise in mind, expecting to make his fortune in one fell swoop. This turns out to have been a costly mistake. The price of adjusting an initial error in the design of the system is multiplied, so that the associates twice pay the cost of installing a number of large machines before running a full-scale test on a single one of them. Thus Lazare's haste and overconfidence magnify the price that must be paid to find out whether the new procedure is really workable. Yet this mistake need not be judged an irrationality, for on a moderate and subjective conception, rationality does not require the agent to be right all of the time, or to be successful in every endeavour. What a moderate conception of rationality requires is that from the agent's own reflective perspective, the action in question is at least as well supported by his or her various reasons for action as the relevant alternatives are. And indeed, given what Lazare knows and believes at the time of his initial decision, the first, overly ambitious step is not necessarily irrational, for he has various reasons for believing that this scheme is far more likely to realize his ambitions than any other project he can think of. After all, it is a matter of applying the recent discovery of a great chemist, who himself believes that the project will work. It is important to note here that even Lazare's partner, who is identified from the start as a man with a good sense of business, agrees to go along with a scheme which he considers overly ambitious. He would prefer a more modest start, but deems the bold approach worth risking.

If Lazare's initial decision to engage in the bold scheme is not irrational (at least in terms of a modest and subjective conception of rationality), then what is the flaw in his practical reasoning? Lazare's error in this episode could be characterized as a species of 'poor planning', an error, moreover, that is instructive in regard to the complex requirements that good planning involves. I shall briefly sketch in some of the basic elements of a contemporary theory of planning, so as to be in a better position to convey the significance of Zola's episode.

In Bratman's words, plans are 'mental states involving an appropriate sort of commitment to action'.[4] Bratman argues that a need for plans concerning future activity is crucial to the success of the purposeful behaviour of human beings and has two basic sources. First of all, a form of deliberation that occurs only at the immediate moment of action would be highly ineffective: 'deliberation requires time and other limited resources, and there is an obvious limit to the extent to which one may successfully deliberate at the time of action. So we need ways to allow deliberation and rational reflection to influence action beyond the present' (p. 2). Secondly, future-oriented intentions figuring within the deliberative structures of planning respond to our pressing needs for co-ordination – the individual's co-ordination of his or her present and future activities, as well as the co-ordination of the actions of more than one agent. If Lazare is to do anything successfully at all, he must co-ordinate his own actions over time; he must also co-ordinate his doings with those of the others with whom he co-operates.

In Bratman's view, intentions – especially future-directed intentions in which an agent resolves to perform some action at a later time – are the building blocks of the plans that play a crucial rôle in our co-ordination and ongoing practical reasoning. One of Bratman's central points, which underscores the originality of his work in relation to previous action theory, is that intentions are not reducible to the agent's other kinds of reasons for action, which in the standard account are all a matter of desires and beliefs. In what way are intentions irreducible to some combination of desire and belief? Various kinds of dispositions are associated with intentions. First of all, unlike desires, intentions are more than potential influences on conduct, but may actually control conduct. Normally, when one has a present-directed intention to do something, one will at the very least try to perform that action. Often, one may form a future-directed intention and simply carry it out when the time comes, without further reflection or deliberation. The same is not true of having a desire to do something, or of believing that one will do something: 'As a conduct-controlling pro-attitude my intention involves a special commitment to action that ordinary desires do not' (p. 16). Moreover, intentions 'resist reconsideration' and have a 'characteristic inertia', so that prior intentions often form an unchallenged background against which future deliberation takes place. Knowledge that one has a prior intention may figure in one's reasoning about what to do next, so that one reasons from the retained intention to further intentions.

Yet this view of the distinctive features of the attitudes known as intentions must be accompanied by an analysis of the kind of practical reasoning that is conducted by agents who engage in planning, and that form of reasoning is not a matter of the blind execution of previously formed schemes. Plans are by necessity partial and incomplete: it is impossible for agents having limited cognitive capacities and information to foresee all of the contingencies of future situations, nor even all of the consequences of their future actions. If an ability to settle on a scheme in advance is crucial to the successful realization of goals, so is the ability to fill in the details of plans at the appropriate moment. Moreover, it would be highly impractical for plans and the future-directed intentions that figure in them to be irrevocable: the inertia and characteristic commitment involved in future-directed intentions does not entail the impossibility of going back on a previous decision: 'plans are not merely executed. They are formed, retained, combined, constrained by other plans, filled in, modified, reconsidered, and so on' (p. 8). In short, the form of reasoning most characteristic of planning agents is described by Bratman as 'reasoning aimed at adjusting and completing prior but partial plans' (p. 10).

A large part of Bratman's theory concerns the conditions under which it is rational to act in keeping with a previously formed intention or plan, and I shall return to this aspect of the theory below. Briefly, this complex issue requires consideration of the conditions under which an agent should or should not engage in deliberative reconsideration of the wisdom of the prior intention. Obviously, if prior intentions have no more weight than present reasons, then the advantages of long-term planning are lost; yet if prior plans become too overpowering, there is a danger of an ineffective rigidity, particularly given the fact that the prior plans are necessarily incomplete, and were not formulated with a view of the details of the present situation. Thus we are led to ask under what conditions it is rational to reconsider the prior intention. A subissue in this regard has to do with whether this deliberation or non-deliberation itself has a reflective or non-reflective basis. Moreover, reconsiderations of a prior intention may lead to the decision to go ahead and act in accordance with that intention, rather than to overrule or alter it, in which case the reconsideration may involve either a change of the reasons that previously supported the action, or simply the preservation or reaffirmation of the same reasons. Although Bratman advocates a view whereby future-directed intentions often have the rôle of controlling rational action, and insists on the fact that rational human agents cannot start their deliberations afresh at every moment, he does not want these emphases to distort our judgement of cases where an irrational decision is carried forward by virtue of the agent's adherence to a plan. Normally, we do not want to say that an irrational decision can be 'bootstrapped' into a rational action by virtue of its place within a plan to which the agent is committed. In this regard, Bratman contrasts what he calls 'internal' and 'external' perspectives on an action or decision, where the former is a deliberation about the rationality of an action conducted in terms of a framework of reasons established by a prior intention and plan, and where the latter refers to a deliberation that is not constrained in this manner by prior commitment to a plan, and involves evaluating the rationality of the action from a different perspective. For now, let us simply underscore the basic idea that the rationality of plans and long-term commitments does not entail the view that what was a bad idea in the first place can become rational simply because of the rationality of sticking to one's prior intentions.

Sometimes it is rational not to deliberate at all about the wisdom of a prior plan, but when the agent encounters a problem 'for' the plan, it may be most reasonable to reconsider it. (Bratman distinguishes between a problem for a plan and a problem posed by a plan (p. 67), where the latter typically is a matter of filling in the means to a particular end, whereas the former involves some major challenge to the feasibility of the overall scheme, or perhaps a significant shift in one's own desires or intentions, where this shift has the effect of calling the prior plan into question.)

In addition to taking up the kind of issues just evoked, Bratman's theory of planning includes reference to two more basic requirements on plans, and these requirements are directly relevant to the case of Lazare. Bratman explains that these two basic demands on plans have a pragmatic rationale, for they state what is normally required of plans if they are to do a good job of co-ordinating and controlling conduct. They are, however, defeasible: 'there may be special circumstances in which it is rational of an agent to violate them' (p. 32). Two kinds of demands are at stake here: demands concerning consistency, and demands concerning the means–ends relations within plans. A first requirement on the rationality of a plan is the demand that it be internally consistent. This means that it must be possible for the entire plan to be successfully executed, without any one part of the plan flatly contradicting or being incompatible with any other part. A second type of coherence that is required of plans demands that they be strongly consistent relative to the agent's beliefs. This means that it should be possible for the plan to be executed successfully given the truth of all of the agent's other beliefs. Suppose that Lazare does not believe it possible to study medicine and music successfully at the same time, but that he none the less plans to undertake both courses of study at once. In that case, his plan is strongly inconsistent relative to his beliefs.

Bratman's requirement concerning what he calls means–end coherence concerns the need for filling in the details of plans that are by necessity schematic and incomplete. Plans are not required to take into account every possible circumstance that might arise, nor need they specify in detail what means must be used to achieve the various ends figuring in the plans. When Lazare decides to become a doctor, he does not have to determine his future specialization in order to have a coherent plan. That is simply a problem posed by the plan, and he can postpone dealing with it until later. Yet means–end coherence does require that 'plans be filled in with specifications that are as detailed' – on the agent's view – 'as needed for their successful execution' (p. 31). And those details that must be filled in can be filled in later, as long as this specification is not put off until too late.

Given these remarks, we are in a position to observe that Lazare's central error in the business endeavour should not be seen as a failure to develop and apply a long-term plan – for indeed he has one – but as a failure to adjust this scheme properly as the events unfold. Successful planning requires extended deliberation that adapts to circumstances, not the automatic application of an initial scheme. When the first design of the machines proves incorrect, Lazare does the right thing by going to Paris to get the chemist's help in readjusting the plans. This is a fine example of means–end coherence, for although he could not have foreseen the situation, he develops a means of saving his plan when it happens to arise. Yet Lazare fails to behave similarly when the large-scale operation does not immediately have the expected results. Instead, he stubbornly insists on investing more and more money in trying to make the original plan work (and this investment is made at a time when he is seriously diminishing his available capital). When this approach fails, he abruptly gives up on the entire enterprise rather than altering his grandiose plan.

The failure of Lazare's reasoning is best illustrated by contrasting his behaviour to the successful operations that his partner performs in what is essentially the same situation. Once Lazare has sold out, Boutigny takes up the business with zeal. He makes the necessary provisional adjustment by abandoning the costly attempt to make the unreliable new method work, and returns to the conventional method of turning seaweed into a valuable commodity. Lazare's initial error – building on a large scale – now pays off, for Boutigny is able to produce the valuable ashes in great quantities. In this manner he begins to realize a fine profit. Later, when he can afford to employ the help of a chemist, he returns to the initial idea of developing the new method, this time with success. Thus, without abandoning the overall intention to make a lucrative business out of the exploitation of seaweed, Boutigny is able to revise the initial conception of what means to that end should be employed, just as he is able later, when conditions change once again, to return to the very same scheme and make it work. His practical cunning amounts to a certain flexibility in his application of different means to a single end.

Lazare, on the other hand, does not respond so coherently. When the basic plan he has taken from his chemical master does not work, he is at a total loss as to what to do, which suggests that his plan suffers from a basic means–end incoherence. Lazare need not have foreseen the exact nature of the difficulty, but in investing such a large amount of money on the scheme, he should have been prepared to deal with the eventuality by being willing to invest time and energy in seeking additional information about ways to deal with problems that arise. Pathetically, he cannot think of any other means to his end, and seems to consult no one else about what to do (save his devious partner and the members of his family). And this problem of means and ends is directly related to the question of his reconsideration of the entire scheme. Finding no further means to his end, he puts the entire project in question, panics, and finally sacrifices his entire investment. Although the enterprise is certainly not developing as he had planned, Lazare in fact had several other options, but instead of rationally deliberating about them, he gives over to a kind of global despair, putting the entire project in doubt (and with it, the whole of science, for Lazare now proclaims his adherence to Schopenhauer's pessimism). Given his inability to come up with a way to deal with the problem that he confronts, Lazare's reconsideration of the entire project is certainly rational, yet his conclusion that the project must be abandoned is not. What Lazare takes to be an unsolvable problem for the entire plan is, from Boutigny's more practical perspective, but a problem arising within the overall business scheme. Where Lazare engages in a fundamental reconsideration of the wisdom of the entire project (and of the initial scheme on which it was based), Boutigny merely readjusts his activity in function of the circumstances that arise, dealing with adversity, while also profiting from an unexpected opportunity – the chance to acquire full ownership of the business when his partner loses his nerve.

That the same kind of error subverts all of Lazare's other major schemes is amply demonstrated by the narrative, for in each occasion we are shown that he fails to adjust his initial plan successfully when confronted with difficulties, and subsequently gives up trying, preferring to transfer his attention to some new project. For example, although Lazare and his cousin have invested quite a lot of money in his project to build a sea-wall, as soon as the young man encounters some obstacles (the workers somehow exasperate him), he calls a halt to the work and immediately begins thinking of new schemes.[5] In short, Lazare is incapable of coherently developing means to the ends he sets for himself, and has an irrational habit of reconsidering and abandoning his own previously established long-term intentions. Such is the basic pattern of irrationality at the heart of each of the major episodes in his career, which is but a series of costly abortions.

Although the theory of planning allows us to describe Lazare's error quite accurately in relation to some basic norms of practical deliberation, the theory does not have anything to say about the reasons why an agent would typically deviate from these norms. Zola's text, however, does include various insightful suggestions along those lines. What, then, does it tell us about the bases of Lazare's irrational behaviour? A first basis would seem to be a discrepancy between Lazare's real desires and the schemes in which he becomes involved. Lazare apparently thinks that he can get what he wants by engaging in a successful business endeavour, but what he really desires is to enjoy a prompt success entirely on the basis of a brilliant and original idea. Just as when he shifted from music to medicine his goal remained the winning of some kind of worldwide fame, so in undertaking the business venture, he still thinks of the project as a way of quickly manifesting his individual genius and singularity. Thus he has a tendency to value only the most extreme and dramatic scenarios, ruling out the modest, mediocre, and time-consuming means to his ends. Here we may have a reason why he never conceives of the idea of making some money for a while by reverting to the old method of turning seaweed into a saleable commodity, even though he has already invested a small fortune, and stands to lose it all. Boutigny is capable of taking recourse to this slower and more ordinary approach, but Lazare is not, and expresses his contempt for the traditional method. Lazare's fundamental interest in the entire venture, then, is to prove to the world that he is a singular and outstanding individual, which is why only an innovative method truly interests him. This may also be why he could never be satisfied with a medical career, and is drawn to a number of different artistic endeavours.

A second, and perhaps more determinant basis of Lazare's error is his inability to sustain the necessary level of confidence in the face of adversity. He is wildly overconfident as long as he thinks he has a brilliant and perfect scheme, but once he is faced with discrepancies between the clean, broad strokes of his scheme and the messy details and circumstances of reality, he loses faith, particularly when it is a matter of reflecting on his own capacities. As the text suggests, when the seaweed factory fails to work as expected, he becomes 'sick with uncertainty' over the ultimate outcome of the project (p. 873), and it is this uncertainty and fear that incapacitate him. His loss of confidence and the related emotions of disgust, anger, and fear vitiate his reasoning about what to do next, turning a problem posed by a plan into an insurmountable problem for the plan.

Here our reading of Zola's text encounters an insight expressed by John Maynard Keynes when he underscores the importance of the degree of confidence that agents have in their various forecasts. On the one hand, then, are the various forecasts that an agent can make, including the one that the agent deems most likely; but on the other hand, there is the agent's second-order confidence in the forecast itself. Keynes suggests that 'the state of long-term expectation, upon which our decisions are based, does not solely depend, therefore, on the most probable forecast we can make'.[6] It also depends on our degree of confidence in that forecast. In a remarkable passage that deserves to be quoted in the present context, Keynes lays great stress on the rôle of confidence in determining the stability and instability of economic activity:

[A] large proportion of our positive activities depend on spontaneous optimism rather than on a mathematical expectation, whether moral or hedonistic or economic . . . Enterprise only pretends to itself to be mainly actuated by the statements in its own prospectus, however candid and sincere. Only a little more than an expedition to the South Pole, is it based on an exact calculation of benefits to come. Thus if the animal spirits are dimmed and the spontaneous optimism falters, leaving us to depend on nothing but a mathematical expectation, enterprise will fade and die; – though fears of loss may have a basis no more reasonable than hopes of profit had before.

It is safe to say that enterprise which depends on hopes stretching into the future benefits the community as a whole. But individual initiative will only be adequate when reasonable calculation is supplemented and supported by animal spirits, so that the thought of ultimate loss which often overtakes pioneers, as experience undoubtedly tells us and them, is put aside as a healthy man puts aside the expectation of death.[7]

Although Keynes's reference to an obscure psychology of the

'animal spirits' signals a theoretical problem rather than a solution, his insistence on the rôle of the agent's degree of confidence in the accuracy of expectations about the future takes us to the heart of what is irrational and destructive in Lazare's disposition. Zola's work certainly shows us a Lazare who has various calculations about different plans of action, and who at times reasons quite well within these planning frameworks. Yet Lazare also thinks about the likelihood of the success of his schemes, and these beliefs – which directly express his degree of confidence – are as unstable as they are puissant. The young man has no terms in which to calculate the likelihood of ever being recognized as a musician of genius, yet when he feels confident about his prospects, he is strongly attracted to this goal and invests everything in the attempt to realize it. Yet when he encounters adversity, he begins to reflect on his chances and suddenly loses confidence in his musical talent. The narrative presents this sudden emotional shift as the crucial factor in his decision to give up his musical career and study medicine. Similarly, the narrative underscores the extent to which it is fear that vitiates Lazare's reasoning at the crucial moment of his business venture. Lazare, then, is at times quite capable of engaging in effective problem-solving behaviour, but when he encounters adversity and begins to reflect upon the chances of his own success, his confidence falters and the ensuing emotional condition and nervous reconsideration subvert the endeavour.

That the key factor is a matter of Lazare's second-order degree of confidence is underscored by the fact that the narrative includes an episode in which Lazare manifests a great deal of first-order courage: on a walk with Pauline, he happens upon the scene of a fire, and without reflecting on the danger, rushes into the flames to save a trapped infant, performing heroically as long as he has no time to deliberate over his chances of success. The incident is significant because it sheds light on another central aspect of the novel's characterization of Lazare, namely, the figure's morbid fear of death. The narrative insists heavily on this tendency of Lazare's, portraying it at times as a simple *idée fixe* that haunts the man like a ghost. Yet when Lazare rushes into the burning flames, risking his life, we see that it is not any simple fear of mortality as such that marks Lazare's personality. Keynes, we have noted, likens the businessman's confidence in his enterprise to the healthy man's ability to put aside the expectation of death, and this analogy suggests a different approach to Lazare's obsession with his own mortality – an obsession that is only manifested, we should observe, after his practical failings have become quite serious. It is not the fear of death that subverts Lazare's practical rationality; rather, it would be more plausible to assume that his practical irrationality, exacerbated by his reaction to the unfortunate events in the house-hold (the father's illness; the mother's sudden demise) is what eventually generates the morbid habit of thought. Thus, a more plausible understanding of the character might be reached by view-ing his morbid fear of death as being in part the extension and symptomatic manifestation of a more basic disposition, namely, his characteristic second-order uncertainty, that is, his chronic lack of confidence in his own ability to foresee and control the future. What disturbs Lazare is not death, nor even the thought of death, but what this thought comes to represent to him after a number of major failures. And in Lazare's mind, the thought of his own death does not stand simply for the absolute limit to his existence. Rather, it stands for the absolute limit and uncertainty of his knowledge. That he will die is certain, which means that there is a point in time – a point impossible to predict with any measure of confidence – beyond which all of his planning and activity is of no avail. In his Schopenhauerian ideology, Lazare uses the thought of death as the ultimate justification of his loss of confidence in his various projects and ambitions: 'What's the use', he reasons, discounting the enter-prises in which he is actually engaged.

Fear of failure, we have argued, plays a fundamental rôle in the subversion of Lazare's practical reasoning, especially at the crucial moment when he must find a way to make his seaweed factory begin to turn a profit. Lazare's fear of failure helps produce his failure, and this fear finds its basis in a characteristic failure to maintain a second-order confidence in his own abilities. Yet is this disposition as mysterious and inexplicable as the 'animal spirits' to which Keynes refers? Zola and his narrators sometimes suggest as much with talk of the mysterious and hereditary nature of the individual, but the narrative in fact shows us something more interesting than this.

To explore this point, let us return to the crucial moment when Lazare is grappling with the factory's failure to turn a profit. The narrator tells us that he is overwhelmed by fear, and clearly this fear contributes to his inability to find a viable scheme. It is at this point that the narrative stresses yet another factor, namely, the rôle of the partner in distorting Lazare's thinking: 'It was Boutigny who had terrified Lazare by giving him a disastrous account of the situation' (p. 880). Boutigny claims that he wants to leave the business in order to take up some brilliant position that is supposed to be waiting for him in Algeria; he shows great reluctance to have anything more to do with what he characterizes as a hopeless factory, and confuses Lazare by presenting the firm's accounts in a needlessly complicated way, emphasizing the debts. Lazare simply capitulates, accepting his partner's offer of 5,000 francs in exchange for the ownership of the entire enterprise, with Boutigny agreeing to assume responsibility for the monies owed by the firm. Obviously, Boutigny is aware of Lazare's loss of confidence and actively exploits this weakness; Lazare, on the other hand, seems blithely unaware of Boutigny's character and intentions, thereby failing to take note of the fact that he is in a strategic situation where his interests require him to formulate expectations about the possible strategic actions of the other party. Lazare trusts Boutigny and adopts what he takes to be the partner's vision of the situation, whereas in fact he is simply being duped by someone who has quite a different plan in mind. Thus we may give a provisional label to the 'animal spirit' that plays a decisive rôle in this transaction: Lazare's overconfidence in the other person.

Another look at the other episodes in Lazare's career suggests that a similar relation to other people consistently plays a decisive rôle in his planning. Zola's narrator at no point makes any explicit comment to this effect, and indeed, the explicit theoretical statements proferred by Zola's narrators are consistently misleading and ill-informed. But the narrative none the less includes the relevant information at each step in the story. First of all, Lazare's meta-ambition, his overarching belief that he must be a stupendous success in some domain, is not an idea that has sprung spontaneously from the depths of his own psyche, but is instead clearly the product of the family's mythology: the family lives modestly near a remote fishing village as a result of an unfortunate financial decline, and the only son is expected to engineer a triumphant reversal of their bad fortune: 'they were waiting for the success of their son, who was suppose to free them from their mediocre plight' (p. 822). Intensely dissatisfied with her own position, Lazare's mother dreams that her son will change her life by become a rich and influential political figure.[8] A forceful and manipulative personality – the narrator refers to her *volontés dominatrices* (p. 821) – she has had years to rehearse this scenario with her son, while the invalid father passively looks on. These years of indoctrination have been successful in so far as Lazare never once doubts that he is destined for some variety of fame and fortune; he has only scorn for more modest (and realistic) schemes. The overarching life theme is in place, then, and only the specific means to that end remain to be filled in: Lazare must choose the domain of activity in which he will demonstrate his brilliance. Here is where one of the young man's other educators introduces an important element: 'At the Lycée in Caen, he had had a violin teacher who, struck by his musical talent, had predicted that he would have a glorious future' (p. 839). Yet this influence is countered by that of his mother, who has no confidence that her scenario is going to be realized in this manner and who regrets that she ever taught her son how to play the piano.[9] She sees her last hopes crumbling, and bitterly opposes Lazare's desire to apply for entrance at the Conservatory in Paris. They quarrel over the issue, and after Lazare's graduation, she gives him until October to abandon his artistic phantasy and choose a serious profession, one worthy of an *honnête homme*. Lazare's cousin Pauline plays a key rôle in breaking the deadlock that summer: 'She ended up by getting him interested in medicine, explaining to him that if she had been born a man, she would find healing people the most exciting thing in the world' (p. 842). Lazare weakly gives in to his mother and cousin.

Although Lazare is initially exalted by his new life among the medical students in the Latin Quarter, during his second year he begins to hate his professors and fails his examinations.[10] It is at this point that Lazare encounters the model who becomes the next decisive influence on his desires – the famous chemist Herbelin, whom the young man eagerly adopts as his 'master'. Medicine is abandoned and chemistry becomes the chosen field. Lazare's first major professional venture is nothing but an attempt to apply one of this master's ideas, and Lazare's mistakes and failures in this scheme result in part from his overly rigid adhesion to the master's plan.

It would seem, then, that Lazare's thinking about different domains and activities is consistently mediated by his relation to particular individuals. Additional evidence of this pattern is presented at the moment in the narrative when Lazare's business ambitions are broken, for he temporarily becomes fascinated with a humble country priest who lives near their home. The priest is a simple-minded and ambitionless being who spends his days calmly gardening and smoking a pipe. Charmed by this model, Lazare acquires a pipe and joins his new mentor daily in the garden, hoping, unsuccessfully, to acquire the old man's simple and unthinking faith as easily as he acquired his taste for tobacco.

The extent to which Lazare is capable of adopting and abandoning a major project in function of the influence that other people momentarily have on him is further underscored by another episode in the novel. As has already been mentioned, Lazare engages himself in designing and building a sea-wall; it is important to note that the basic idea is a long-standing scheme of his father's and that it is cousin Pauline who encourages Lazare to commit himself to the endeavour. Yet when the plan does not simply spring into reality without the least bit of trouble, Lazare tires of the business and leaves the construction half finished. That part of the structure that has already been put in place when Lazare gives up is destroyed by the waves of the very next storm (pp. 984–5). Important elements in this episode are the villagers' sarcastic and overtly cruel reaction to Lazare's scheme, and the latter's rather painful awareness of their feelings. Far from supporting his efforts and expressing any gratitude or confidence, they clearly prefer not to be protected from the ocean by the efforts of someone whom they take to be a pretentious bourgeois: 'they would laugh the day when the sea would sweep away his beams like straws. The sea could destroy the whole place, but it would be amusing just the same' (pp. 909–10). The villagers gather to cheer the waves that destroy the sea-wall, cruelly mocking Lazare's efforts, while he stands dejected, a few feet away.[11] Yet Lazare's public humiliation on this occasion does not satisfy them, and the villagers continue to challenge him to do something about the ocean's steady advance – although none of them thinks for a second that it is really possible to stop the ocean waves. The narrator tells us that when the fishermen complain about the plight of the village and ask Lazare for his help, what they are really expressing is their pride in the ferocity of the ocean.[12] Irritated by the villagers' jibes, Lazare avoids going to the village so as to be spared their painful remarks. One day, however, one of the locals happens to meet him when he is on his way to visit the priest, and 'with a malicious laugh in the corner of his eyes', asks Lazare for permission to make firewood of the beams that have been thrown up on the beach. Although Lazare has apparently long since decided to abandon the project, in a moment of anger, 'without even having thought about it', he suddenly responds to the villager that the wood cannot be used for firewood because the work on the sea-wall is going to be resumed the very next week (p. 1015). The villagers hear of this and gossip maliciously, delighted to know that they will be able to see the 'dance' another time. Two weeks pass, however, without Lazare taking any action, and the fishermen cruelly ask him if he is having trouble finding someone willing to do the work. Lazare finally does take up the project once more, but the narrator tells us that in doing so he is only 'giving in to his cousin', who wants him to have something to occupy him, but who does not want him to move away (p. 1016). Lazare makes a new design for the structure and spends more of his cousin's dwindling inheritance on the work, hoping to get additional financing from a local council – but when an engineer files a highly negative report on the project, these funds are denied, and the project is abandoned. At this point we have come full circle: Lazare's father, as mayor of the village, has for years being trying to get money in support for a project to protect the village from erosion, and it was Lazare's cousin Pauline who encouraged Lazare in the first place to get involved in the project. In short, Lazare's initiative was on loan from others, and when the others no longer support the project, his interest in it vanishes.

The episode of the sea-wall falls within a larger pattern that may be traced in Lazare's actions. He tends to shift wildly between moments of supreme, and indeed foolhardy, confidence in each new project, and moments of uncertainty in which he doubts the value and viability of the very schemes in which his previous confidence has led him to invest. The evidence just surveyed allows us to add that these irrational shifts are not due simply to some mysterious inner process within the character's psyche, but are directly related to his interaction with other agents. The moments of confidence, then, occur when Lazare is under the sway of the influence of a model who seems to him to point the way to the realization of his desires for success and personal distinction. The moments of uncertainty occur when Lazare no longer believes himself guided by such a model, either because he has lost confidence in the agent in question, or when he for other reasons believes himself thrown back on his own resources – resources which he judges, at such moments, to be grossly inadequate. Thus we may note that Lazare only experiences great confidence in his own projects when he believes them anchored firmly to the direction and guidance of a superior and more expert model or personal mediator. Lazare's thinking about this or that sphere of activity, plan, or problem is not direct, then, but is mediated through the emotions and ideas he has in regard to some other person, who either points the way or bars the path to the desired goal. It is this mimetic disposition that vitiates his reckoning of means and ends when actively engaged in the planning and execution of his various schemes, for his overconfidence in the other's expertise leads him to attach far too much weight to whatever he takes that person's opinion to be. For example, the authority that Herbelin enjoys in Lazare's eyes makes it impossible for Lazare to listen to Boutigny's suggestion about a more modest and less risky way to get their seaweed business started. But when Herbelin has been discredited in Lazare's mind, Boutigny becomes the unchallenged expert, and Lazare disastrously accepts the man's self-interested and blatantly deceptive account of the state of affairs. At crucial points in Lazare's life, his cousin Pauline gives him advice which is not particularly sound, yet he acts on it without seeming to engage in any serious reflection and deliberation. It is Pauline who gets him to abandon music for medicine, just as it is Pauline who discourages him from moving to Caen to start his own newspaper, and gets him to work on the seawall so that he can be 'occupied' without needing to move away from the family home. It is Lazare's mother who, when the dowry has been consumed, insists on postponing Lazare's marriage to Pauline, effectively destroying their romance, and it is his mother who actively encourages Louise to supplant Pauline (p. 931). Thus Lazare's inconstancy, his inability to sustain a second-order confidence in his own projects and forecasts, would appear to be functionally linked to the actions of other persons with whom he has contact.

The pattern that has just been sketched recalls the opposition that has sometimes been drawn between two kinds of explanatory approaches: on the one hand, an approach that emphasizes the rational decision making of the individual, and on the other, an approach that underscores the rôle of 'social influence' in determining people's actions. Robert Abelson develops such a dichotomy, suggesting that both epistemic and practical forms of the individual agent's rationality are often subordinated to social influence. Rationality, Abelson contends, corresponds to an idealization that is never matched by psychological reality; it is a pre-emptive and presumptive concept, and instead of looking for something that is not really there, we would be better advised to orient research towards the forms of social influence that are actually operative: 'searching for the idealization that isn't there is a less productive strategy than finding out what *is* there'.[13] Thus an individual psychology based on the notion of rationality should be abandoned in favour of social psychology, the central message of which is that *'individuals are very much more susceptible to the social influence of peers or authority figures than they are ordinarily aware'*.[14] Abelson adds, however, that social psychology can agree to a 'limited subjective rationality' in the form of some personal system of principles applied to reasoning over an imperfect belief set.

Reference to Zola's depiction of Lazare may help us to clarify these issues, which are anything but simple. In some highly significant and important instances, Lazare's practical reasoning is wholly inadequate and indeed irrational. This judgement is based on normative standards of rationality that are quite moderate and subjective, for it is a matter of saying that given his own goals and reflective beliefs, Lazare behaves incoherently. Indeed, what the novel tells us about Lazare's own self-reflective judgements wholly confirms this perspective, for he is severe in condemning his own failures (e.g. pp. 1014–15). Certain forms of social influence, we have suggested, are central to this irrationality, which could indeed suggest that the story of Lazare's failures may be better understood in terms of a network of social relations and interactions than in terms of Lazare's personal reasoning. For example, the narrative states that as a result of a villager's remark, Lazare immediately and impulsively claims – without even having thought about it – that he is going to renew the project for building a sea-wall. What is worse, it is his cousin's influence that causes him to make good on this impetuous promise. Clearly it is a matter here of someone who is easily swayed by other people's words and actions.

Yet it is also important to note that 'social influence' is not a term standing for some kind of process that is totally irreducible to further analysis and that has no conditions and elements at the level of the cognition and motivation of the individuals involved. 'Social influence' is not a social or group phenomenon that vitiates Lazare's rationality from without, in some kind of mechanical fashion; nor should his tendency to be influenced by others be understood as something that emerges from a separate compartment within his psyche, a compartment having no contact with the rest of his thinking. Thus it should not be a matter of drawing a sharp contrast between an analysis based on a theory of individual rationality and an analysis based on some sort of a-rational social-psychological symptomology, comprised of unthinking impulses or 'forces'. Nor is it sufficient to contrast two forms of rationality (such as the 'instrumental' versus the 'charismatic' or 'traditional'), thought to stand in a wholly mysterious relation to each other.

Instead, the phenomena that may be associated with the idea of 'social influence' themselves require explanation in terms of the internal functional relations between the individual agent's attitudes. This is the case because the influence or impact that others may have on Lazare is necessarily mediated through Lazare's perceptions of these others' behaviours, as well as through his other various beliefs about them. If Lazare is capable of being influenced by what other agents tell him, it is because he has certain beliefs about these agents and certain desires in relation to them. For example, he initially takes Herbelin to be a genuis who embodies some kind of infallible scientific wisdom, and it is this poorly founded and simplistic belief that shapes Lazare's planning. When the plan falters, Lazare considers that he now has evidence of the falsehood of his former attitude, and the chemist (and along with him, the whole of science) is divested of authority. The difference resides in Lazare's perception of the situation, which shifts from an unreasonable and unfounded inflation of Herbelin's status, to an equally unreasonable and unfounded deflation of all scientific authority. And these shifts have their basis in Lazare's own assumptions and desires, not in the objective truth of the world.

Social influence, then, is not a non-rational process, or one that is detached from the individual agents' practical reasoning and beliefs. Nor is it solely or primarily a source of distortions and irrationality, as is shown by those instances where social influence is a useful part of an agent's rational planning and action. For example, the same narrative that depicts Lazare as a creature led to his ruin by his manner of reacting to others informs us that

Boutigny relies on the expertise of a bright young chemist when he successfully exploits the new method of treating seaweed. Presumably this means that Boutigny thinks that the chemist knows something that he does not know himself; the astute businessman follows the chemist's advice, adopting his ideas concerning which means should be adopted in order to achieve certain ends. Relying on the chemist's authority enhances Boutigny's probability of success in achieving his own goals.[15] Here we see that it would be simplistic to think that Lazare's distortions and irrationalities can be explained by the presence of 'social influence', while Boutigny's efficiency is explained by its absence. After all, it is Lazare who gets Boutigny involved in the seaweed business in the first place.

Lazare's irrationality should be discussed in terms of the incoherent and ineffective forms of reasoning that orient and distort his interactions with others, transforming them consistently into a source of irrationality and failure. The key point, then, is not that Lazare simply engages in no practical reasoning whatsover in his dealings with Boutigny, Pauline, and the others, his behaviour being instead oriented by 'animal spirits' or some other opaque and mysterious causes. Rather, in dealing with these others he consistently engages in a highly inadequate form of practical reasoning, which, far from being a total renunciation of his own beliefs and desires in favour of external influence, is in fact Lazare's habitual manner of trying to advance his own interests. Lazare consistently makes extremely naïve judgements about the motives and capacities of others. More specifically, his thinking involves a tendency to attach far too much weight to what may be called erroneous 'tutelary beliefs'. This means that in making his own plans, he frequently assumes that the information needed is all in the hands of some single authoritative individual and can easily be acquired from that person. Lazare then directly models his own attitudes on what he thinks the authority believes and prefers, for in this manner, Lazare assumes, he will win the desired rewards – which should fall to him the way he receives candy from his mother.

As the example of Boutigny's employment of the chemist suggests, relying on another person's authority is sometimes part of the recipe for rational planning. Yet there are many situations where a mimetic strategy is highly unlikely to be successful, so the rational agent has to be in a position to exercize some reflective control over the adoption of the beliefs and preferences gleaned from a model. Quite obviously, if the mimetic agent is to be rational, he or she must have some good reasons to believe that the potential model or mediator's beliefs and preferences truly are in some way superior to the policies that the imitator is capable of generating without reference to the model's example. The example of Lazare shows as well that the imitative agent must have good reason to expect that he or she will be capable of successfully imitating the model's practices: some of Lazare's failures result, not from an error in choosing the model, but from his inability to demonstrate the requisite talent in executing the scheme that had been mimetically adopted.

There is another category of situations where the mimetic strategy is unlikely to be successful, namely, those where the imitative agent has no good reason to assume that he or she truly has access to the potential model's desires and beliefs. It may in some cases be wise to base one's decisions and actions on the policy adopted by a more authoritative and accomplished individual, but such wisdom becomes folly when the policy adopted in this manner is in reality only a strategic deception. Thus a mimetic strategy is least likely to succeed in cases where the model is engaged in deceitful behaviour in dealing with the imitator, for the simple reason that the imitator does not have any direct and simple access to what the model really believes and desires. Some of Lazare's major errors take this form, for he copies other people's actions and follows their advice without reflecting on the hidden assumptions and desires that motivate them. For example, Lazare does not really understand what Boutigny believes and wants until it is too late, just as Lazare never understands that his mother's life-long desire is a public recovery of her imagined distinction and superiority, not his own acquisition of autonomy and success. In short, Lazare's error is at times his unawareness of the first premise of all strategic thinking, which Sir Winston Churchill – a man of no small experience in these matters – expressed as follows: 'one should always try to put oneself in the position of what Bismarck called "the Other Man". The more fully and sympathetically a Minister can do this the better are his chances of being right. The more knowledge he possesses of the opposite point of view, the less puzzling it is to know what to do.'[16]

The analysis of Lazare's irrationalities does not terminate here, however, for one may wish to enquire about the origins of the self-defeating habits of reasoning that we have identified in Lazare. How could someone come to have the attitudes and dispositions that lead them to engage in these kinds of unsuccessful and ill-founded forms of mimetic belief and desire? Zola's novel clearly does not provide the kind of detailed evidence that a thorough investigation of this problem would require, yet it does present a few important hints which make possible a rough sketch of an argument along these lines. Briefly, then, our reading of the text suggests that in discussing the possible origins of Lazare's dispositions, it is crucial to study the character of his mother, for this woman is depicted as being largely responsible for creating the environment in which the young man has learned to envision the world, himself, and other people. Madame Chanteau's vision of things is twisted by the discrepancy between her beliefs about her proper place in the social order and the reality of her situation, and this discrepancy is a source of no small bitterness. The discrepancy in question is in part the product of her own imagination, for although she imagines herself to have been a distinguished creature of society who married beneath herself, the narrator identifies her to us as an orphaned school teacher, an '*orpheline de hobereaux ruinés de Cotentin*' (p. 821). She delusively blames her husband for their modest existence, 'wilfully forgetting' her own responsibility in the mismanagement of their resources. She shows herself in the course of the novel to be an unscrupulous, self-serving, and intensely manipulative individual, who wittingly or unwittingly casts a deceptive rhetorical veil over each of the unfair and manipulative actions she adopts in her dealings with others. She conceals her offences behind a smokescreen of accusations, loudly proclaiming that the very people she is exploiting are the aggressive and guilty parties. She cherishes her memory of the days when she supposedly enjoyed a distinguished social position in Caen, and has invested heavily in her phantasy of a dramatic reversal, which she hopes to engineer by manipulating her son's career. Lazare reveres this mother who has nourished him with an incessant stream of propaganda; he takes many of her statements at face value, and seems generally innocent of any knowledge of his mother's strategic and manipulative policies. Unquestioningly obeying her exhortations and failing to reflect on the prejudices and interests that orient her actions, Lazare enjoys in return the promise that he will win the distinction of being the darling saviour of this unquestioned parent. Although Lazare does try to oppose his mother in regard to the initial choice of his career, his resistance is short-lived and pathetic, particularly given the fact that she is largely responsible for the form of his ambitions – as well as for his earlier initiation to the art of music. It is hardly surprising under these circumstances that a person raised by a woman whose chief characteristic is the will to dominate should have a tendency to model his plans on the opinions of some central and dominant individual. And as we have seen above, such is the basic attitude that the young Lazare extends into his dealings with the other salient figures in his hapless career. Beyond these rather sketchy remarks about the formative years of Lazare's development, however, the novel does not permit us to go.

CHAPTER 6

Science, reason, and society

In the last three chapters I have explored some ways in which readings of literary narratives can help us to clarify, challenge, and improve concepts of rationality emerging within a range of disciplines, including philosophy, the social sciences, and psychology. Various narratives, I have argued, usefully illustrate the shortcomings of reductionist models of agency and atomistic conceptions of rationality, and in each case I have stressed the relevance and value of an agential perspective on rationality. Yet it may be objected here that although these hypothetical revisions of atomistic concepts of rationality are a step in the right direction, they still do not go far enough. At the heart of the agential conception of rationality – or so the objection would run – is an essentially 'individualist' prejudice, the result being a failure to account for supraindividual social realities: if we grant that individual beliefs, desires, intentions, and actions should be evaluated in the larger context of the agent's long-term reasons and interests, we should conclude as well that the latter should be viewed in a larger framework, namely, the interpersonal and social context where they are situated. Otherwise, we would be forced to allow that an agent and her actions could be rational even when they contribute to an essentially irrational social action or situation.

This is a difficult and important issue. In keeping with the approach adopted in the rest of this study, I shall address myself to this problem by seeking connexions between theoretical and narrative sources. My central text will be Lem's thought-provoking fictional characterization of a collective scientific research project in *His Master's Voice* (trans. of *Głos pana*, first published in 1968). Lem's narrative in *His Master's Voice* begins with a fictive 'Editor's Note' purporting to inform the reader about the circumstances surrounding the publication of the text to follow. A manuscript, we read, has been found among the papers of the great scientist, Peter E. Hogarth. Although the manuscript was unfinished, lacked a title, and included a fragmentary afterword or preface in rough draft form, Hogarth's colleague has decided that it should be published, and with the help of publishers and assistants has given the text its final finish. This kind of description of the conditions surrounding the discovery and publication of a manuscript is, of course, a well-known framing device. In the present instance the fictive preface serves to underscore a theme that will be stressed throughout Lem's narrative (and indeed, from the first page on) for it points to the fact that the fate of an individual's work – here, Hogarth's manuscript – is shaped by circumstances and agents standing outside that agent's control. Although the manuscript is an autobiography, the outcome is not entirely Hogarth's own doing; his authorship of the story is incomplete, and not even the title is his own. It is thus all the more appropriate that he declares in his second paragraph that 'It was as a result of circumstances beyond my control that I become involved in the events that I wish to relate here' (p. 3). Both the events and their telling have an essentially social nature, for their final shape emerges from the complex inter-relations between individual action and social factors.

Lem has Hogarth begin his narrative with some remarks about the genre to which he is about to contribute – the autobiography – and about its relation to another genre – biography and, more specifically, biographies about scientists. The latter genre, Hogarth complains, sacrifices reality to stereotype and convention. Typically, myths about the nature of scientific genius lead the writers of such biographies to depict scientists as pristine seekers after the truth. Artists may be portrayed as spirits chained to flesh, but the scientist is always portrayed as an instance of the contrary metamorphosis. The result, Hogarth pursues, is that none of his twenty-eight biographers has told his true story; consequently he remains 'completely unknown'. His own manuscript, then, will serve to fill in this lacuna, just as it will relate the unknown facts about the momentous His Master's Voice project in which Hogarth was a leading figure. Hogarth promises, then, to give us 'the inside story', but he adds a little proviso, one that we would be wise to take quite seriously as we go on to read the rest of his narrative:

Which is not to say that I believe a man who is the subject of biographies possesses any greater knowledge of himself than his biographers do. Their position is more convenient, for uncertainties may be attributed to a lack of data, which allows the supposition that the one described, were he but alive and willing, could supply the needed information. The one described, however, possesses nothing more than hypotheses on the subject of himself, hypotheses that may be of interest as the products of his mind but that do not necessarily serve as those missing pieces. (p. 5)

We will indeed have the occasion to observe in what follows that at key moments, the hypotheses proclaimed by our brilliant and knowledgeable first-person narrator can be rather misleading.

Lem's narrator Hogarth presents his tale, then, as a corrective to the 'official story' that is typically told about the scientific genius. As such, it contacts interestingly (and in some ways anticipates) certain trends in the study of science, namely, the shift away from positivist and logical-empiricist accounts, which focus on the logical features of the products of successful science, viewed in an abstractive context of 'justification' – as opposed to the psychological and social context of actual discovery. Moreover, not only does Hogarth dwell on the blind and irrational features of the latter context, but he insists repeatedly on the fact that the scientists' results are as much inventions and constructions as they are discoveries.[1] Thus, many of the elements in Hogarth's narrative converge to form a typically 'post-modern' perspective on scientific rationality. Or, more accurately, what one modern perspective hailed as scientific rationality is apparently reduced to a series of irrational and non-rational determinants and conditions, of which two varieties move to the fore: those at work within the psychology of the individual researcher, and those extending beyond these psychic confines to a network of socio-cultural, political, and historical factors. A – if not the – central theme of Hogarth's descriptions and explanations of his life of research, then, is the *Gebundenheit des Denkens* – the bounded nature of thought, its finitude as well as its crucial and formative links to causes that are neither thought nor reason. In this vein, Hogarth eloquently proclaims that 'Our civilization, in its "advanced" scientific part, is a narrow construct, a vision repeatedly constricted by a historically stiffening conglomeration of multiple factors' (p. 26).

Hogarth's narrative moves back and forth between two kinds of factors that go into the conglomerate, namely, the social and psychological determinants that fashion the 'narrow construct' of scientific reason. I shall follow these movements for a moment before beginning to probe a little deeper into the complexities of the text, which is much more interesting than the simple shift from 'modern' to 'post-modern' views of science would allow. We may begin with some of the psychological determinants. Hogarth detests psychoanalysis, which he considers dogmatic and circular. His own auto-analysis certainly does not adopt the terms and concepts of any identifiable variety of psychoanalysis, but none the less remains a psychodynamic narrative in which the conscious will struggles against destructive and blind impulses (thus he includes a murky discussion of his childhood experience of his mother's death). Hogarth's account of his graduate work in mathematics highlights the unconscious interpersonal factors at work in his own motivation, factors that not only heightened his desire to succeed, but that led him down a particular avenue of research and caused him to prefer a certain type of finding. Hogarth tells us that as a graduate student at Berkeley he had resented the fact that his mathematics professor favoured a sycophantic student who followed the teacher's lead in deciding which area of the field to cultivate. Hogarth thus set out to prove his teacher wrong:

I do not think I ever finished any larger paper in all my younger work without imagining Dill's eyes on the manuscript. What effort it cost me to prove that the Dill variable combinatorics was only a rough approximation of an ergodic theorem! Not before or since, I daresay, did I polish a thing so carefully; and it is even possible that the whole concept of groups later called Hogarth groups came out of that quiet, constant passion with which I plowed Dill's axioms under. (p. 110)

The great mathematician's progress would seem to have been animated, then, by a species of mimetic desire, for he is propelled by his desire to win the recognition denied him by a teacher, who in the same stroke becomes the life-long mediator whose approval and praise stand as an overarching source of value. Public success is in fact sought after as the external sign of victory in an interpersonal (and in many ways imaginary) competition. Yet this very success leads to the destruction of the myth that had inspired and guided the quest in the first place. The mediator, formerly 'hawklike, hale, seemingly ageless' in Hogarth's mind, is discovered to be a rank-and-file professor of mathematics: 'There were dozens like him in the States. But such rational arguments would not have helped me, especially since at that time I had not acknowledged even to myself the meaning and aim of the idiosyncrasies in my ambition.' As long as he was still the aspiring young mathematician, Hogarth could only be momentarily lucid about his relation to Dill. But eventually the distant mediator and rival was surpassed and revealed as a mediocre, 'shrunken, pot-bellied old man with dull eyes and a slack jaw'. Hogarth continues:

For some time afterward, I felt an emptiness, as if after the loss of someone very close. That kind of stimulating challenge, demanding the concentration of all one's mental power, was suddenly gone. Probably the Dill that followed me constantly and looked over my shoulder at the marked-up manuscripts never existed. When I read, years later, of his death, I felt nothing. But there long remained in me the wound of that vacated place. (pp. 111–12)

Hogarth informs us, then, that the source of his mathematical ambition was a competitive relation to someone whom he had consistently misrepresented to himself. His research was propelled and oriented by a kernel of irrational tutelary beliefs, beliefs immune to rational arguments and blind to their actual basis. Yet the old Hogarth intimates that the young Hogarth should have known better, for the intermittent moments of lucidity surely contradicted the driving beliefs in the tutor's superiority and importance. Yet these unreasonable notions about another human being none the less fuelled and oriented Hogarth's mathematical discoveries, the result being that he successfully made good on his demand for recognition, replacing the teacher's axioms with his own. And it is this same theory of Hogarth groups, invented in a swerve away from the trajectory of a rival, that Hogarth subsequently imposes on the neutrino recordings when he makes his first attempt to study the message being investigated by the His Master's Voice project.

Once he has attained success and maturity, the scientist no longer works in the distorted shadow of his former teacher. Yet this does not mean that his rational cognitive faculties have become freed from their former mimetic bonds and now operate in an autonomous pursuit of knowledge. The truth about the actual context of discovery remains a story about unreasonable interpersonal relations. At the time when Hogarth is asked to join the His Master's Voice (HMV) project, he is conducting a summer seminar as a guest lecturer at a university in New Hampshire, where he has been invited by a former classmate. His reason for accepting the invitation? The seminar is to cover a branch of mathematics in which he is not up to speed, a branch, moreover, that has recently been attracting a lot of attention; in Hogarth's own words, 'phenomenal discoveries were in the air'. Hogarth comments in the same context that 'every man, it seems, must envy another', and it is his envy of those at the 'mathematical front line' that leads him to accept the summer appointment (pp. 50–1). The chance to teach in the unfamiliar area is valuable to him because it represents an opportunity to work in the limelight and once more impose himself on the community of scholars. Instead of guiding his research in function of the imagined attitudes of a single, personal model, Hogarth now thinks in terms of a larger community of researchers, informing his desires in terms of a concept of a collective mediator. The quest for a socially defined notoriety and success remains at the heart of the professor's research, giving him not only a motive but an orientation for his work. Thus the interpersonal factors concern not only the context but the content of Hogarth's discoveries, in both his youthful and mature research.

Although Hogarth works within organizational structures granting him what would seem to be a great deal of personal freedom (even as a graduate student he is allowed to choose which branch of mathematics he wishes to explore), there are important external and internal constraints on this freedom. If this acclaimed scientist seems to range 'freely' from topic to topic, these movements are in fact determined by his own emulative passions. The most important external constraint on his autonomy is set by the nature of his practical goal, which is to win the recognition and acclaim of his teachers and scientific peers. This means that he must work on the 'mathematical front line', for it is in this manner that he will demonstrate the importance of his contributions, and along with that, the superiority of his genius. When he wants to swerve away from his teacher's ideas and establish his own theory, he must do so by proving that Dill's results can be subsumed beneath a new approach that can 'plow them under'. Hogarth is bitterly aware of the extent to which the system of recognition effectively limits his autonomy, and complains that his efforts to apply statistical analysis to anthropology have been unjustly ignored by the specialists, whose background or 'paradigmatic' assumptions made them incapable of recognizing the value of Hogarth's breakthroughs.

Many aspects of Hogarth's story, then, could seem to suggest that the background determinants of scientific work render its epistemic rationality somewhat illusory. What makes the scientist seek a new theory, and what makes the scientist prefer this new theory over previous ones, is not entirely a matter of good, epistemic reasons, such as the belief that the new theory constitutes progress over the old in accordance with such aims and standards as truth, explanatory power, probable knowledge, verisimilitude, and so on. Instead, what makes the scientist seek and prefer a new theory is his rivalrous relationship to competitors in the field, or to the scientific community at large. Yet these rivalrous relationships require the scientist to adopt a strategy that sometimes limits the innovative nature of the new theory, which must after all be recognized and valued by those working within previous theories. In those instances when a radically different theory is developed and recognized, the reasons for such success are not purely epistemic. Thus, the rationality of scientific discovery and progress are apparently vitiated by the interpersonal and social bases of the scientists' motivations and background beliefs.

The text's treatment of the theme of the relation between science's epistemic rationality and science's non-rational and irrational determinations climaxes in Hogarth's ruminations over the story's central episode – humankind's apparent encounter with a signal transmitted by an extra-terrestrial civilization. Detected as a result of a bizarre series of accidents and contingencies (and not as the result of rationally oriented enquiry), the signal represents a formidable challenge to a science graven in the image of human experience, interests, and conditions. In Hogarth's view, the predictable result is humanity's failure to understand the message. Far from being an investigation of the message's true contents and provenance, the research project is 'a kind of psychological association test, a particularly complex Rorschach test' (p. 32). The various hypotheses that the scientists concoct on the subject of the senders' intentions are drawn between the two poles of all sacred mythologies: the extra-terrestrial Other is imagined to be either perfectly maleficent or beneficent, a hideous destroyer or a powerful benefactor. Hogarth cleverly mocks this tendency and points out that it is the stuff of bad science fiction, yet his own sentimental thinking about the message falls squarely within the same religious framework, for he consistently imagines the senders to be incredibly advanced and benign beings, whose qualities are the inverse image of everything that the misanthropic Hogarth dislikes about his fellow creatures. Although Hogarth claims that his computational analysis of the message proves very little – using his theory of Hogarth groups, he establishes what he calls the formal 'closure' of the message's organization – he fiercely defends his sentimental intuitions about the benign intentions of the senders. Most importantly, he dogmatically insists that the neutrino beam must be interpreted as the artefact of the communicative action of extraterrestrial beings, even after some of his colleagues present a strong rival hypothesis to the effect that the apparently 'codified' beam is but the product of a purely natural cosmological event. In Hogarth's mind, there simply had to be a sender, and the sender had to have sent the message with the intent that it be received by members of another civilization; moreover, the intent itself was meant to be recognized, the proof of all this being that this neutrino recording has a highly improbable degree of informational redundancy. To defend his opinion, Hogarth levels the charge of circularity against the rival hypothesis, yet he offers no independent support of his own conviction that the neutrino phenomenon must be the trace of an alien intelligence's communicative intent. Nor can Hogarth hope to find any evidence for the idea that an unknown civilization would have invested huge resources (a consumption of power of the order of an entire sun) in order to broadcast a message that could only be received, thousands of years later, by another unknown civilization. That the beam seems to have the effect of stimulating the emergence of living organisms may provide some semblance of a rationale for such a costly, one-way activity, but this conjecture does not make the entire hypothesis any less speculative and metaphysical. Yet in Hogarth's own circular thinking, the mysterious aspects of the signal are simply proof of the sublime and superior intelligence of the beings who sent it – and by the same stroke, proof of the inferiority and baseness of the humans who fail to grasp its hidden truths. Hogarth concludes, then, that 'receiving the message from the stars, we did with it no more than a savage who, warming himself by a fire of burning books, the writings of the wisest men, believes that he has drawn tremendous benefit from his find!' (p. 27). And in another of the scientist's images, the researchers are only ants stumbling over the corpse of a philosopher.

Hogarth's dogmatic attachment to the hypothesis of the sender has the consequence of his belittling the actual findings made in the course of the project. He is eloquent about the project's inability to grasp the sender's message and to reply to it adequately, yet comments in passing that the actual discoveries resulting from the investigations have been 'put to good use, so the millions from the budget did not go to waste' (p. 198). The presence of this remark in Hogarth's narrative has far-reaching implications, and sheds new light on his other statements about the irrational nature of scientific work. More specifically, it would appear that although Hogarth is lucid about the many kinds of non-reasonable conditions that make possible the activity of enquiry, the story does not consistently support the conclusion that this enquiry never results in the attaining and recognition of discoveries that realize a certain epistemic progress relative to anterior views. In particular, the project has two concrete achievements, discovered independently by its biochemistry and biophysics departments, in the form of the creation of a previously unknown form of self-organizing colloid (pp. 89-91). In Hogarth's own terms, the production of this unique artefact is not a collective delusion or construct, but is an intersubjectively verifiable reality. Whatever the project's non-rational and irrational determinations may have been, these factors have not prevented the researchers from independently arriving at new cognitive and practical results. The science depicted in Lem's narrative, then, achieves at least a moderate form of realism. In fact, Hogarth's biggest criticism of science's efforts seems to be that it is not realistic enough, that is, that it does not result in realism with a capital 'R'. In other words, the scientist is disappointed because science does not answer the whole riddle in one fell swoop, offering the single true and complete description of the universe, or a map that perfectly reduplicates the territory. Hogarth's narrative usefully suggests, then, that at least some of the grounds for doubting science's epistemic rationality are in fact religious, for it is a matter of complaining that piecemeal scientific enquiries and discoveries fail to get at the 'whole' of Reality, or worse still, the secret message intended by some sacrosanct Sender or other ersatz deity. Remove this sort of exaggerated assumption about the goal of scientific enquiry, and its actual achievements stand in a rather different light. Scientific rationality certainly must fail when its goal is defined as the achieving of a rather stupendous epistemic result (the perfect map, the one the Sender meant), but the evaluation runs differently when a more modest aim is assumed. Moreover, to acknowledge that individual scientists are moved by competitive and non-epistemic reasons does not entail the conclusion that all of their efforts give rise to no epistemically superior results. Hogarth's critique of his teacher's theory may have been fuelled and even oriented by a form of irrational mimetic desire, yet the resulting theory has a genuine cognitive superiority, and will be recognized as such as long as it withstands similar efforts made by the young researchers who in turn emulate Hogarth. The point, then, is that although scientists may be motivated by, and oriented towards, many different kinds of non-epistemic goals, their success as scientists requires that they successfully meet norms which, although they are to some extent a socially conditioned and 'narrow' construct, do effectively guarantee a significant degree of genuinely epistemic progress.[2]

I have just suggested that Hogarth's narrative sounds decidedly post-modern in its critique of science's epistemic claims, but that a closer look reveals a perspective that grants a modicum of epistemic rationality to scientific research. Yet this conclusion may be inadequate in so far as many of Hogarth's sharpest criticisms of science do not have the epistemic rationality of science as their object. What they focus on would be better characterized as the practical rationality of the scientist. Here the essential idea would seem to be that the individual scientist's rational goal of producing superior scientific explanations (a goal pursued, perhaps, in order to achieve such non-epistemic aims as career advancement, victory over a rival, social recognition, glory, etc.) is irrational, and indeed immoral, to the extent that the actual consequences of the scientist's activities amount to a contribution to irrational and destructive social situations. In short, the scientist may very well possess some significant measure of individual, epistemic rationality, but this is no admirable thing because its exercise only contributes to a collective, practical irrationality. Such a view explains the rather bleak tone of Hogarth's narrative, which ends with lines from Swinburne that express gratitude for death's oblivion.

Yet what does it mean to speak of a collective irrationality? A brief theoretical aside will put us in a better position to appreciate what Lem's novel has to say about the scientist's practical predicament.

Early in the present study, I suggested that we should apply concepts of rationality only to entities that we deem to be capable of purposive, intentional behaviour. Such a stipulation implies that the rationality heuristic should not be applied to any number of simple objects lacking the extremely complex physical (and biological) properties that make intentional attitudes possible. The same is true of events: outside of animistic mythologies, a leaf falling from a tree is not an intentional action, and is thus neither rational nor irrational. The case of human artefacts is more complex, for it often seems to make very good sense to understand and evaluate the latter in terms of their rationality. Yet a closer look reveals that it is a matter here of a shift of attention in which the traits of agents' attitudes and actions are figuratively extended to the features of objects made and used by these agents. This point bears illustration here, for it has important implications for the question of what constitutes collective rationality and irrationality. Suppose, for example, that I purchase a non-refillable pen that has a unique and pleasing kind of fine point, but runs out of ink very quickly. I may think of this object as an inefficient and irrational thing. But the pen itself has no goals, intentions, or other attitudes, so I cannot literally deem it to be irrational. It would make much more sense to ask questions about the rationality of the pen's makers, in which case I may discover that a certain kind of greedy calculation effectively shaped the decision about how long the pen's supply of ink was going to last: it was reckoned that many consumers would choose the pen with an innovative point over pens having a larger supply of ink, in which case designing the new pen so that it will quickly run out of ink has the desired result of increasing sales. There is a sense (a very narrow sense, I think) in which this is a perfectly rational calculation: making the commodity this way serves some people's profit-making ends quite effectively. But it may also make good sense to deem it irrational of me to go on purchasing this brand of pen once I know about its small supply of ink – unless, of course, I have some good reasons for deeming the trade-off worthwhile.[3] There is also a larger contextual perspective in which the ecological consequences of the 'throw-away' mode of production and consumption reveal the bankruptcy of the entire business. The point highlighted by the example is that talk about the rationality of artefacts is better understood as talk about the rationality of makers and users, and that there are probably many interesting cases where judgements about these different agents' rationality will diverge.

Talk of the rationality or irrationality of social facts raises

similar, but even more complex, issues. In the words of one philosopher, 'At present our intuitions about group rationality are weak,
at best.'[4] As Elster puts it, 'The very notion of "collective rationality" might appear to be suspect, or if not, trivial.'[5] Elster explains
that such talk is suspect when it involves an appeal to a personified
collectivity over and above the individuals who make it up. On the
other hand, the notion is trivial when it simply refers distributively
to the individuals in a group. Yet in spite of this apparent dilemma,
there are cases in which people do have strong, convergent intuitions about the rationality of certain social realities. For example, a
stock market crash or 'panic' is universally decried as irrational.
But at the same time, it is not entirely clear what the real basis and
meaning of such judgements are. Many questions are left dangling:
do groups, institutions, and social events literally have goals and
purposes? Is a market crash irrational because it thwarts the 'real
purpose' of the institution, in which case the institution can be said
to be 'incoherent' or 'contradictory'? Does an 'institution' really
have a purpose, or is such a usage always a matter of a figurative
extension, similar to the case of the artefact that has its intentional
features 'on loan' from the actual agents who make and use it? In
the case of talk of 'group minds' and 'collective consciousness', such
questions are easily answered, but the more interesting cases cannot be sorted out quite so readily.

If statements about the rationality of social realities cannot
literally be about features of supra-individual intentional states or
attitudes (because there is no group brain to instantiate any such
attitudes), what are they literally about? Given the ontological
lesson of methodological individualism, the most promising answer
to that question seems to be that such judgements refer to relations
between different agents' attitudes (and/or actions).[6] We may be
warranted in being realists about such relations when we are warranted in being realists about the relata: if there are minds and if
two of these minds stand in two attitudes, then there is also a
situation in which these attitudes bear a particular relation to each
other. Yet this rather general remark hardly serves to identify the
specificity of social forms of rationality and irrationality: an
external observer may correctly identify any number of relations
between other agents' attitudes and/or actions, but not all such
relations are social in any interesting sense of the word. For example, Tom believes p and Ivan believes not-p, and thus their beliefs

taken together are incoherent, but we do not necessarily have here the ingredients of a contradictory – and hence irrational – social belief system. Why not? Only an unrealistic and angelic standard of social order would require that there be no contradictions between any of the agents' beliefs (indeed, moderate theories of individual rationality do not even impose such a requirement on the beliefs of a single agent); and it is conceivable that under certain circumstances both Tom and Ivan could stand to gain from the fact that someone else represents a rival point of view. Moreover, the example remains hopelessly atomistic until it is demonstrated that the relation between the agents and attitudes in question has a more robust social quality, on some satisfactory definition of the latter.[7]

What, then, are the elements of a situation of social rationality or irrationality? Perhaps a good way to approach the problem is to take what most people would deem to be a fairly uncontroversial case of social irrationality and to look for the basis of such a judgement. I shall now evoke two such cases, the first corresponding to a variety of 'weakly' social irrationality, the second to a 'strongly' social variety. Corresponding cases of social rationality can easily be imagined.

Let us imagine, first of all, the case of a traffic jam, which surely deserves to be cursed as an irrational social situation. None of the individuals had the intention, when they made their plans to drive somewhere, to contribute to a traffic jam; indeed, it is possible that none of them even thought that there was any chance of getting involved in such a mess. The other cars and drivers did not even figure in their plans, and these plans could have been realized perfectly well had all the others stayed home. Yet the seemingly 'accidental' consequence of all of these individual actions is a decidedly social situation, a situation desired by no one, a situation, moreover, that effectively thwarts all of their desires to speed along towards their individual destinations. The outcome is a 'perverse effect', a social situation that is irrational precisely because it was desired by no one and because it effectively thwarts the realization of everyone's individual desires.[8] A corresponding example of social rationality would be a situation where everyone's purely individualistic and selfish strivings jointly combine to produce additional, 'emergent' benefits for all. In one case, then, an invisible hand chokes the social body, while in the other, it culls fruits cultivated by no one. To put a stop to undesirable emergent effects, everyone (or perhaps some percentage of the group's members) would have to become aware of the phenomenon and behave differently – unless by some happy coincidence, another emergent effect happens to offset the first one.

The example is a case of 'weakly' social rationality because its social elements are entirely external or additive, in the sense that the individuals do not take each other into account in formulating their plans of action. (In Weber's terms, there is no 'functional orientation towards the other', a necessary component in properly social action.[9]) A form of 'strongly' social irrationality or rationality can be generated, on the contrary, by giving the individuals' reciprocal orientations towards each other a greater rôle. In this manner, we move from the domain of 'parametric' to that of 'strategic' rationality.[10] Here we return to the basic intuitions of game theory's analyses of strategic situations, that is, those characterized by significant degrees of interdependence of outcomes and decisions.[11] In such situations, the individual rationality of the agents involved does not necessarily give rise to the best possible outcome. As Elster puts it, 'When two or more rational individuals interact, they may do much worse for themselves than they could have done.'[12]

In order to illustrate how interdependence may be linked to 'collective irrationality', let us imagine a situation where agents freely commit themselves to a conflictual plan of action in spite of the fact that this very commitment has disadvantageous consequences for all parties concerned. This apparently self-defeating commitment, however, is individually rational in so far as the parties concerned have reason to fear an even worse evil should they fail to commit themselves to the conflictual strategy. In the paradigmatic example, although both parties want peace, they none the less engage in costly preparations for war because they deem such preparation less costly than the danger of suffering an attack when unprepared.

How is such a situation specifically social, and in what sense is it irrational? The situation is social in a strong sense because it arises from a non-trivial relation between the two parties' attitudes, and more specifically, from their reciprocal expectations about what the other party might do. In fact, it is uncertainty about what the other party will do that leads each to adopt a strategy that is, by their own lights, in a real sense inferior to another salient possibility. If I knew for sure that the other party would behave peacefully, I would do the same; but I do not know that the other will not attempt a successful 'first strike', and I also know that the other has no way of being sure that I will not do the same. Moreover, my knowledge of the other party's uncertainty about my own actions gives me reason to assume that the other will feel insecure and prepare for war, which is in turn a reason for doing the same myself. I can also reckon that the other party performs precisely the same calculation in regard to my uncertainty about his action. In short, both parties reason that uncertainty requires them to adopt the strategy that makes an unarmed peace impossible, in spite of the fact that the latter would be the preferred solution were the uncertainty removed. Both parties are led by their rationality to adopt this strategy.

A key point to note here is that the relationship that emerges is not the one that each party would have chosen in isolation, and clearly it is in reference to this latter preference that the actual choices that emerge in the situation may be deemed irrational. The example is a case where social irrationality arises from the difference between the preferences that agents have when taken individually, and the choices and outcomes that emerge as a result of their expectations about the other's possible influence on the interaction. Knowledge that the other's choice can have consequences for oneself – and that the other knows the same – plays a crucial rôle in determining the strategies adopted by both self and other. Typically, we want to say that this factor is a source of irrationality whenever it leads the agents to adopt a solution that does not even correspond to their initial, well-considered preferences. Instead, their knowledge of their interdependence vitiates their preferences and leads them to adopt a costly strategy.

The example just evoked is clearly social in a strong sense because a determinant rôle is played by reciprocal expectations and mutual (or 'loop') beliefs. The latter is a concept that enables us to distinguish strongly social beliefs from other possibilities, including a purely contingent form of consensus (Tom and Ivan happen to believe the same thing), pluralistic ignorance (Tom and Ivan believe the same thing, but do not know it), and false consensus (Tom and Ivan wrongly think they believe the same thing).[13] There is, on the contrary, genuine mutual belief to the degree that the members of the group believe (a) *p*, (b) that the members of the group believe p, and (c) that the members of the group believe that the members of the group believe p.[14]

The two examples of irrational social situations that I have evoked are really quite different: in one case, thoughts about the other's possible actions lead the agents to adopt a certain strategy, whereas in the other case, the outcome is the consequence of actions planned without thinking about the other's actions. Yet there is a common element in the two examples, albeit a very general one, valuable not as a technical definition or theory of social (ir)rationality, but as a pointer for further analysis: these two irrational social situations are both cases where the agents, as a result of their own rational doings, find themselves in situations that none of them would have chosen had the choice been left up to them alone.

With these issues in mind, let us return to Lem's narrative and to what it has to say about the ways in which individual scientific rationality may contribute to collective irrationality. A central theme in Hogarth's 'inside' account of the HMV project concerns precisely the extent to which the scientist's epistemic aims are made to contribute to objectionable military ambitions. The cosmic message, he complains, merely provides material for a scientific project wholly directed and determined by partisan, militaristic interests, the context that shapes the orientations and organization of the project – as well as the use of its findings – being the arms race between the superpowers. Rather than being studied by an open, international forum of scientists, the tapes of the 'neutrino broadcast' are whisked away to a former atomic test site in the United States, where a large group of specialists study them in secrecy. At the same time, this team of isolated civilian scientists is 'doubled' by a parallel group, so that the leaders in Washington can observe and compare the results gathered by its twin units, who 'compete' without even knowing of each other's existence. Government propaganda prevents the international community of scientists – and the American public as a whole – from having any inkling of the message's discovery. Once he has joined the project, the researcher finds himself a member of a bureaucratically governed organization, under direct (and covert) governmental and military supervision (the scientists' quarters are bugged, and a military supervisor sits on the project's governing committee). One of his colleagues in the project expresses the scientist's situation in a rather unflattering comparison:

He once read me an excerpt from a nineteenth-century volume describing the raising of pigs trained to find truffles. It was a nice passage, telling, in an elevated style typical of that age, how man's reason made use – in keeping with its mission – of the avid gluttony of the swine, to whom acorns were tossed each time they unearthed a truffle.

This kind of rational husbandry, in Rappaport's opinion, was what awaited scientists; it was in fact already being put into practice in our own case. He made me this prediction in all seriousness. The wholesale dealer takes no interest in the inner life of the trained pig that runs about for the truffles; all that exists for him are the results of the pig's activity, and it is no different between us and our authorities. (p. 61)

Scientific rationality, then, would seem to be but another chapter in the dialectics of enlightenment, an episode in which the modicum of reason alloted to a gifted individual is converted into a mere instrument, an instrument, moreover, put to purposes that flatly contradict not only the purposes of knowledge sought 'for its own sake', but all truly reasonable human ends. So that even if the story of the individual scientist's rationality were not really a tale of lust, ambition, envy, and the like, but instead an account of an encounter between a pristine intellect and the world, this latter tale would be contradicted by the facts of the individual's place in a larger scheme of things, the social truffle hunt known as science. At times in his narrative, Hogarth indeed seems to forget the sordid facts about his own motives and focuses instead on the tension between his own putatively noble interests and aims and the collective set-up within which he finds himself imbricated. In this vein, we read that Hogarth wants to collaborate with other specialists in an effort to arrive at a genuine, non-instrumental understanding of the message from the stars: the goal is not fame, social rewards, or any sort of domination, but knowledge, a knowledge valued out of curiosity and a pious desire to heed the lessons of a 'higher' civilization (it being assumed that any civilization capable of the 'neutrino broadcast's' tremendous technology, and of putting it to the 'disinterested' use of long-term intergalactic signalling, must necessarily be more advanced than our own). Or such, at least, is Hogarth's manner of presenting his ambitions in his 'finer' moments. Continuing in this same vein, he complains that the authorities who organize the project hope, on the contrary, that the team's analyses of the message will yield technically useful knowledge, and in particular, knowledge capable of military applications that will allow them to win the nuclear arms race.

In spite of these noble attitudes, Hogarth freely abandons his teaching duties and research activities to participate in a project that he knows to be controlled by the military. How does he justify or rationalize that seeming contradiction? The topic is first treated in a brief passage that runs as follows:

It was one of those typical situations of the scientist of our time – zeroed in on and magnified, a prime specimen. The easiest way to keep one's hands clean is the ostrich-Pilate method of not involving oneself with anything that – even remotely – could contribute to increasing the means of annihilation. But what we do not wish to do, there will always be others to do in our place. Yet this, as they say, is no moral argument, and I agree. One might reply, then, with the premise that he who consents to participate in such work, being full of scruples, will be able to bring them to bear at the critical moment, but even should he be unable, no such possibility would exist if in his place stood a man who was devoid of scruples.

But I have no intention of defending myself in that way. Other reasons prompted me. If I know that something is happening that is extremely important but at the same time a potential menace, I will always prefer to be at that spot than to await the outcome with a clear conscience and folded hands. In addition, I could not believe that a civilization incommensurably above us would send out into the Cosmos information convertible to weaponry. If the people of the Project thought otherwise, that did not matter. And, finally, this chance that had suddenly opened up before me was totally beyond anything I could still expect from life. (p. 53)

Hogarth's account of these reasonings gives a plausible justification for his having followed what are essentially selfish motives (revealed in talk of his own preferences and chances): there was no good reason to believe that the analysis of the neutrino broadcast could have military implications, and hence his rationality and conscience remained intact. At the end of the tale, Hogarth turns out to have been right. Yet developments along the way make it look as if the situation will evolve rather differently, and for a while Hogarth himself is a 'prime specimen' of the scientist's dilemma to which he refers. This episode begins when a colleague in the project named Donald Prothero secretly informs Hogarth about some results pointing the way to the discovery of a manner of causing nuclear explosions to occur at any distance and with pinpoint accuracy. This so-called TX effect would make possible the invention of a weapon guaranteeing nothing less than world domination to the party controlling it. Hogarth and Prothero consider the tactic of simply burying the dangerous hypothesis by discontinuing the work leading in that direction, but reflect that they do not in fact control the future course of the entire project's work. On the contrary, Prothero informs Hogarth that he has seen the plan of another group's research for the coming year, and it is clear that they intend to perform the very experiments that led Prothero to the discovery of the TX effect in the first place: 'The equipment is all automatic. They will take a few thousand photographs a day, and the effect will stand out like a sore thumb' (p. 137).

Thus it seems unlikely that by discontinuing their own research, Hogarth and Prothero can prevent the dangerous discovery from being duplicated. They decide to go on with the investigation, but conspire to do this work in secrecy. Neither Hogarth nor Prothero is certain about what they will be able to do should they discover that the construction of the deadly device is indeed possible, but they intend to try to prevent this knowledge from being put to the wrong use. Hogarth and Prothero work in secret, then, feverishly trying to develop and confirm a destructive discovery when their real desire is that no such discovery ever be made. Is this behaviour rational? On the face of it, it seems quite literally preposterous or backwards: if you want peace, prepare for peace, not war; and if you want to prepare for peace, do not invent weapons. Reflecting back on the situation, Hogarth deems their strategy to have been neither rational nor irrational, but an instance of mindless reflex behaviour:

When I look back now, I see how foolishly we both behaved – how mindlessly, even. I still do not know what ought to have been done, but that conspiratorial activity – there is no other way to say it – served only to preserve the illusion that our hands were clean. We got in deeper and deeper. We could neither hide our progress nor – in the face of the pointlessness of keeping the secret – suddenly one day announce it. The announcing had to be done either immediately after the discovery of TX – or never. Both of these ways out, logical though they were, were closed to us. The awareness that the biophysicists, in another quarter, would be moving onto that 'hot' ground made us hurry. Our fear for the fate of the world – because nothing less, after all, was at stake – caused, truly by reflex, our concealment of the research. (p. 152)

Elsewhere in his narrative, Hogarth comments that if he and his co-conspirator were guilty of anything, 'it was of illogic' because in one way or another their secret research eventually had to be grist for the Project's official mill.

Here is an instance in which Hogarth's autobiographical narrative would seem to be less than wholly accurate, for he fails to give a convincing account of his motivation in secretly pursuing a discovery that would bring a devastating weapon into the world. It is wholly implausible that such behaviour can be deemed literally 'mindless', a non-rational 'reflex', directly 'caused' by the emotion of fear. The conspiracy was instead the product of intentional action pursued over a period of days, and Hogarth's later, contradictory comments about 'reflex' and 'illogic' merely conceal the complexities involved in the problem of evaluating his former emotions and reasons.

The question of the rationality of Hogarth's scheme breaks into two parts. First of all, it is necessary to evaluate two contrasting views concerning the rationality of contributing to the military effort of one camp in the global arms race; secondly, there is the question of the rationality of Hogarth's efforts, given his stance on the first issue.

Hogarth deems the nuclear arms race an instance of irrationality and does not want his research to contribute to it in any way. He presents his reasoning as follows:

Every world crisis can be viewed in strategic terms, as long as the consequence of that approach was not our potential destruction as a biological species. But when the fate of the species became one of the members of the equation, the choice had to be automatic, a foregone conclusion, and appeals to the American way, the patriotic spirit, to democracy, or anything else lost all meaning. Whoever was of a different opinion was, as far as I was concerned, a candidate for executioner of humanity. (p. 141)

Hogarth reasons that the players should jointly refuse to adopt a strategy that involves the danger of their mutual destruction. He does not want to contribute to an irrational, runaway competition which, because it involves the risk of the destruction of all of the competitors, gives the rationality of the individual strategists a rather dubious status. Hogarth's co-conspirator, Prothero, has presented similar arguments to the military directors of the project. Increasing the American government's military potential, he contends, merely enhances the global danger of annihilation. The only way to forestall the danger of conflict is to have each side's weaponry offset the other's. Thus, if arms-related research is to be pursued, it should not be conducted in secrecy, so that the precarious equilibrium of forces – the balance of terror known as MAD (mutually assured destruction) – can be maintained. The generals' response to Prothero is that it is indeed necessary to maintain the strategic equilibrium. Yet they disagree as to what that entails. In their view, it remains necessary to act as before, because neither side can know whether the other is conducting research that could upset the balance of power. The American scientists' eventual discoveries will not necessarily disturb the balance of power; on the contrary, they could have the consequence of restoring it, and in the absence of complete information about the research being conducted by the other side, it is impossible to know which outcome will be the case. As long as no such knowledge is available, the safest card to play is continuous, secretive research aimed at the invention of the most formidable weapons.

The contrast between the military strategist's reasoning and that of the scientist could not be more striking, and highlights the difference between their underlying assumptions. The general assumes that it is necessary to place the greatest weight on his side's uncertainty about the other side's intentions and capacities; consequently, only the strategy of escalation is rational, even if it can only lead to continued risk and the high cost of armament. Hogarth and Prothero would ideally like to see the weapons research discontinued entirely by their side, the assumption presumably being that the other camp would do the same, or would not act aggressively should their own research win them a decisive advance in weaponry. Essentially, these two scientists do not believe that the superpowers are necessarily locked in an irrational, strategic relationship; on the contrary, a co-operative solution should be possible, and making scientific knowledge a common property is one means to that end. Co-ordinating their actions, the two parties should be able to choose the situation that is most advantageous to both. But that solution requires that the mutual beliefs of uncertainty and suspicion be replaced by confidence in mutual beliefs having the opposite content, namely, reciprocally held beliefs in the pacific intention of the other side. In so far as such an outcome is deemed to be within reach, actions undertaken with that end in view are rational and not suicidal.[15]

Yet even if the correctness of Hogarth's position in this regard were to be granted, there remains the problem of how it is to be applied in the context at hand. Ideally, the scientists would abandon and conceal their lethal discovery. Yet the research project in which the two rational scientists are engaged is collective and differentiated, the result being that no two individuals can actually guarantee that a particularly salient line of enquiry will be neglected. Their strategy, then, is to continue their work, hoping to divulge their findings to the international community so as to avoid upsetting the balance of power by placing the decisive weapon in the hands of their military overseers. Yet given the setting of their research, this strategy is highly uncertain, for their very movements are controlled by the government. Is the strategy they adopt irrational, then? The core of the problem is that of comparing the relative likelihoods of two eventualities. On the one hand, there is the chance that, should Hogarth and Prothero cease their work, the deadly TX effect will be discovered by other scientists in the project and given over to the American military, the result being an upsetting of the strategic balance and hence an increased likelihood of global conflict and total devastation. On the other hand, there is the likelihood that should Hogarth and Prothero manage to complete their discovery in secret, they will somehow find a way to divulge their results internationally, thereby forestalling any upsetting of the strategic equilibrium. Hogarth and Prothero are clearly in a situation of genuine uncertainty here, for it is impossible to assign accurate measurements of probability to the two 'lotteries' between which they must choose. Given their firm, and seemingly well-substantiated belief that the biophysicists will inevitably discover the TX effect, Hogarth and Prothero's secretive action is coherent and rational, even if it is a scheme that in their own opinion has only a small chance of succeeding. Thus we must disagree with Hogarth when he accuses himself of having behaved illogically, for there is a defensible rationale behind his behaviour.

Yet one other avenue for criticizing his action is open, and although I do not find it compelling, I think it worth developing briefly. Namely, it could be suggested that what really motivates this scientist to work eagerly and secretly at developing the hideous TX effect is not the reasonable strategy just outlined, but a more egotistical and reprehensible motive, namely, his constant desire to outstrip the scientific community and have his name associated with any discovery that will be recognized as a world-historical breakthrough. This is the Hogarth who never fails to stand up to combat his scientific rivals at the group sessions, contesting everyone else's views and asserting his own, not, as he pretends, 'because it was expected of [him]' (p. 188), but because he wants most of all to impose himself on others, to emerge as the victor in the contest of genius. What Hogarth hates most is the idea that the biophysicists will get credit for a discovery made by Prothero and himself. Many elements in the novel's depiction of Hogarth correspond to such a hypothesis about his motivations, including his own statements about the reason for his initial involvement in the HMV project. In that case, the overly hasty dismissal of the 'ostrich-Pilate strategy' (in fact a rigorous stance of non-participation in military research) merely conceals the selfish individual's avid desire to be at the 'front line' of scientific work, a desire that never ceases to hold sway, even when the military connotations of the expression take on a rather literal meaning. Hogarth leaps into the trenches, then, not to be the one to defuse the bomb, but to make sure he gets credit for its invention. In that case, Hogarth's epistemic rationality, however magnificent, is forever at the service of a piggish urge to be hailed as the very best finder of truffles. And in so far as the gathering of these particular truffles is a form of collective madness, the scientist's piggish reason converts to unreason. Hogarth's real reason for resenting his military overseers has no genuine ethico-political basis, but amounts to another manifestation of the same will to power: what he really dislikes is having superiors, be they political or intellectual. Moreover, Hogarth's tangled position has one last twist: since his entire objection to the military leader's strategy rests on the possibility of a non-aggressive attitude towards others, his views are contradicted by his own consistent, life-long career of aggressive and competitive action. In other words, if the members of the other side are like Hogarth, then Hogarth and his team should continue working on developing better and better weapons!

Although the line of reasoning just sketched certainly corresponds to aspects of the novel's depiction of Hogarth, it is rather caricatural and fails to take into account other important elements in the text. There are genuine reasons to believe that Hogarth would do whatever possible to prevent the TX effect from having a dangerous political impact, beginning with his enormous desire to prevail over the politicians and generals he loathes so much. Hogarth might very well like to win credit for an important discovery, but he has already experienced that particular satisfaction, and would be more likely to prefer the chance of a truly heroic exploit – that of playing the mediator between the superpowers. Indeed, he at one point indulges in a Jules Verne fantasy of using the weapon to impose peace upon the world. That the TX effect fails to have the destructive potential first imagined relieves him, in any case, of his political burden.

To conclude, we may return now to our question about the collective rationality and irrationality of science. In this regard, I think it important to observe that the narrative suggests the value of a nuanced view, namely, one that eschews the extremes of a sterile debate between 'post-modern' and 'positivist' perspectives. Individual scientists' actions, aimed at both epistemic and practical goals, do not always, or necessarily, contribute to irrational social situations, that is, situations that have the undesired consequence of thwarting the goals of the group's members. Sometimes scientists' actions may have this consequence, but it is far from clear that the most reasonable way of dealing with such cases is the condemnation of all scientific research. Moreover, in many instances, scientific practices stand as robust examples of collective rationality, in both the weak and strong senses evoked above. This is a major theme requiring lengthy development, and only a few suggestive remarks will be offered here. Quite clearly, the duplication and differentiation of scientific tasks across a large number of individuals leads to the emergence of beneficial, unintended epistemic consequences.[16] Moreover, that scientists are sometimes guided by their mutual beliefs about each other's future goals and actions can have desirable effects, such as a tendency to challenge and test one's own views before presenting them to others. In this manner, scientists' mutual beliefs sometimes do effectively instantiate the norms and attitudes that have been referred to as a special 'ethos' in favour of certain epistemic virtues.[17] These virtues are not a matter of so many noble traits of the scientist's special personality, traits detached from any social basis and circumstances. Instead, they are traits encouraged and instituted by the social nature of the individual researcher's activity, as well as by the resistance that reality sets up to a human action and thought that are anything but omnipotent. Lem's novel, then, evokes a science that is neither the manifestation of pure, individual genius, nor the tool of blind libido; it is not a universal panacea, the highest or only value; nor is it uniquely an instrument of destruction, held by no one, yet working away always at our doom. A fallible endeavour having varied conditions and effects, the science depicted by Lem calls for a perspective on research that would be capable of tracing the multiple causes and effects of individual and collective reason.

I shall conclude this chapter with a brief recapitulation of the main points that have emerged in the textual analyses of the last three chapters. I have contended that in spite of their reductive, naturalist features, Dreiser's narratives (like many others) rely implicitly on a psychological model in which practical reasoning and related notions of agential rationality play an irreducible rôle. In spite of proclamations to the contrary, the stories cannot be understood without applying the basic rationality heuristic to the character's fictional behaviour, which is thereby revealed to be a matter of actions comprehensible in terms of the agent's various reasons (motives, beliefs, intentions, etc.). What is more, the characterizations rest on a number of assumptions about the rationality of action and thus do not successfully manifest a purely mechanical or a-rational model of agency. More specifically, my readings of these narratives suggest – but of course do not prove – that desire is not a blind mechanism sealed off from intention, belief, and reasoning, but interacts with the latter in complex ways. Moreover, aspects of Dreiser's depictions of his characters underscore the interest of evaluating even genuinely non-intentional behaviour in the context of the agent's rational and irrational plans and actions. This point belongs to the larger theme of the superiority of an agential as opposed to an atomic perspective on the meaning and status of particular attitudes and instances of behaviour. The two perspectives simply do not converge in all cases: sometimes what is coherent and subjectively rational from an atomic perspective turns out to be incoherent and irrational within the broader context of an agential perspective. This latter approach embraces the agent's memory of previous reasons as well as the agent's projection of long-term intentions and plans. It also embraces the agent's crucial second-order beliefs about the status of other attitudes and behaviour. Yet the agential perspective for which I have argued remains a modest and subjective approach to rationality. The agential approach makes it possible to elucidate important intuitions about rationality without having recourse to objective criteria or substantive norms, and thus makes possible immanent critiques of an agent's deliberations and actions. Such critiques are not equivalent to complete assessments of the moral, ethical, and political status of an agent's doings, but the conclusions these critiques support are often of direct and crucial significance to such assessments. My reading of a Zola narrative led to the formulation of a hypothesis about a possible source of irrationality in long-term planning, namely, the way in which decisions can be vitiated by shifts in second-order confidence linked to the agent's reliance on an unsound mimetic strategy whereby the agent adopts both ends and means from a privileged model. Yet the agent's confidence, and with it, the agent's ability to deliberate and act successfully, shift irrationally in function of an undue inflation and deflation of the model's perceived authority. Such an approach is particularly prone to error in contexts where the model's actual desires and schemes are not known to an imitator who is unaware of the strategic aspects of the situation. Finally, Lem's narrative suggests that in spite of a tendency to assume that purely epistemic ends are always overdetermined by non-epistemic practical motives – which would put in question the very possibility of a purely cognitive form of scientific rationality – agents may in fact locally achieve modest epistemic goals supported by modest epistemic reasons, conclusions to the contrary deriving their appeal from properly theological impulses and assumptions. Similarly, although it is sometimes tempting to conclude that collective situations systematically convert individual rationality into irrationality, such conclusions are overly extreme and fail to take account of alternative possibilities.

CODA

Der Bau

Franz Kafka was not Jean de La Fontaine, and his stories do not end with tidy statements of a moral. None the less, I shall conclude the present study by drawing a few lessons from a reading of 'The Burrow', a fable that conveys a remarkable characterization of a small and limited creature's reasonings.[1]

At the outset of the narrative, the owner of the burrow reviews the various calculations that have gone into the design of his dwelling: 'I have completed the construction of the burrow and it seems to be successful.' Now that the construction is finished, there are brief moments of tranquility and confidence when the animal relaxes and enjoys the advantages of his dwelling. Most of the time, however, the animal frets anxiously over the possible flaws in the construction. For example, although the burrow's single entrance is cleverly concealed, it could still be found by hostile creatures, who might enter the burrow and take its owner by surprise. The animal ponders possible ways of increasing the overall security of the dwelling, but confronts the fact that many of the construction's basic structural features are the best that he can devise. Others could only be altered at the cost of great risk and protracted labour, with only a minimal – and perhaps wholly imaginary – advantage to be gained. Yet the animal lingers over the possible flaws in the burrow and remains obsessed with the impossibility of changing its basic plan.

Tortured by his uncertainty about the security of his home, the creature ventures forth and hides outside the opening, trying to make crucial observations that will determine how safe he is inside the burrow. Yet such observations, the animal reflects, cannot yield any absolutely certain results: to be perfectly accurate, the experimental observations would have to be made under the right conditions. All other things must be equal. In the case at hand, this clause is taken to mean that an experiment designed to test the safety enjoyed by an animal inside his burrow cannot be conducted with an empty burrow; the animal concludes that he must be back inside the dwelling at the time of the observation. Yet it is impossible simultaneously to sit inside the burrow and to measure its security from the outside! Consequently, the experiments are said to be only 'half-experiments or even less'. In his desire to measure the safety of the burrow, the animal considers the possibility of enlisting some other creature's aid. Perhaps this confederate could make the necessary observations from the external perspective and report on the results. Yet could these reports be trusted? 'If I trust someone when we are eye to eye, can I also trust him just as fully when I cannot see him?' The animal reflects that it might be possible to trust a confederate acting under his direct supervision – or a confederate who could in principle be directly supervised – but it is impossible, while on the inside, to trust anyone who is outside the burrow. Not only could the confederate prove to be dishonest, but it is also possible that other causes could make the confederate's reports unreliable: even a trustworthy confidant might be prevented from doing his duty as a result of 'the countless accidents of existence' (*alle die unzähligen Zufälle des Lebens den Vertrauensmann hindern können, seine Plicht zu erfüllen*). The animal concludes that it is impossible to measure the security of the burrow from the outside, or to have it done by some other means, and must return to his burrow without obtaining the infallible knowledge that he desires. Yet getting back into the burrow is yet another problem, for the animal fears that he is particularly vulnerable to attack at this moment. The animal conducts other experiments in an attempt to find an infallible method of making a safe return; these experiments, however, yield no 'universal law or infallible method of descent' (*ein allgemeines Gesetz oder ein unfehlbare Methode finde ich aber nicht*).

The creature's thoughts about the burrow move on a number of distinct levels arriving at rather different conclusions. A first level may be defined as comprising everything that the animal believes about the real conditions under which the burrow was conceived and constructed, as well about the objective advantages and protection the construction may be expected to afford its occupant. This is the level at which the creature admits that the construction seems 'successful', that it can protect the dweller's life perfectly well, offering 'a great deal of security'. This is also the level at which the animal knows that life in the burrow is definitely to be preferred to a nomadic existence, for he speaks of his former life on the outside as 'comfortless', as wholly lacking in security, and as an 'indiscriminate succession of dangers'. Any decision to abandon the burrow for such a life would 'certainly be total folly', the creature asserts. Similarly, although the animal details the dangers caused by the present disposition of the burrow's entrance, he knows that he cannot in fact conceive of any truly superior or safer scheme to replace this entrance, and comments at the outset that the entrance is 'secured as securely as anything in this world can be secured'. It is possible that some terrible enemy may happen upon the entrance, manage to make its way through the maze linking the entrance to the main part of the burrow, and fall upon the burrow's inhabitant. At the same time, however, the burrow's owner must also anticipate the danger that an attack may come from another direction – the burrow being large, there is the chance that some adversary may burrow blindly into one of its far-flung passages. With the latter danger in mind, the creature deems it necessary to have a way of making a quick exit from the burrow, and thus reluctantly concludes that the precarious entrance, covered only by a movable layer of moss, is a necessary precaution. Prudence, he remarks, requires that this risk be taken (*die Vorsicht verlangt, wie leider so oft, das Risiko des Lebens*). The 'flaw' in the structure – its fallible nature, the element of risk that remains – is dictated by the objective conditions, as is unfortunately so often the case. Yet even should an attack happen to occur, the animal would still not be left defenceless. The burrow-dweller has the advantage of knowing the plan of the dwelling, and the invading robber could easily turn out to be the creature's victim – and a tasty one at that – the animal reflects.

These and similar reckonings give the creature ample reason to feel safe in the burrow: he has quite a lot of knowledge about the burrow's construction, about the kinds of enemies that exist outside, and about the kinds of invasions and dangers that could be expected. Yet his attitudes are not all situated at this same level. The creature not only has an understanding of the burrow's strengths and weaknesses, as well as various beliefs about the possibilities of invasion and defence; he also has a number of reflective attitudes about the adequacy and inadequacy of these beliefs. The creature has his prospectus or forecast, on the one hand, and his degree of confidence in that forecast, on the other. By the creature's own report, this degree of confidence is low in the sense that the animal rarely experiences any relief from his anxieties about the possibility of attack, and is tortured by the doubts he has about the actual security of the plan. These worries have a partial basis, or better, a pretext or starting point, in a conclusion yielded by the reasoning at the first level: the construction is known to be fallible. Not only is it possible that dangers foreseen as remote possibilities could be realized, but it is also possible that some wholly unforeseen and unforeseeable event, entirely missing in all of the animal's plans and previous experience, could occur, bringing with it the creature's ruin. 'Anything might happen' (*Ach was könnte nicht alles geschehen!*) the creature exclaims, and with this expression of radical uncertainty, with this emphasis on the openness of the animal's constructions and calculations to a realm of unforeseeable contingency (a life of 'countless accidents' having 'incalculable consequences') the door is open to endless speculation, at once sceptical and paranoiac, about the inadequacies of all of the animal's actions and beliefs. Thus realistic and prudent deliberations about how to deal with potential invaders – the insects and other unthreatening creatures that are most likely to intrude upon the burrow – give way to fearful thoughts of legendary enemies hidden in the bowels of the earth (the rodent's equivalent of ghost stories). 'They are beings of the inner earth, and not even the legends have ever been able to describe them.'[2]

It is important to observe that Kafka's creature evaluates his own plans, actions, and achievements in terms of an unrealistic and idealized standard of infallibility and certainty. In his desire for absolute security, the animal clings to an ideal of perfect, infallible rationality of both action and knowledge. The *angst* he experiences arises from a habit of stressing the differences between this ideal standard and the modest rationality of which the creature is actually capable. Although he knows himself to be committed to a scheme that is in many respects more than satisfactory (indeed, by his own lights, this scheme is the best that could have been chosen given the objective conditions), the animal continues to question the adequacy of the initial plan, even though in the animal's own most reflective beliefs, this policy of constant reconsideration cannot lead to any improvement of the initial plan and only brings unnecessary torment. Thus an excessive doubt concerning the achievements of fairly successful instances of practical reasoning introduces a real element of irrationality. The animal's irrational fear and doubt not only cause anguish, but lead to dangerous behaviour and unnecessary risks (for example, the moments when the animal hovers nervously outside the entrance to the burrow).

The animal's views are irrational, then, in those moments when he indulges in excessive doubts about the viability of actions and plans that he has good reason to trust. Although actually committed to a long-term plan of action, the creature has an irrational disposition to engage in pointless and at times dangerous reconsiderations of the scheme. Moreover, in judging the latter features of the animal's behaviour irrational, we are expressing an evaluation that is based on some of the animal's own beliefs. It is the animal himself that concludes that the idea of building a second entrance, to be used to survey the security of the first entrance, is in fact superfluous; it is the animal who asserts that the truth of the matter is that the burrow is quite secure and that the tendency to reconsider the plan points more to the occupant's own flaws than to any actual weakness in the design of the real burrow. In other words, at such moments, the animal understands that some of his own reflections involve inappropriate and self-defeating judgements of the calculations that were produced at the first level. The estimation of the rationality of the construction should not be determined by placing inordinate weight on the most unlikely and fantastic contingencies. Such contingencies may always be conceived of in relation to any scheme that is not 'completely perfect' and infallible, yet no real burrow could ever embody such ideals. Yet an irrational and nervous reconsideration of the wisdom of his own wisdom leads the animal to engage in the pointless exercise of trying to evaluate the reliability of the burrow from some God's eye perspective.[3] To assume that rationality requires belief and action to be perfectly grounded and absolutely sure leads to the erroneous conclusion that actual beliefs and actions, which surely lack such qualities, are irrational. Yet only an unrealistic and idealized idea of rationality underwrites such a conclusion. Discounted and overlooked as a result are the limited, fallible, and prudent forms of enquiry, and with them, the modest knowledge to which these enquiries may in fact give rise. The moral of my story?

> He that dwells on reason's sleep
> taints the dwelling reason keeps.

Notes

INTRODUCTION

1. For references to work on rationality, see chapter 1 and bibliography.
2. In a ruling of the Ontario Court of Appeal, Justice Patrick Galligan upheld the acquittal of a sleepwalking man who had killed his mother-in-law and injured his father-in-law. 'When asleep, no one reasons, remembers or understands', Judge Galligan argued (*The Globe and Mail*, June 2, 1990, p. A10). For a discussion of less unusual ways in which attributions of mental attitudes influence our decisions about responsibility and blame, see Shaver (1985).
3. Ed. Nordal (1933), vol. 2, pp. 174–75; trans. Pálsson and Edwards (1976), p. 150.
4. See Lönnroth (1976, 1980) for an exemplary pragmatic analysis.
5. Boyer (1987), p. 1549 n. 2.
6. Wilensky (1983) develops this argument at length.
7. Barthes (1970), p. 25.

1 RATIONALITY

1. De Sousa (1980), pp. 128–30. Similarly, Bunge comments that the conditions of purposiveness are 'freedom, learning, expectation, and valuation' (1981), p. 82.
2. A tangled debate surrounds the use of the causal idiom in the analysis of action. An influential causal account is proposed by Davidson (1980); for commentary, see Lepore and McLaughlin (1985), and Vermazen and Hintikka (1985). A causal approach is also defended by Bishop (1990), and by Dretske (1988, 1990); for comments on the latter, see Bratman (1990). Problems with the causal theory are presented in detail in Wilson (1989). For an anti-causal, functionalist view, see Cummins (1983).
3. Such a conception is explicit, for example, in Frank H. Knight's *Risk, Uncertainty, and Profit*, when he writes that 'The universal form of conscious behavior is thus action designed to change a future situation inferred from a present one' (1921), pp. 201–2. This same kind of

assumption is carried forward in the extensive contemporary literatures on 'rational choice', 'decision theory', 'problem solving', and 'action'. For a start on philosophical action theory, the complexities of which are hardly hinted at in my summary remarks here, see Audi (1989), Brand (1984), Elster (1983a, 1983b), and Føllesdal (1980). Some important, more technical works are Aune (1977, 1988), Binkley, Bronaugh and Marras (1971), Brand and Walton (1976), Danto (1973), Ginet (1990), Goldman (1970), Grice (1986), Gustafson (1986), Pettit (1986), Rescher (1968), Thalberg (1977, 1985), Tuomela (1977), Velleman (1989), and Wilson (1989). For historical background, see Audi (1989) and Nussbaum (1978). Unfortunately, action theory and social scientific work on rationality are rarely mentioned in discussions of literature and narrative; some useful exceptions, however, are Altieri (1981), Beaugrande (1980), Boruah (1988), Caserio (1987), van Dijk (1976a), Margolin (1986), McCormick (1988), and Schmidt (1982). Many literary scholars who feel a need for a theory of individual psychology work with some version of psychoanalysis. My search for alternatives to that prevalent strategy is motivated by a number of doubts concerning the adequacy of the basic tenets of past and contemporary psychoanalytic theories; for a sampling of important criticisms of psychoanalysis, see Castoriadis (1978), Eagle (1983), Erwin (1981), and Grünbaum (1984).

4. This point is made by Benn and Mortimore (1976b), pp. 2–3, and by Szabados (1979), p. 388.

5. For some general discussions of rationality and anthologies on the topic, see Agassi and Jarvie (1987), Benn and Mortimore (1976b), Bennett (1964), Bunge (1987), Elster (1979, 1983b, 1985a, 1986b, 1986c, 1989b), Føllesdal (1981, 1988), Hogarth and Reder (1986), Hollis (1977, 1987), Lukes (1967), Margolis, Krausz and Burian (1986), Rescher (1988), Simon (1983), Stich (1990), Tamny and Irani (1986), and Wilson (1970). For additional sources, see bibliography.

6. For an example of this line of reasoning, see Godzich (1985), p. xxi.

7. B. H. Smith (1988), pp. 144, 214 n. 38.

8. See P. Churchland (1981), pp. 89–90, and P. S. Churchland (1986). For a valuable survey of positions in the philosophy of mind, see P. Churchland (1984), and for a number of important contributions, Block (1980). An application to literary theory is Ponech (forthcoming). Excellent arguments about the self-defeating nature of eliminativism are presented in Baker (1987).

9. Dennett (1987) and Baker (1987).

10. J. Levin (1988), pp. 206–7.

11. For a detailed discussion of variants of this basic schema of practical reasoning, see Audi (1989), chapter 4; see also P. Churchland (1970), and von Wright (1971, 1983).

12. Davidson (1985), p. 352. Similarly, Ginet comments that it is wrong

to imagine a theory of an 'agent' that never acted to satisfy its antecedent desires or to carry out its antecedent intentions. Nothing, he adds, 'can count as a person unless rational agency, acting for reasons, is characteristic of it' (1990), pp. 3–4. See also Davidson (1982a, 1982b, 1990a, 1990b), Church (1987), Føllesdal (1982), Henderson (1990), Loar (1981), Pettit (1986), and Pylyshyn (1984).

13. Cherniak (1986), p. 9.

14. For philosophical standards of personal identity, see Perry (1975) and Parfit (1986).

15. Cherniak does not mention the relations between his proposal and Popper's much discussed rationality principle, and I shall not try to do justice to that complex topic here. See Popper (1957, 1967, 1969), and for commentaries, Koertge (1975, 1979), Glück and Schmid (1977), Hands (1985), Lagueux (forthcoming), Lallement (1987), Latsis (1972, 1976, 1983), Marshall (1981), Rex Martin (1977), Nadeau (1990), Pépin (1990), Schmid (1988), and Watkins (1970). In thinking about Popper's rationality principle, I have been helped by two talks on the topic given by Alain Boyer.

16. A particular target is Hintikka's (1962) work on epistemic logic, but some of Cherniak's remarks would also be accurate in relation to more recent work, such as Gärdenfors (1988).

17. Distinctions between practical and epistemic rationality, or between the rationality of action as opposed to that of belief, are common in the literature. For examples, see Benn and Mortimore (1976b), Kekes (1988), Mortimore and Maund (1976), and Walliser (1988).

18. Again, a distinction of this sort is frequently evoked in the literature. See, for example, Benn and Mortimore (1976b), p. 5; the idea is developed at some length by Foley (1987). For additional background, see Dancy (1985).

19. Bicchieri (1987), p. 502.

20. Lukes (1967) points the way to some of these different options when he identifies three basic senses in which a particular action may be called rational: (a) 'rational' meaning simply that the behaviour is goal-directed; (b) 'rational' meaning that this action is the most efficient means to a given end; and (c) 'rational' as a way of saying that one thinks the end that an action achieves is the right one (where presumably this latter end is not prized because of its rôle as a means to some other end). These distinctions make it possible to specify that the present discussion focuses on different positions that are taken in regard to topics (a) and (b).

21. Von Mises (1949) p. 12, cited by P. S. Cohen (1976), p. 142.

22. De Sousa (1987), pp. 159–60.

23. L. Jonathan Cohen (1981), p. 322.

24. See Simon's (1957, 1976, 1978, 1983), and for a useful commentary on Simon's work, Mongin (1988a). See also Slote (1989).

25. For an example, see Acham (1984), p. 32. For background, see Weber (1968a, 1968b); for some commentaries, see Castoriadis (1988), Lash and Whimster (1987), Schluchter (1980), and Schutz (1967).
26. Mortimore (1976), p. 93; see also Føllesdal (1988), p. 206.
27. Elster (1983b), p. 15 (Elster's italics). The present study follows Elster's lead in this respect. For a fine survey of some of Elster's work, see Mongin (1988b).
28. Foley (1987), p. 131.
29. Hollis (1979), p. 14.
30. For a range of views and a bibliography, see Marks (1986a); see also Alston (1967), Brandt and Kim (1963), Lewis (1988), Locke (1982), Pettit and Price (1989), Platts (1986), Price (1989), Stampe (1987), and Wilkerson (1986).
31. Marks (1986b).
32. Baier (1986), and Davis (1986).
33. Davidson (1980), pp. 3–4.
34. Here I follow the important arguments presented in Bratman (1987). On the issues surrounding various senses of 'intention' and the notion's rôle in explanations of action, see also Adams and Mele (1989), Anscombe (1958), Audi (1973, 1988), Harman (1976, 1983, 1986), McCann (1986), Meiland (1970), Mele (1988, 1989a, 1989b, 1989c), and Wilson (1989).
35. Bratman (1987), pp. 16, 18.
36. See Ben-Zeev (1987), De Sousa (1987), Elster (1985b), Greenspan (1988), Lyons (1980), Rorty (1980).
37. In what follows, I draw primarily on Abelson and Levi (1983) and Gärdenfors and Sahlin (1988a). My goal here is a highly schematic and non-technical presentation aimed at making some of the basic features of this kind of theory tangible to literary readers, and thus many technical elements and problems are skipped over (for example, I do not delve into the different possible assumptions about utilities). This restriction is justified in the present context because the discussion of rationality undertaken in this study does not work with the assumptions that make the standard mathematical models of decision possible. As Simon puts it, 'human beings have neither the facts nor the consistent structure of values nor the reasoning power at their disposal that would be required, even in these relatively simple situations, to apply SEU principles' (1983), p. 17. For excellent overviews and criticisms of the basic theory, see Schoemaker (1982) and Hollis (1987). Other sources include Allais (1953), Benn and Mortimore (1976c), Coats (1976), Elster (1983a, 1986b), Hollis and Nell (1975), Hogarth (1980), Janis and Mann (1977), Jeffrey (1965), Lee (1971), Levi (1986), Scholz (1983), Sen (1979, 1985), Shackle (1961, 1972), and von Wright (1963, 1972). I thank André Orléan for his generous help on conceptions of rationality in economics.

38. We may observe here that even in regard to people's desire for money, a commodity that by definition has a quantitative form, this assumption is already an important oversimplification. Note as well that utility is not simply measured in dollars. To simplify my exposition, I ignore this point in what follows.

39. As suggested above, this is a highly schematic presentation of the theory. For more details, see Gärdenfors and Sahlin (1988a). Roughly, the 'expected utility' of a given alternative a_i is defined as follows: $EU(a_i) = P(s_1) \times u(o_{i1}) + P(s_2) \times u(o_{i2}) + \ldots + P(s_m) \times u(o_{im})$. Intuitively, this means that in determining the expected value of any given alternative action, the decision maker has to sum up the particular values associated with each of the action's possible outcomes, these particular values being a function of the likelihood of the outcome and the utility attached to that outcome. The underlying assumption is that the agent's global rational preference corresponds to a linear model in which one merely multiplies each component preference by its appropriate weight and adds the products.

40. This basic distinction between risk and uncertainty is central to economic models of rationality, and may be found in Knight (1921) and Keynes (1973). See also Borch (1968) and Levi (1986). For an overview of varieties of uncertainty, see Howell and Burnett (1978).

41. For this point, which is more controversial than the schematic elements presented so far, see Gärdenfors and Sahlin (1988b), pp. 313-34.

42. Stigler (1961).

43. Orléan (1985, 1987, 1989b).

44. On this theme see Elster (1986b), pp. 10-11, and Hollis (1987).

45. Bratman (1987), pp. 29, 79.

46. See Elster (1983b, 1986b, 1989a, 1989b, 1989c); and Partridge, Benn, and Mortimore (1976).

47. Adelman, Arnold, Bamber, et al. (1989), p. 78; the passage is part of a critique of Levin (1988); for Levin's trenchant response, see his (1989).

48. Relevant sources include Ben-Zeev (1982), Black (1982), Brandt (1979), Donagan (1977), Elster (1985a), Gewirth (1978), Gibbard, (1985, 1990), Harsanyi (1983, 1985), Nathanson (1985), Sen (1987), and Suppes (1981).

2 AGENCY, RATIONALITY, AND LITERARY KNOWLEDGE

1. For background to my remarks on literature and literary scholarship, see my (1988).

2. A useful survey is Aron (1984); I have found Todorov (1977, 1987) especially helpful.

3. A superb overview and critique of critical theory's tendency to lean on the illusory foundations of a certain linguistics has been provided recently by Pavel (1988).

4. R. W. Miller (1987), pp. 499–501.

5. The play is a 'tipica commedia d'intreccio influenzata da teatro dell 'maschere' italiano' D'Amico (1959), vol. 6, p. 360. For background to my other sample statements, see Albjerg (1978), Argetsinger (1983), Argetsinger and Rossel (1990), Bamberger (1983), Billeskov Jansen (1974), Brix (1942), and Holberg (1969). Some of the sample claims actually have been made by critics, and some are probably correct, yet that is not my present concern.

6. See Hollier (1989).

7. For valuable arguments along these lines, see Altieri (1981), chapter 2.

8. A critic who claims, on the contrary, that character should be understood entirely as an effect of the discursive tissue is Hamon, who none the less reintroduces the language of action and attitudes under the rubric of the 'theory of modalities'. The latter, he notes in passing, is the branch of narrative research that has contributed most to our understanding of the structures of narrative and stories in general (1983), p. 237, yet no reason is given why that might be so. An even more extreme and untenable relativist and textualist approach to literary agency is set forth in Cixous (1974, 1975). For what I take to be more promising approaches to literary character, see Hochman (1985), Margolin (1983, 1986, 1987), and Phelan (1989).

9. On this question, see Johnson-Laird (1983). Of particular interest in this context are Beaugrande and Colby (1979), Black and Bower (1980), von Dijk (1980, 1985), Hobbs (1990), Prince (1987), Stein (1982), and Wilensky (1983).

10. Balloons: *Le Ballon rouge*, Albert Lamorisse's 1956 film; cockroaches (and cockroach analogues): Kafka's '*Die Verwandlung*' (1915), of course, but more recently, Weiss (1990); constellations of computers: 'The Washing Machine Tragedy' in Lem (1981).

11. Examples are Cascardi (1986), Crisman (1988), Havard (1983), Khatchadourian (1980), and Wright (1981).

12. Federman suggests that Murphy's reliance on a dubious astrology is Beckett's way of mocking Cartesian doctrines, and adds, quite significantly, that Murphy is 'not capable of maintaining himself in the permanent state of hallucination, irrationality, and chaos' that he hoped to achieve, and thus 'never sinks completely into absurdity and irrationality' (1965), pp. 79, 85, 93. Another critic, Dearlove, comments that the 'paradox of Murphy's quest is that it, like all Beckettian quests, is impossible and doomed to failure' (1982), p. 28.

13. The original reads: 'Il se voulut reculer et il tomba à la renverse sur un homme qui était derrière lui et le renversa, lui et son siège, sur le

malheureux Ragotin, qui fut renversé sur un autre, qui fut renversé sur un autre, qui fut aussi renversé sur un autre, et ainsi de même jusqu'où finissaient les sièges, dont une file entière fut renversée comme des quilles'(1973), p. 269.

14. Lem's character survives, then, by virtue of the kind of rational self-binding that Elster (1979) foregrounds.

15. For a careful exposition of the view that works can be identified with types of inscriptions, see Goodman and Elgin (1988); for interesting counterarguments, see Currie (1989) and Davies (1979, forthcoming). See also Matthews (1981). My thanks to David Davies for his discussion of these matters.

16. Currie (1989), esp. pp. 66–73. For an example that lends support to these general claims, see Close (1990).

17. Interesting issues may be introduced when we consider the potential complexities of our understanding of computer-generated discourse. A valuable source on this question is the discussion of 'bitic' literature in Lem's *Imaginary Magnitude* (1985).

18. See Breton (1973), and Nadeau (1964) for background.

19. Tuomela (1984).

20. For a development of this view on the status of linguistic entities, see Bunge (1984). For an amusing description of post-structuralists' tendency to attribute action to texts, see Levin (1990).

21. Von Wright (1971), p. 67.

22. See Bratman (1987), and Elster (1979, 1983b).

23. Literary critics have not drawn systematically on the insights of game theory, and this in spite of the fact that Lewis's much-discussed theory of conventions (1969, 1975) – which several critics have tried to employ – is essentially a game-theoretic model. On game theory, see Elster (1989b), Harsanyi and Selten (1988), Luce and Raiffa (1957), von Neumann and Morgenstern (1944), Schelling (1960), Shubik (1982), and Ullmann-Margalit (1977). For a systematic discussion of the application of game-theoretical insights in a literary context, with reference to a sample analysis, see my (forthcoming:a). For texts in which aspects of Lewis's notion of convention are employed in literary analyses, see Mailloux (1982), Pavel (1986), and Reeves (1986a, 1986b); two other critics who draw on concepts of games are Hutchinson (1983) and Lanham (1973).

24. For a detailed exploration of these issues and of concepts of strategy in general, see Hjort (forthcoming:b).

25. See Harsanyi and Selten (1988), pp. 30–3.

26. Pavel (1986), p. 22. Central essays in the polemic are Derrida (1977a, 1977b) and Searle (1977); for additional bibliography, see Dasenbrock (1989), pp. 247–53.

27. Poe (1978), pp. 1024–42. Henceforth I shall refer to this volume as *Works*, giving page numbers in the text. An earlier exploration of the

theme of mesmerism was Poe's 'A Tale of the Ragged Mountains', written in 1843. For a discussion of Poe's sources, see Lind (1947); for an elucidation of his ideas about mesmerism, see Falk (1969). For background on Poe, see Allen (1926), Moss (1963), Quinn (1941), and Wagenknecht (1963).

28. Baudelaire (1974), p. 286.

29. In a letter to George W. Eveleth of 11 March 1847, Poe writes that the case 'was a hoax, of course' (*Works*, p. 1232). In another letter, Poe similarly stated that 'Hoax *is* precisely the word suited to M. Valdemar's case . . .' (*Works*, p. 1231).

30. Editorial note published in *The Broadway Journal* of 13 December 1845; cited in Poe (1984), p. 1106.

31. Williams (1988), p. xvi. An earlier version of this kind of reading is Thompson (1973), who none the less admits that the sceptic and perpetual ironist was 'fascinated' with the metaphysical ideas that were supposedly the target of his ironies.

32. Thus Ketterer (1979), p. 214, and Allen (1969), p. 88, have no doubt that Poe was genuinely interested in the possibility that his metaphysical notions could be true.

33. Barthes (1973), pp. 53–4.

34. See Barthes (1973), p. 30 for the claim that codes are what make meanings possible, as well as the famous passage in his (1966), pp. 56–8, where Barthes refers explicitly to the possibility of imitating Chomsky's programme. For indications concerning what would be involved in backing up such claims, see Johnson-Laird on the concept of an 'effective procedure' (1983), pp. 6-8.

35. Barthes (1973), p. 50; cf. his (1970), pp. 27–28.

36. For an excellent study that supports my statement, see Allen (1969), especially chapter 7, 'Poe's Inconsistencies', pp. 113–28. See also Siebers (1984) for some interesting hypotheses about the pragmatics of fantastic literature.

37. Poe (1984), p. 870.

38. For excellent versions of the kind of approach I have in view, see Currie (1985), and Schmidt (1976, 1982). For a useful critical discussion, see McCormick (1988). An interesting document is Pratt (1981).

39. Searle (1983), pp. 79–111.

40. See Charlton (1988), Curtis (1989), Demos (1960), Dunn (1987), Elster (1986a), Martin (1985), McLaughlin and Rorty (1988), Mele (1987), and Pears (1984).

41. See Altieri (1981), and Lindauer (1974) for discussions of this issue.

42. Simon (1983), pp. 32–3.

43. For more on this approach, see my (1988), pp. 195–267.

3 NATURALISM AND THE QUESTION OF AGENCY

1. *The Financier* was originally published in 1912, and again in a revised edition in 1927. Page numbers given in the text refer to the Apollo edition (1974a) of the 1927 text. 'Concerning Mycteroperca Bonaci' and 'The Magic Crystal' are on pp. 501–3. For a discussion of differences between the 1912 and 1927 editions, see Wilkinson (1965); for background on Dreiser's life, see Lingeman (1986).
2. See Kaye (1986), and Rose, Lewontin, and Kamin (1984).
3. For a sample, see Loeb (1964; first published 1912).
4. (1883), Vol. 1, p. 16. *De l'Intelligence* was first published in 1870, but the passage in question figures among the revisions made by the author on the occasion of the publication of the 4th edition. The French text reads:

   Plus un fait est bizarre, plus il est instructif. A cet égard, les manifestations *spirites* elles-mêmes nous mettent sur la voie des découvertes, en nous montrant la coexistence au même instant, dans le même individu, de deux pensées, de deux volontés, de deux actions distinctes, l'une dont il a conscience, l'autre dont il n'a pas conscience et qu'il attribue à des êtres invisibles. Le cerveau humain est alors un théâtre où se jouent à la fois plusieurs pièces différentes, sur plusieurs plans dont un seul est en lumière. Rien de plus digne d'étude que cette pluralité foncière du moi; elle va bien plus loin qu'on ne l'imagine.

5. See Nordau (1896), and Strindberg (1912–20); an excellent source on these matters is Lindström (1952).
6. Dreiser (1981a), pp. 20, 399. All subsequent page numbers given in the text refer to this popular Signet Classic edition.
7. Dreiser (1977) is a useful collection of the author's earnest philosophizing. The citation is from p. 206. For additional materials, see Dreiser (1920, 1974b).
8. For useful background on Dreiser's sources, see Moers (1969) and Hussman (1983).
9. For documentation on the relations between the life of Yerkes and the Cowperwood character, see Gerber (1973).
10. An example of the standard reading is Wirzenberger, who claims that the novel pivots on the selfish interests of its protagonist just as the planets revolve about the sun (1955), p. 126. Matthiessen (1951) reaches essentially the same conclusion. An early attack on Dreiser's naturalism, first published in 1915, is Sherman (1981). For a broad range of reactions to Dreiser's work, see Boswell (1986). Dreiser's 'inconsistency' as a mechanist was signalled by Vivas (1981). I wholly agree with Michaels, who says of the lobster and fish episode that it is 'curiously inapplicable to the events of *The Financier* itself' (1982), p. 289.
11. Dreiser exploited the same motifs in an essay called 'A Lesson from

the Aquarium', published in *Tom Watson's Magazine* in 1906; cited in Pizer (1981), p. 138.

12. It is curious that C. S. Smith (1976), a critic who attempts an uncritical amplification and rebroadcasting of the 'financier as artist' theme, fails to make any mention of the artistic businessman's dealings with his aesthetic models, while straining the text carefully for minor details seeming to lend support to the idea of Cowperwood's artistic nature. Michaels (1982), gives good reasons for doubting the narrator's line about how Cowperwood valued art for art's sake, but does not mention the rôle of Ellsworth and the other advisers.

13. The *locus classicus* is, of course, Aristotle's *Poetics*, 1448b 5–9; for commentary, see Else (1957).

14. Caillois (1963), Owen (1982), and Wickler (1968).

15. For an overview of theories of imitation and social learning, see Bandura (1986, 1989). For a discussion of Bandura's approach and for a development of my point about the role of imitation in motivational processes, see my *Models of Desire* (forthcoming:b).

16. The literature on motivation suggests that even in regard to the most basic organismic needs – and this even among as 'lowly' a species as the rat – motivational states do not strictly obey the simple logic of depletion–repletion (meaning that once a certain internal threshold is crossed, the animal immediately and necessarily experiences hunger, thirst, etc., and then is compelled to act on that motivational state). See Toates (1986); for background on motivational theory, see Alston (1967), Cormier (1986), Geen, Beatty and Arkin (1984), Madsen (1974), Satinoff and Teitelbaum (1983), Toates and Halliday (1980), Weiner (1980, 1986).

17. Dretske (1988), pp. 127–31.

18. Additional support for this claim is provided by the fact that psychologists have found it worthwhile to investigate the implicit theory of personality in Dreiser's fiction; see Rosenberg and Jones (1972).

4 AGENT'S RATIONALITY

1. The editorial history of *Sister Carrie* is itself quite a story, but this is not my present topic. Briefly, the original edition of 1900 included numerous revisions required by the publishers; an unexpurgated edition based on the original typescript was only published in 1981. I shall be referring to the latter, citing page numbers in the Penguin edition. For background to the editorial history of the work, see West (1985).

2. Kahneman, Slovic, and Tversky (1982).

3. Critics have hardly been oblivious to the interest of this passage. Howard, for example, comments:

The series of events that precipitates Hurstwood's flight from Chicago with

Carrie is one of Dreiser's most famous dissections of the forces acting in what we call "choice." His irresistible impulse to pursue Carrie has put him in an intolerable situation with his wife when, by chance, he finds his employer's safe open and an unusually large sum inside. He does not *decide* to steal the money; rather he is pushed and pulled by fear and desire . . . As Donald Pizer comments, it is a remarkable "dramatization of the ways in which chance and subconscious desire blend into event." In a sense Hurstwood chooses, but in classically determinist fashion the internal and external forces that shape his actions make nonsense of the notion of free will. (1985, p. 44)

A critic attuned to the question of Dreiser's model of agency is Mitchell (1989), whose book I discovered while completing my final revisions.

4. See Bratman (1987); for his discussion of spontaneous, unreflective behaviour, p. 126. Mele's (1989b) remarks on default intentions and *akrasia* are also relevant: Mele would probably agree that since Hurstwood's motivations are not in line with any unqualified best judge-judgement – or even a considered judgement – about what he should do, the gesture of closing the safe would be judged subjectively irrational even if we should happen to think it intentional in some sense.

5. This judgement that Hurstwood is irrational in lying to Carrie is probably based on standards external to his own sense of his framework of values and preferences: at no point in the text are we given any evidence that he thinks honesty is an important element in a romantic relationship, and Hurstwood systematically lies to Carrie once they are together in New York.

6. For Bratman's rigorous formulation of the principle of deliberative rationality that Hurstwood in this regard obeys, see his (1987), p. 85.

7. I shall not discuss here the fascinating question concerning the conditions under which suicide is a rational action, nor shall I speculate on the rationality of Hurstwood's behaviour in this regard. For background on the general issue, see Mayo (1986).

8. Let me repeat here that my claim is not that references to a fictional character in a novel somehow stand as empirical evidence for or against any hypotheses about human behaviour. Yet in so far as reading about fictional characters and actions can help us to complexify and develop intuitions about types of behaviour, literary examples can contribute to the process of hypothesis formation.

9. For a valuable discussion of the rôle of second-order attitudes in the constitution of personhood, see Frankfurt (1988).

10. On this notion, see Elster (1983b), who defines it as a case of irrational belief formation where affect is the source of the distortion.

11. For a detailed discussion of these matters, see Foley (1987), chapter 5.

12. In a version of the notation of situation semantics developed in Barwise and Perry (1983, 1985), this first option would be described as follows: $<l<Dr,A,S>^1,<Dr,A,S>^0>$.

13. In the previous notation: $<l<Dr,A,\{<l'<r,x>^1,<r,x>^0>\}>^l>$.
14. This point is made, for example, by Simon (1983), p. 11.
15. The basic assumption has been expressed by Bunge and Ardila as follows: 'The concept of a value system has remained rather vague in the anthropological, psychological, and philosophical literature. It can be elucidated in a clear and simple manner by assuming that *what organisms value is being in certain states*. Consequently they only value external items (things or events) insofar as they are instrumental in attaining those internal states' (1987), p. 172. I should add that this is not Bunge's ultimate position on the status of values.
16. Elster (1983b).

5 PLANS AND IRRATIONALITY

1. Zola (1964), vol. 3, p. 840. All subsequent references given in the body of the text are to page numbers in this edition. For a discussion of Zola's planning of this novel, see Franzén (1958); for bibliographies of sources on Zola in general, see Baguley (1982), Nelson (1982). Basic background on Zola is ably presented in Mitterand (1986); a recent, theoretically motivated reading of interest is Bell (1988).
2. 'Une nouvelle fièvre l'emportait, il s'était donné entier, fougueusement, à l'idée d'être un médecin de génie, dont l'apparition bouleverserait les mondes' (p. 848).
3. Although my goal in this context is not to make an argument in the general context of Zola scholarship (which does not in any case constitute anything resembling a unified and well-defined programme or context of research), I would like to mention in passing some of the published critical remarks about Lazare that I have seen. Critics seem invariably to share the very general intuition that Lazare is an irrational creature, a fact that is significant in my context. Yet some of their remarks about him are descriptively inaccurate. Thus Kuhn (1976) makes an ill-defined 'ennui' the hidden cause of all of Lazare's actions, while wrongly stating that Lazare's decision to abandon his medical studies is motivated by a desire to write poetry. Borie (1973) sets his psychoanalytical industry to work in order to produce a Lazare who suffers from 'oral sadism' and other violent neuroses, which are only plausible if one ascribes to an unspecified psychoanalytical dogma. In a similar pseudo-clinical vein, Nelson (1983) describes 'a dilettante whose morbid inactivity is also portrayed as the consequence of Schopenhauerian pessimism compounded by advanced hypochondria and an obsession with death' (p. 197, n. 19). Nelson wrongly states that the local villagers 'place hope' in Lazare's scheme to stop the ocean waves – whereas in fact the villagers are delighted when Lazare – to them a cursed *gringalet de bourgeois* (p. 909) – fails miserably. I return to this point below.

4. Bratman (1987), p. 29. In what follows, page numbers given in the text are to this volume.

5. 'Son équipe d'ouvriers l'avait exaspéré, il venait de se débarrasser des travaux ainsi que d'une corvée trop lourde, sans goûter la joie de voir enfin son idée debout. D'autres projets l'occupaient, des projets confus d'avenir, des places à Caen, des ouvrages destinés à le pousser très haut. Mais il ne faisait toujours aucune démarche sérieuse . . . (p. 941).

6. Keynes (1973), p. 148.

7. Keynes (1973), pp. 161–2.

8. Madame Chanteau, we read, 'reporta sur cet enfant son espoir d'une haute fortune, le mit au lycée, le fit travailler elle-même chaque soir . . . on attendrait les succès du fils, qui devait les tirer de leur vie médiocre . . . le courage lui venait de faire des économies, avec l'idée entêtée d'opérer plus tard une rentrée triomphale à Caen, lorsque son fils y occuperait une grande position' (pp. 821–2). And when Lazare decides to study medicine, 'Ce fut une grande joie pour Mme Chanteau. Elle aurait préféré son fils dans l'administration ou dans la magistrature; mais les médecins étaient au moins des gens honorables, et qui gagnaient beaucoup d'argent' (p. 843).

9. 'Dire que c'était elle qui lui avait appris le piano! Rien que la vue d'une partition l'exaspérait aujourd'hui. Son dernier espoir croulait : ce fils qu'elle avait rêvé préfet ou président de cour, parlait d'écrire des opéras; et elle le voyait plus tard courir le cachet comme elle, dans la boue des rues' (p. 823).

10. 'Il avait échoué à son examen de juillet, il était aigri contre les professeurs, toute la soirée il déblatéra contre eux, des ânes dont il finissait par avoir plein le dos, disait-il' (p. 851).

11. The scene amounts to a cruel public humiliation of Lazare, for unaware of his presence, the villagers do not conceal their contempt for him and for his scheme:

> Elle s'en moque un peu, de ses allumettes, à ce jeune homme! Des ricanements accueillaient ces paroles. Tout Bonneville était là, les hommes, les femmes, les enfants, trés amusés par les claques énormes que recevaient les épis. La mer pouvait écraser leurs masures, ils l'aimaient d'une admiration peureuse, ils en auraient pris pour eux l'affront, si le premier monsieur venu l'avait domptée, avec quatre poutres et deux douzaines de chevilles. Et cela les excitait, les gonflait comme d'un triomphe personnel . . . Dommage qu'il ne soit pas là, le jeune homme! dit la voix goguenarde de ce gueux de Tourmal. Il pourrait s'accoter contre, pour les renforcer . . . Lazare ne leur pardonnait pas leurs rires imbéciles. Blessé au coeur par cette débâcle qui était pour lui une défaite, il eut un geste de colère . . . (pp. 984–6)

12. 'Et, dans leurs doléances, dans la façon dont ils le suppliaient de ne pas laisser le pays sous les vagues, il y avait une goguenardise féroce de matelots, fiers de leur mer aux gifles mortelles' (p. 1015).

13. Abelson (1976), p. 61. It should be noted that these criticisms of the concept of rationality are attenuated in Abelson and Levi (1983), where the following comment is appended to the remark just cited: 'In retrospect, this critique is perhaps too strong: departures from rationality certainly provoke attention, which may spur the research effort to find what "is there"' p. 235.

14. Abelson (1976), p. 60; Abelson's italics.

15. Following Orléan (1986, 1988), an even stronger point may be made. In some contexts, it is rational for an agent to adopt (copy or imitate) the beliefs or preferences of another agent, even when the imitator has no compelling evidence that the model's behaviour is in fact a good or adequate solution to a problem. More specifically, in some cases, when an agent has good reason to believe that he or she does not possess the knowledge required to formulate a successful plan of action, it can be rational to assume that some other agent may have the lacking information, and hence to imitate that agent's action.

16. Churchill (1950), vol. 3, p. 455.

6 SCIENCE, REASON, AND SOCIETY

1. For more details on this shift, see my (1988) and the many references given there, as well as Albert (1987), Barnes (1972), Harold I. Brown (1988), James Robert Brown (1984, 1989), Diamond (1988), Doppelt (1988), Giere (1988), Haller (1981), Hilpinen (1980), McMullin (1988), and Shapere (1988). A valuable source on post-positivist philosophy of science is R. W. Miller (1987).

2. Although my primary aim here is not to make an argument about Lem's conscious intentions or more general attitudes, I think it worthwhile to point out that it is unlikely that he holds any kind of radical social constructivist position on scientific knowledge. Some 'external' evidence for this is provided by his remarks about his involvement in the Lysenko affair. Lem was compiling surveys of scientific periodicals for the Polish monthly *Zycie Nanki* ('Life of Science'), and was accused of having written an overly tendentious synopsis of the controversy: 'I held Lysenko's doctrine of the inheritance of acquired characteristics to be ridiculous, and I was proved right after several years, but my taking this position had rather painful consequences for our monthly' (1984), p. 16. Perhaps I have missed a stitch, but I think that an objection to Lysenko's stance entails disbelief in the view that scientific 'knowledge' is totally over-determined by ideology, as does the very idea that one could be 'proved right'. For background on Lem, see Marzin (1985), Rodnianskaia (1986), and Ziegfeld (1985). For a fine reading of *His Master's Voice*, see Hayles (1986). My thanks to Peter Swirski for his comments on this chapter.

3. Is it possible to imagine a class of artefacts that are objectively and inherently rational (or irrational) in that they are such that they infallibly serve (or fail to serve) the purposes of their maker(s) and all of their users? Yet even the existence of such godlike (or infernal?) items would not make talk of an artefact's rationality any less relational and figurative: the goals are still on loan from the actual agents.

4. Sarkar (1983), p. 196.

5. Elster (1983b), p. 26; see also Partridge, Benn and Mortimore (1976).

6. For expositions of the notion of methodological individualism, see Agassi (1973), and Elster (1989b).

7. The violence and absurdity of a purely statistical and global perspective on human activity taken 'as a whole' is brilliantly demonstrated in Lem's *One Human Minute* (1986). This text usefully traces a limit to our ability to think constructively about the global rationality or irrationality of human life.

8. Boudon (1977, 1988), Merton (1936).

9. Weber (1968a), vol. 1, p. 4. For a detailed development of a range of concepts of social influence and interaction, see Tuomela (1984), chapter 9; see also Tuomela and Seebass (1985). A useful survey of sociological theories of interaction is provided by Turner (1988).

10. For this distinction, see Elster (1983a).

11. A technical discussion would be out of place here. For background, see the items listed in note 23 of chapter 2. I recommend Elster (1989b) to literary readers who want a clear and succinct introduction of the basic intuitions.

12. Elster (1989b), p. 28.

13. See Scheff (1967).

14. See Bach and Harnish (1979), p. 269. In these authors' definition of the notion, only three levels are included, but in some versions, the beliefs go on indefinitely. In recent discussions, much has been made of this point, and some thinkers even deem it a decisive objection to challenge the psychological realism of a concept requiring an infinity of levels of belief. Bach and Harnish take up this issue in a passage that deserves citing:

> Higher-level beliefs are in principle possible, and indeed among spies or deceptive intimates there could be divergence at level four or higher without divergence at the first three levels, but we think such higher-level beliefs are not possible for a whole community or large group. Nevertheless, to allow for this possibility our definition could be amended to require that no higher-level belief, if there are any, be false. (p. 309, n.1)

Does this remark open the door to the objection that the amendment requires the believers to conduct an indefinite search for false higher-level beliefs – thereby violating the requirement of psychological realism? Perhaps psychological realism tells us that human comprehension stalls quickly after level four or five, so that the amendment should be weakened, or is not even necessary.

15. Lem discusses the arms race in various texts. Of particular interest is his 'Upside-Down Evolution' (1986), presented as a factual account of the military history of the twenty-first century, when the development of insect-like swarms of weapons replaces traditional forms of combat and, more importantly, strategizing, by blurring the very line between intentional, bellicose action and natural catastrophes. In that context, Lem's narrator, who presents himself as the prophetic author of a book called *His Master's Voice*, seems to echo the reasoning of Professor Hogarth, commenting as follows: 'Although the danger of atomic warfare increased whenever "equality" was lessened, and therefore the rational thing would seem to have been to preserve that equality under multinational supervision, the antagonists did not reach an agreement despite repeated negotiations' (p. 41). For some background on assessments of rationality of deterrence strategies in a nuclear context, see Brams (1985) and Maclean (1984).

16. See Sarkar (1983) and Thagard (1988) for treatments of this theme. The recent emphasis on computational analogies (the collective organization of science is said to be like parallel processing) amounts to a kind of social amnesia, for ideas about these forms of organization first emerged in social thought (one need only think of the notion of 'unsociable sociability' developed by Kant in his 'Idea for a Universal History from a Cosmopolitan Point of View' the second thesis of which is that human reason is developed only in the race, not in the individual (1963, first published in 1784), pp. 11–26).

17. Merton (1973).

CODA

1. (1969; written in 1923/24); English trans., Muir (1952). In what follows, translations are my own, but I have found the Muir translation helpful. As it is a matter here of a text that is in many respects as labyrinthine as the burrow that it describes, it should be understood that what follows is a highly selective interpretation of the document. For some other interpretations of the work readers may consult Boulby (1982), Gelus (1982), Sussman (1977), and Thiher (1987). For a bibliography of secondary studies on Kafka, see Caputo-Mayr (1987).

2. In a reading of Kafka's text, Sussman construes the object of the animal's worries as 'consciousness itself', and thus finds it convenient to assert that the only enemies to which the creature refers are those of legend (1977), p. 112. This is inaccurate, however, for the animal refers explicitly to external enemies as well as to the legendary ones (p. 413). If the external world is entirely in the animal's head, where then is the animal?

3. In the final part of the text, the creature's habitual deliberations about the security of the dwelling are interrupted and reoriented by a

new event: the animal hears, or imagines hearing, a strange and unrecognizable sound, interpreted first as the buzz produced by a swarm of insects, then as the sound emitted by the approach of some singular and deadly invader. Yet the end of Kafka's story has been lost, and the extant text breaks off without identifying the source of the sound, or informing the reader about the outcome of this episode, so that we are – perhaps quite appropriately – forever situated in a position of radical uncertainty in regard to this entire aspect of Kafka's story.

Bibliography

Note: This bibliography refers to editions used, not always indicating the original date and place of publication.

LITERATURE, CRITICISM, CRITICAL THEORY, AESTHETICS

Adelman, Janet, Margaret J. Arnold, Linda Bamber, et al. (1989). Letter. *PMLA*, 104, 76–78.

Albjerg, Asger (1978). *Ludvig Holbergs poetiske Maskerade*. Copenhagen: Vinten.

Allen, Hervey (1926). *Israfel: The Life and Times of Edgar Allan Poe*. 2 vols. New York: George H. Doran.

Allen, Michael L. (1969). *Poe and the British Magazine Tradition*. New York: Oxford University Press.

Altieri, Charles (1981). *Act and Quality: A Theory of Literary Meaning and Humanistic Understanding*. Amherst: University of Massachusetts Press.

Argetsinger, Gerald S. (1983). *Ludvig Holberg's Comedies*. Carbondale: Southern Illinois University Press.

Argetsinger, Gerald S., and Sven H. Rossel, eds. *Jeppe of the Hill and other comedies by Ludvig Holberg*. Carbondale: Southern Illinois University Press.

Aron, Thomas (1984). *Littérature et littérarité: un essai de mise au point*. Paris: Belles Lettres.

Baguley, David (1982). *Bibliographie de la critique sur Emile Zola, 1971–1980*. Toronto: University of Toronto Press.

Bamberger, Angelika (1983). *Ludvig Holberg und das erste dänische National-theater*. Frankfurt: Haag and Herchen.

Barthes, Roland (1966). *Critique et vérité*. Paris: Seuil.
  (1970). *S/Z*. Paris: Seuil.
  (1973). 'Analyse textuelle d'un conte d'Edgar Poe', in *Sémiotique narrative et textuelle*, ed. Chabrol, 29–54.

Baudelaire, Charles (1974). 'Introduction à "La Révélation magnétique"', in *Baudelaire*, ed. Richard, 285–86.

Beaugrande, Robert de (1980). 'The Pragmatics of Discourse Planning', *Journal of Pragmatics*, 4, 15–52.

Beaugrande, Robert de, and Benjamin N. Colby (1979). 'Narrative Models of Action and Interaction', *Cognitive Science*, 3, 43–66.

Beckett, Samuel (1938). *Murphy*. New York: Grove.

—— (1970). *Le Dépeupleur*. Paris: Minuit.

Bell, David F. (1988). *Models of Power: Politics and Economics in Zola's Rougon-Macquart*. Lincoln: University of Nebraska Press.

Bergson, Henri (1940). *Le Rire: essai sur la signification du comique*. Paris: Presses Universitaires de France.

Billeskov Jansen, F. J. (1974). *Ludvig Holberg*. New York: Twayne.

Black, John B., and Gordon H. Bower (1980). 'Story Understanding and Problem Solving', *Poetics*, 9, 223–50.

Borie, Jean (1973). *Le Tyran timide: le naturalisme de la femme au XIXe siècle*. Paris: Klincksieck.

Boruah, Bijoy H. (1988). *Fiction and Emotion: A Study in Aesthetics and the Philosophy of Mind*. Oxford: Clarendon.

Boswell, Jeanetta (1986). *Theodore Dreiser and the Critics, 1911–1982*. Metuchen, N.J.: Scarecrow.

Boulby, Mark (1982). 'Kafka's End: A Reassessment of "The Burrow"', *German Quarterly*, 55, 175–85.

Boyer, Régis, ed. and trans. (1987). *Sagas islandaises*. Paris: Gallimard. Bibliothèque de la Pléiade.

Breton, André (1973). *Manifestes du surréalisme*. Paris: Gallimard.

Brix, Hans (1942). *Ludvig Holbergs Komedier: den danske Skueplads*. Copenhagen: Gyldendal.

Caputo-Mayr, Maria Luise (1987). *Franz Kafka: eine kommentierte Bibliographie der Sekundärliteratur, 1955–1980, mit einem Nachtrag 1985*. Bern: Francke.

Cascardi, Anthony J. (1986). *The Bounds of Reason: Cervantes, Dostoevsky, Flaubert*. New York: Columbia University Press.

Caserio, Robert L. (1987). 'Story, Discourse, and Anglo-American Philosophy of Action', *Journal of Narrative Technique*, 17, 1–11.

Chabrol, Claude, ed. (1973). *Sémiotique narrative et textuelle*. Paris: Larousse.

Cixous, Hélène (1974). *Les Prénoms de personne*. Paris: Seuil.

—— (1975). 'The Character of "Character"', *New Literary History*, 5, 383–402.

Close, Anthony (1990). 'The Empirical Author: Salman Rushdie's *The Satanic Verses*', *Philosophy and Literature*, 14, 248–67.

Cogny, Pierre, ed. (1978). *Le naturalisme*. Paris: U.G.E.

Crisman, William (1988). 'The Status of Adult Rationality in Tieck's Fairy Tales', *Colloquia Germanica*, 21, 111–26.

Currie, Gregory (1985). 'What is Fiction?' *Journal of Aesthetics and Art Criticism*, 43, 385–92.

—— (1989). *An Ontology of Art*. New York: St. Martin's.

D'Amico, Silvio, ed. (1959). *Enciclopedia dell Spettacolo*. Rome: Le Maschere.

Dasenbrock, Reed Way, ed. (1989). *Redrawing the Lines: Analytic Philosophy Deconstruction, and Literary Theory*. Minneapolis: University of Minnesota Press.

Davies, David (1979). 'The Aesthetic Relevance of Artistic Acts: An Examination of Recent Contributions to the Theory and Metatheory of Art.' Unpublished M.A. Thesis, University of Manitoba.

(forthcoming). 'Text, Context, and Character: Goodman on the Literary Artwork.' *Canadian Journal of Philosophy*.

Davies, Stephen (1983). 'The Rationality of Aesthetic Reponses', *British Journal of Aesthetics*, 23, 38–47.

Dearlove, J. E. (1982). *Accommodating the Chaos: Samuel Beckett's Nonrelational Art*. Durham: Duke University Press.

Dijk, Teun A. van (1976a). 'Philosophy of Action and Theory of Narrative', *Poetics*, 5, 287–338.

(1976b). *Pragmatics of Language and Literature*. Amsterdam: North-Holland.

(1980). 'Story Comprehension: An Introduction', *Poetics*, 9, 1–21.

ed. (1985). *Discourse and Literature*. Amsterdam: John Benjamins.

Dreiser, Theodore (1920). *Hey Rub-a-Dub-Dub*. New York: Boni and Liveright.

(1974a). *The Financier*. New York: Thomas Y. Crowell, Apollo Edition.

(1974b). *Notes on Life*. Ed. Marguerite Tjader and John J. McAleer. Birmingham: University of Alabama Press.

(1977). *Theodore Dreiser: A Selection of Uncollected Prose*. Ed. Donald Pizer. Detroit: Wayne State University Press.

(1981a). *An American Tragedy*. New York: Signet Classic.

(1981b). *Sister Carrie*. New York: Penguin.

(1984). *The Genius*. New York: Signet Classic.

Else, Gerald F. (1957). *Aristotle's Poetics: The Argument*. Cambridge, Mass.: Harvard University Press.

Falk, Doris V. (1969). 'Poe and the Power of Animal Magnetism', *PMLA*, 84, 536–46.

Feagin, Susan L. (1980). 'Motives and Literary Criticism', *Philosophical Studies*, 38, 403–18.

Federman, Raymond (1965). *Journey to Chaos: Samuel Beckett's Early Fiction*. Berkeley: University of California Press.

Franzén, Nils-Olaf (1958). *Zola et La Joie de vivre: la genèse du roman, les personnages, les idées*. Stockholm: Almqvist and Wiksell.

Gelus, Marjorie (1982). 'Notes on Kafka's "Der Bau": Problems with Reality', *Colloquia Germanica*, 15, 98–110.

Gerber, Philip L. (1973). 'The Financier Himself: Dreiser and C. T. Yerkes', *PMLA*, 88, 112–21.

Godzich, Wlad (1985). 'Foreword: Where the Action Is', in *The Poetics of Plot: The Case of English Renaissance Drama*. Thomas G. Pavel. Minneapolis: University of Minnesota Press, vii–xxii.

Goodman, Nelson, and Catherine Z. Elgin (1988). *Reconceptions in Philosophy and Other Arts and Sciences*. Indianapolis: Hackett.

Hamon, Philippe (1983). *Le Personnel du roman: le système des personnages dans Les Rougon-Macquart d'Emile Zola*. Geneva: Droz.

Havard, Robert G. (1983). 'The Ironic Rationality of *Razón de amor*. Pedro Salinas: Logic, Language and Poetry', *Orbis Litterarum*, 38, 254–70.

Hayles, N. Katherine (1986). 'Space for Writing: Stanislaw Lem and the Dialectic "That Guides My Pen"', *Science-Fiction Studies*, 13, 292–311.

Hjort, Anne Mette, ed. (forthcoming:a). *Rules and Conventions*. (forthcoming:b). *The Strategy of Letters*.

Hobbs, Jerry R. (1990). *Literature and Cognition*. Stanford: Center for the Study of Language and Information.

Hochman, Baruch (1985). *Character in Literature*. Ithaca: Cornell University Press.

Holberg, Ludvig (1969). *Værker i tolv bind*. Ed. F. J. Billeskov Jansen. Copenhagen: Rosenkilde and Bagger.

Hollier, Denis, ed. (1989). *A New History of French Literature*. Cambridge, Mass.: Harvard University Press.

Howard, June (1985). *Form and History in American Literary Naturalism*. Chapel Hill: University of North Carolina Press.

Hussman, Lawrence E. (1983). *Dreiser and his Fiction: A Twentieth-Century Quest*. Philadelphia: University of Philadelphia Press.

Hutchinson, Peter (1983). *Games Authors Play*. London: Methuen.

Kafka, Franz (1969). 'Der Bau', in *Sämtliche Erzählungen*. Frankfurt: Fischer, 412–44. 'The Burrow.' Trans. Willa Muir and Edwin Muir. In *Selected Stories of Franz Kafka*. New York: Modern Library, 1952, 256–304.

Ketterer, David (1979). *The Rationale of Deception in Poe*. Baton Rouge: Louisiana State University Press.

Khatchadourian, Haig (1980). 'Rational/Irrational in Dostoevsky, Nietzsche and Aristotle', *Journal of the British Society for Phenomenology*, 11, 107–15.

Kuhn, Reinhard (1976). *The Demon of Noontide: Ennui in Western Literature*. Princeton: Princeton University Press.

Lanham, Richard A. (1973). *Tristram Shandy and the Games of Pleasure*. Berkeley: University of California Press.

Lem, Stanislaw (1978). *The Chain of Chance*. Trans. Louis Iribarne. New York: Helen and Kurt Wolff Books, Harcourt Brace Jovanovich.

(1981). *Memoirs of a Space Traveler: Further Reminiscences of Ijon Tichy*. Trans. Joel Stern and Maria Swiecicka-Ziemianek. New York: Helen and Kurt Wolff Books, Harcourt Brace Jovanovich.

(1983). *His Master's Voice*. Trans. Michael Kandel. New York: Helen and Kurt Wolff Books, Harcourt Brace Jovanovich.

(1984). *Microworlds: Writings on Science Fiction and Fantasy*. Ed. Franz Rottensteiner. New York: Helen and Kurt Wolff Books, Harcourt Brace Jovanovich.

(1985). *Imaginary Magnitude*. Trans. Marc Heine. New York: Helen and Kurt Wolff Books, Harcourt Brace Jovanovich.

(1986). *One Human Minute*. Trans. Catherine S. Leach. New York: Helen and Kurt Wolff Books, Harcourt Brace Jovanovich.

Levin, Richard (1988). 'Feminist Thematics and Shakespearean Tragedy', *PMLA*, 103, 125–39.

(1989). Reply to Letter to the Editor, *PMLA*, 104, 78–79.

(1990). 'The Poetics and Politics of Bardicide', *PMLA*, 105, 491–504.

Lewis, Matthew Gregory (1952). *The Monk*. New York: Grove.

Lind, Sidney E. (1947). 'Poe and Mesmerism', *PMLA*, 62 (1947), 1077–94.

Lindauer, Martin S. (1974). *The Psychological Study of Literature: Limitations, Possibilities, and Accomplishments*. Chicago: Nelson-Hall.

Lindström, Hans (1952). *Hjärnornas Kamp: Psykologiska Idéer och Motiv i Strindbergs Åttiotalsdiktning*. Uppsala: Appelbergs.

Lingeman, Richard R. (1986). *Theodore Dreiser: At the Gates of the City, 1871– 1907*. New York: G. P. Putnam's Sons.

Livingston, Paisley (1988). *Literary Knowledge: Humanistic Inquiry and the Philosophy of Science*. Ithaca: Cornell University Press.

(forthcoming:a). 'Convention and Literary Explanations', in *Rules and Conventions*, ed. Hjort.

Lönnroth, Lars (1976). *Njáls Saga: A Critical Introduction*. Berkeley: University of California Press.

(1980). 'New Dimensions and Old Directions in Saga Research', *Scandinavica*, 19, 57–61.

McCormick, Peter (1988). *Fictions, Philosophies, and the Problems of Poetics*. Ithaca: Cornell University Press.

Mailloux, Steven (1982). *Interpretive Conventions: The Reader in the Study of American Fiction*. Ithaca: Cornell University Press.

Margolin, Uri (1983). 'Characterization in Narrative: Some Theoretical Prolegomena', *Neophilologus*, 67, 1–14.

(1986). 'The Doer and the Deed: Action as a Basis for Characterization in Narrative', *Poetics Today*, 7, 205–25.

(1987). 'Introducing and Sustaining Characters in Literary Narrative: A Set of Conditions', *Style*, 21, 107–24.

Markels, Julian (1961). 'Dreiser and the Plotting of Inarticulate Experience', *The Massachusetts Review*, 2, 431–48.

Marzin, Florian F., ed. (1985). *Stanislaw Lem: An den Grenzen der SF und darüberhinaus*. Meitingen: Corian.

Matthews, Robert J. (1981). 'Literary Works and Institutional Practices', *British Journal of Aesthetics*, 21, 39–49.

Matthiessen, F. O. (1951). *Theodore Dreiser*. London: Methuen.

Michaels, Walter Benn (1980). 'Sister Carrie's Popular Economy', Critical Inquiry, 7, 373–90.

(1982). 'Dreiser's Financier: The Man of Business as a Man of Letters', in American Realism, ed. Sundquist, 278–96.

(1987). The Gold Standard and the Logic of Naturalism: American Literature at the Turn of the Century. Berkeley: University of California Press.

Mitchell, Lee Clark (1989). Determined Fictions: American Literary Naturalism. New York: Columbia University Press.

Mitterand, Henri (1986). Zola et le naturalisme. Paris: Presses Universitaires de France.

Moers, Ellen (1969). Two Dreisers. New York: Viking.

Moss, Sidney P. (1963). Poe's Literary Battles: The Critic in the Context of his Literary Milieu. Durham: Duke University Press.

Nadeau, Maurice (1964). Histoire du surréalisme suivie de documents surréalistes. Paris: Seuil.

Nelson, Brian (1982). Emile Zola: A Selective Analytical Bibliography. London: Grant and Cutler.

(1983). Zola and the Bourgeoisie: A Study of Themes and Techniques in Les Rougon-Macquart. London: Macmillan.

Nordal, Sigurdur, ed. (1933). Egils saga Skalla-Grímssonar. Islenzk fornrit. Vol. 2. Reykjavík: Hid íslenzka fornritafélag.

Nordau, Max (1896). Paradoxe. Leipzig: Glischer.

Nystrand, Martin (1986). The Structure of Written Communication: Studies in Reciprocity between Writers and Readers. New York: Academic.

Pálsson, Hermann, and Paul Edwards, ed. and trans. (1976). Egil's Saga. Harmondsworth: Penguin.

Pavel, Thomas G. (1986). Fictional Worlds. Cambridge, Mass.: Harvard University Press.

(1988). Le Mirage linguistique. Paris: Minuit. Trans. (1989). The Feud of Language: A History of Structuralist Thought. Oxford: Basil Blackwell.

Phelan, James (1989). Reading People, Reading Plots: Character, Progression, and the Interpretation of Narrative. Chicago: University of Chicago Press.

Pizer, Donald, ed. (1981). Critical Essays on Theodore Dreiser. Boston: G. K. Hall.

Poe, Edgar Allan (1978). Collected Works of Edgar Allan Poe, vol. 3, Tales and Sketches, 1843–1849. Ed. Thomas Ollive Mabbott. Cambridge, Mass.: Harvard University Press.

(1984). Essays and Reviews. Ed. G. R. Thompson. New York: Library of America.

Ponech, Trevor (forthcoming). 'Literary Criticism and the Philosophy of Mind.'

Pratt, Mary Louise (1981). 'The Ideology of Speech-Act Theory', Centrum, 1, 5–18.

Prince, Gerald (1987). A Dictionary of Narratology. Lincoln: University of Nebraska Press.

Quinn, Arthur Hobson (1941). *Edgar Allan Poe: A Critical Biography*. New York: D. Appleton-Century.

Reeves, Charles Eric (1986a). '"Conveniency to Nature": Literary Art and Arbitrariness', *PMLA*, 101, 798–810.

(1986b). 'The Languages of Convention: Literature and Consensus', *Poetics Today*, 7, 3–28.

Richard, Claude, ed. (1974). *Baudelaire*. Paris: l'Herne.

Rodnianskaia, Irina (1986). 'Two Faces of Stanislaw Lem: On *His Master's Voice*', *Science-Fiction Studies*, 13, 352–9.

Scarron, Paul (1973). *Le Roman comique*. Paris: Garnier.

Schmidt, Siegfried J. (1976). 'Towards a Pragmatic Interpretation of "Fictionality"', in *Pragmatics of Language and Literature*, ed. van Dijk, 161–79.

(1982). *Foundation for the Empirical Study of Literature: The Components of a Basic Theory*. Trans. Robert de Beaugrande. Hamburg: Helmut Buske.

(1989). *Die Selbstorganisation des Sozialsystems Literatur im 18. Jahrhundert*. Frankfurt: Suhrkamp.

Sherman, Stuart P. (1981). 'The Naturalism of Mr. Dreiser', in *Critical Essays on Theodore Dreiser*, ed. Pizer, 4–12.

Siebers, Tobin (1984). *The Romantic Fantastic*. Ithaca: Cornell University Press.

(1988). *The Ethics of Criticism*. Ithaca: Cornell University Press.

Smith, Barbara Herrnstein (1988). *Contingencies of Value: Alternative Perspectives for Critical Theory*. Cambridge, Mass.: Harvard University Press.

Smith, Carl S. (1976). 'Dreiser's *Trilogy of Desire*: The Financier as Artist', *Canadian Review of American Studies*, 7, 151–62.

Stein, Nancy L. (1982). 'The Definition of a Story', *Journal of Pragmatics*, 6, 487–507.

Strindberg, August (1912–20). *Samlade Skrifter*. Stockholm: Bonniers.

Sundquist, Eric J., ed. (1982). *American Realism: New Essays*. Baltimore: The Johns Hopkins University Press.

Sussman, Henry (1977). 'The All-Embracing Metaphor: Reflections on Kafka's "The Burrow"', *Glyph*, 1, 100–31.

Thiher, Allen (1987). 'The *Nachlass*: Metaphors of Gehen and Ways Toward Science', in *Kafka and the Contemporary Critical Performance*, ed. Udoff, 256–65.

Thompson, G. R. (1973). *Poe's Fiction: Romantic Irony in the Gothic Tales*. Madison: University of Wisconsin Press.

Todorov, Tzvetan (1977). *Théories du symbole*. Paris: Seuil.

(1987). *La Notion de littérature et autres essais*. Paris: Seuil.

Udoff, Alan, ed. (1987). *Kafka and the Contemporary Critical Performance*. Bloomington: Indiana University Press.

Vivas, Eliseo (1981). 'Dreiser, An Inconsistent Mechanist', in *Critical Essays on Theodore Dreiser*, ed. Pizer, 30–37.

Wagenknecht, Edward (1963). *Edgar Allan Poe: The Man Behind the Legend.*
New York: Oxford University Press.
Weiss, Daniel Evan (1990). *Unnatural Selection.* Chicago: Black Swan.
West, James L. W. III (1985). *A Sister Carrie Portfolio.* Charlottesville:
University Press of Virginia.
Wilkinson, Robert Edwin (1965). 'A Study of Theodore Dreiser's *The
Financier.*' Unpublished Ph.D. Diss., University of Pennslyvania.
Williams, Michael J. S. (1988). *A World of Words: Language and Displacement
in the Fiction of Edgar Allan Poe.* Durham: Duke University Press.
Wirzenberger, Karl-Heinz (1955). *Die Romane Theodore Dreisers.* Berlin:
V.E.B., Deutscher Verlag der Wissenschaften.
Wright, A. M. (1981). 'Scientific Method and Rationality in Dürrenmatt',
German Life and Letters, 35, 64–72.
Ziegfeld, Richard E. (1985). *Stanlisaw Lem.* New York: Ungar.
Zola, Emile (1964). *Les Rougon-Macquart.* 5 vols. Ed. Henri Mitterand.
Paris: Gallimard. Bibliothèque de la Pléiade.

ACTION, AGENCY, AND RATIONALITY

Abelson, Robert P. (1976). 'Social Psychology's Rational Man', in *Ration-
ality and the Social Sciences,* ed. Benn and Mortimore, 58–89.
Abelson, Robert P., and Ariel Levi (1983). 'Decision Making and Deci-
sion Theory', in *Handbook of Social Psychology,* ed. Lindzey and Aron-
son. vol. I, 231–309.
Acham, Karl (1984). 'Über einige Rationalitätskonzeptionen in den
Sozialwissenschaften', in *Rationalität,* ed. Schnädelbach, 32–69.
Adams, Frederick, and Alfred Mele (1989). 'The Role of Intention in
Intentional Action', *Canadian Journal of Philosophy,* 19, 511–32.
Adorno, Theodor W., Ralf Dahrendorf, Harald Pilot, et al. (1969). *Der
Positivismusstreit in der deutschen Soziologie.* Neuwied and Berlin: Her-
mann Luchterhand.
Agassi, Joseph (1973). 'Methodological Individualism', in *Models of
Individualism and Collectivism,* ed. O'Neill, 185–212.
Agassi, Joseph, and Ian Charles Jarvie, eds. (1987). *Rationality: The Criti-
cal View.* Dordrecht: Martinus Nijhoff.
Albert, Hans (1987). 'Science and the Search for Truth', in *Rationality: The
Critical View,* ed. Agassi and Jarvie, 69–82.
Alchian, Armen A. (1950). 'Uncertainty, Evolution and Economic
Theory', *Journal of Political Economy,* 58, 211–21.
Allais, Maurice (1953). 'Le Comportement de l'homme rationnel devant
le risque: critique des postulats et axiomes de l'école américaine',
Econometrica, 21, 503–46.
Alston, William P. (1967). 'Motives and Motivation', in *The Encyclopedia of
Philosophy.* Ed. Paul Edwards. New York: Macmillan, vol. 5, 399–409.
Anscombe, G. E. M. (1958). *Intention.* Oxford: Basil Blackwell.

Audi, Robert (1973). 'Intending', *Journal of Philosophy*, 70, 387–403.
  (1986). 'Action Theory as a Resource for Decision Theory', *Theory and Decision*, 20, 207–21.
  (1988). 'Deliberative Intentions and Willingness to Act: A Reply to Professor Mele', *Philosophia*, 18, 243–45.
  (1989). *Practical Reasoning*. London: Routledge.
Aune, Bruce (1977). *Reason and Action*. Dordrecht: Reidel.
  (1988). 'Action and Ontology', *Philosophical Studies*, 54, 195–213.
Bach, Kent, and Robert M. Harnish (1979). *Linguistic Communication and Speech Acts*. Cambridge, Mass.: M.I.T. Press.
Baier, Annette C. (1986). 'The Ambiguous Limits of Desire', in *The Ways of Desire*, ed. Marks, 39–61.
Baker, Lynne Rudder (1987). *Saving Belief: A Critique of Physicalism*. Princeton: Princeton University Press.
Bandura, Albert (1986). *Social Foundations of Thought and Action: A Social Cognitive Theory*. Englewood Cliffs, N.J.: Prentice-Hall.
  (1989). 'Human Agency in Social Cognitive Theory', *American Psychologist*, 44, 1175–84.
Barnes, Barry, ed. (1972). *Sociology of Science: Selected Readings*. Harmondsworth: Penguin.
Barrett, Robert B., and Roger F. Gibson, eds. (1990). *Perspectives on Quine*. Oxford: Basil Blackwell.
Barwise, Jon, and John Perry (1983). *Situations and Attitudes*. Cambridge, Mass.: M.I.T. Press.
  (1985). 'Shifting Situations and Shaken Attitudes. An Interview with Barwise and Perry,' *Linguistics and Philosophy*, 8, 105–61.
Becker, Gary S. (1976). *The Economic Approach to Human Behavior*. Chicago: University of Chicago Press.
Benn, Stanley I., and Geoffrey W. Mortimore, eds. (1976a). *Rationality and the Social Sciences: Contributions to the Philosophy and Methodology of the Social Sciences*. London: Routledge and Kegan Paul.
  (1976b) 'Introduction', in *Rationality and the Social Sciences*, ed. Benn and Mortimore, 1–7.
  (1976c) 'Technical Models of Rational Choice', in *Rationality and the Social Sciences*, ed. Benn and Mortimore, 157–95.
Bennett, Jonathan (1964). *Rationality: An Essay Towards an Analysis*. London: Routledge and Kegan Paul.
Ben-Zeev, Aaron (1982). 'Who Is a Rational Agent?' *Canadian Journal of Philosophy*, 12, 647–61.
  (1987). 'The Nature of Emotions', *Philosophical Studies*, 52, 393–410.
Bicchieri, Cristina (1987). 'Rationality and Predictability in Economics', *British Journal for the Philosophy of Science*, 38, 501–13.
Binkley, Robert, Richard Bronaugh, and Ausonio Marras, eds. (1971). *Agent, Action, and Reason*. Toronto: University of Toronto Press.
Bishop, John (1989). *Natural Agency: An Essay on the Causal Theory of Action*. Cambridge: Cambridge University Press.

Black, Max (1982). 'Why Should I Be Rational?' *Dialectica*, 36, 147–68.

Block, Ned, ed. (1980). *Readings in the Philosophy of Psychology*. 2 vols. Cambridge, Mass.: Harvard University Press.

Boër, Steven E., and William G. Lycan (1986). *Knowing Who*. Cambridge, Mass.: M.I.T. Press.

Borch, Karl Henrik (1968). *The Economics of Uncertainty*. Princeton: Princeton University Press.

Borger, Robert, and Frank Cioffi, eds. (1970). *Explanation in the Behavioural Sciences*. Cambridge: Cambridge University Press.

Boudon, Raymond (1977). *Effets pervers et ordre social*. Paris: Presses Universitaires de France.

   (1988). 'Rationalité et théorie de l'action sociale', in *Penser le sujet aujourd'hui*, ed. Guibert-Sledziewski and Vieillard-Baron, 139–63.

Brams, Steven J. (1985). *Superpower Games: Applying Game Theory to Superpower Conflict*. New Haven: Yale University Press.

Brand, Myles (1984). *Intending and Acting: Toward a Naturalized Action Theory*. Cambridge, Mass.: M.I.T. Press.

Brand, Myles, and Douglas Walton, eds. (1976). *Action Theory: Proceedings of the Winnipeg Conference on Human Action*. Dordrecht: Reidel.

Brandt, Richard B. (1979). *A Theory of the Good and the Right*. Oxford: Oxford University Press.

Brandt, Richard, and Jaegwon Kim (1963). 'Wants as Explanations of Actions', *Journal of Philosophy*, 60, 425–35.

Bratman, Michael E. (1987). *Intention, Plans, and Practical Reason*. Cambridge, Mass.: Harvard University Press.

   (1990). 'Dretske's Desires', *Philosophy and Phenomenological Research*, 50, 795–800.

Brown, Harold I. (1988). *Rationality*. London: Routledge.

Brown, James Robert, ed. (1984). *Scientific Rationality: The Sociological Turn*. Dordrecht: Reidel.

   (1989). *The Rational and the Social*. London: Routledge.

Bunge, Mario (1981). *Scientific Materialism*. Dordrecht: Reidel.

   (1984). 'Philosophical Problems in Linguistics', *Erkenntnis*, 21, 107–74.

   (1987). 'Seven Desiderata for Rationality', in *Rationality: The Critical View*, ed. Agassi and Jarvie, 5–15.

Bunge, Mario, and Rubén Ardila (1987). *Philosophy of Psychology*. New York: Springer.

Caillois, Roger (1963). *Le Mimétisme animal*. Paris: Hachette.

Castañeda, Hector-Neri (1975). *Thinking and Doing: The Philosophical Foundations of Institutions*. Dordrecht: Reidel.

Castoriadis, Cornelius (1978). *Les Carrefours du labyrinthe*. Paris: Seuil.

   (1988). 'Individu, société, rationalité, histoire', *Esprit*, 135, 89–113.

Charlton, William (1988). *Weakness of Will: A Philosophical Introduction*. New York: Basil Blackwell.

Cherniak, Christopher (1986). *Minimal Rationality*. Cambridge, Mass.: M.I.T. Press.

Church, Jennifer (1987). 'Reasonable Irrationality', *Mind*, 96, 354–66.

Churchill, Winston (1950). *The Second World War*. 5 vols. London: Cassell and Co.

Churchland, Patricia Smith (1986). *Neurophilosophy: Toward a Unified Science of the Mind/Brain*. Cambridge, Mass.: M.I.T. Press.

Churchland, Paul (1970). 'The Logical Character of Action-Explanations', *Philosophical Review*, 79, 214–36.

(1981). 'Eliminative Materialism and the Propositional Attitudes', *Journal of Philosophy*, 68, 67–90.

(1984). *Matter and Consciousness*. Cambridge, Mass.: M.I.T. Press.

Classen, Emil M., ed. (1967). *Les Fondements philosophiques des systèmes économiques*. Paris: Payot.

Coats, Alfred W. (1976). 'Economics and Psychology: The Death and Resurrection of a Research Programme', in *Method and Appraisal in Economics*, ed. Latsis, 43–64.

Cohen, L. Jonathan (1981). 'Can Human Irrationality Be Experimentally Demonstrated?' *Behavior and Brain Sciences*, 4, 317–33.

Cohen, P. S. (1976). 'Rational Conduct and Social Life', in *Rationality and the Social Sciences*, ed. Benn and Mortimore, 132–54.

Cohen, R. S., and Larry Laudan, eds. (1983). *Physics, Philosophy and Psychoanalysis*. Dordrecht: Reidel.

Cohen, Robert S., and Marx W. Wartofsky, eds. (1983). *Epistemology, Methodology and the Social Sciences*. Dordrecht: Reidel.

Cormier, Stephen M. (1986). *Basic Processes of Learning, Cognition, and Motivation*. Hillsdale, N.J.: Lawrence Erlbaum.

Cummins, Robert (1983). *The Nature of Psychological Explanation*. Cambridge, Mass.: M.I.T. Press.

Curtis, Rebecca C., ed. (1989). *Self-Defeating Behaviors: Experimental Research, Clinical Impressions, and Practical Implications*. New York: Plenum.

Dallmayr, Fred (1988). 'Habermas and Rationality', *Political Theory*, 16, 553–79.

Dancy, Jonathan (1985). *An Introduction to Contemporary Epistemology*. Oxford: Basil Blackwell.

Danto, Arthur C. (1973). *Analytic Philosophy of Action*. Cambridge: Cambridge University Press.

Davidson, Donald (1980). *Essays on Actions and Events*. Oxford: Clarendon.

(1982a). 'Paradoxes of Irrationality', in *Philosophical Essays on Freud*, ed. Wollheim, 289–305.

(1982b). 'Rational Animals', *Dialectica*, 36, 317–27.

(1984). 'First Person Authority', *Dialectica*, 38, 101–12.

(1985). 'Incoherence and Irrationality', *Dialectica*, 39, 345–54.

(1990a). 'The Structure and Content of Truth', *Journal of Philosophy*, 87, 279–328.

(1990b). 'Meaning, Truth, and Evidence', in *Perspectives on Quine*, ed. Barrett and Gibson, 68–79.

Davis, Wayne A. (1986). 'The Two Senses of Desire', in *The Ways of Desire*, ed. Marks, 63–82.

Demos, Raphael (1960). 'Lying to Oneself', *Journal of Philosophy*, 57, 588–95.

Dennett, Daniel C. (1978). *Brainstorms: Philosophical Essays on Mind and Psychology*. Cambridge, Mass.: M.I.T. Press.

(1987). *The Intentional Stance*. Cambridge, Mass.: M.I.T. Press.

Derrida, Jacques (1977a). 'Signature Event Context', *Glyph*, 1, 172–97.

(1977b). 'Limited Inc. a b c . . .', *Glyph*, 2, 162–254.

De Sousa, Ronald (1980). 'The Rationality of Emotions', in *Explaining Emotions*, ed. Rorty, 127–52.

(1987). *The Rationality of Emotion*. Cambridge, Mass.: M.I.T. Press.

Diamond, Arthur M. Jr. (1988). 'Science as a Rational Enterprise', *Theory and Decision*, 24, 147–67.

Donagan, Alan (1977). *The Theory of Morality*. Chicago: University of Chicago Press.

Doppelt, Gerald (1988). 'The Philosophical Requirements for an Adequate Conception of Scientific Rationality', *Philosophy of Science*, 55, 104–33.

Dretske, Fred (1988). *Explaining Behavior: Reasons in a World of Causes*. Cambridge, Mass.: M.I.T. Press.

(1990). 'Reply to Reviewers', *Philosophy and Phenomenological Research*, 50, 819–40.

Dunn, Robert (1987). *The Possibility of Weakness of Will*. Indianapolis: Hackett.

Eagle, Morris N. (1983). 'The Epistemological Status of Recent Developments in Psychoanalytic Theory', in *Physics, Philosophy and Psychoanalysis*, ed. Cohen and Laudan, 31–55.

Elster, Jon (1979). *Ulysses and the Sirens: Studies in Rationality and Irrationality*. Cambridge: Cambridge University Press.

(1983a). *Explaining Technical Change: A Case Study in the Philosophy of Science*. Cambridge: Cambridge University Press.

(1983b). *Sour Grapes: Studies in the Subversion of Rationality*. Cambridge: Cambridge University Press.

(1985a). 'Rationality, Morality, and Collective Action', *Ethics*, 96, 136–55.

(1985b). 'Sadder but Wiser? Rationality and the Emotions', *Social Science Information*, 24, 375–406.

ed. (1986a). *The Multiple Self*. Cambridge: Cambridge University Press.

ed. (1986b). *Rational Choice*. Cambridge: Cambridge University Press.

(1986c). 'Rationality', in *Contemporary Philosophy*, ed. Fløistad, vol. II, 113–31.

(1988). 'Economic Order and Social Norms', *Journal of Institutional and Theoretical Economics*, 144, 357–66.

(1989a). *The Cement of Society: A Study of Social Order*. Cambridge: Cambridge University Press.

(1989b). *Nuts and Bolts for the Social Sciences*. Cambridge: Cambridge University Press.

(1989c). *Solomonic Judgements: Studies in the Limitations of Rationality*. Cambridge: Cambridge University Press.

Erwin, Edward (1981). 'The Truth About Psychoanalysis', *Journal of Philosophy*, 78, 549–60.

Farrell, Daniel M. (1980). 'Jealousy', *Philosophical Review*, 89, 527–59.

(1989). 'Intention, Reason, and Action', *American Philosophical Quarterly*, 26, 283–95.

Faust, David (1984). *The Limits of Scientific Reasoning*. Minneapolis: University of Minnesota Press.

Fløistad, Guttorm, ed. (1986). *Contemporary Philosophy*. Vol. 2: *Philosophy of Science*. Dordrecht: Martinus Nijhoff.

Fodor, Jerry A. (1968). *Psychological Explanation*. New York: Random House.

(1975). *The Language of Thought*. New York: Crowell.

(1980). *Representations*. Cambridge, Mass.: M.I.T. Press.

Foley, Richard (1987). *The Theory of Epistemic Rationality*. Cambridge, Mass.: Harvard University Press.

(1990). 'Skepticism and Rationality', in *Doubting*, ed. Roth and Ross, 69–82.

Føllesdal, Dagfinn (1980). 'Explanation of Action', in *Rationality in Science*, ed. Hilpinen, 231–48.

(1981). 'Understanding and Rationality', in *Meaning and Understanding*, ed. Parret and Bouveresse, 154–68.

(1982). 'The Status of Rationality Assumptions in Interpretation and in the Explanation of Action', *Dialectica*, 36, 301–16.

(1988). 'Hva er rasjonalitet?' *Norsk Filosofisk Tidsskrift*, 4, 203–12.

Frankfurt, Harry G. (1988). *The Importance of What We Care About: Philosophical Essays*. Cambridge: Cambridge University Press.

Gärdenfors, Peter (1988). *Knowledge in Flux: Modeling the Dynamics of Epistemic States*. Cambridge, Mass.: M.I.T. Press.

Gärdenfors, Peter, and Nils-Eric Sahlin, eds. (1988a). *Decision, Probability, and Utility: Selected Readings*. Cambridge: Cambridge University Press.

(1988b). 'Unreliable Probabilities, Risk Taking, and Decision Making', in *Decision, Probability, and Utility*, ed. Gärdenfors and Sahlin, 313–34.

Gasché, Rodolphe (1988). 'Postmodernism and Rationality', *Journal of Philosophy*, 85, 528–40.

Geen, Russell G., William W. Beatty and Robert M. Arkin (1984). *Human Motivation: Physiological, Behavioral, and Social Approaches*. Boston: Allyn and Bacon.

Geraets, Theodore, F., ed. (1979). *Rationality Today*. Ottawa: University of Ottawa Press.

Gewirth, Alan (1978). *Reason and Morality*. Chicago: University of Chicago Press.

Gibbard, Allan (1985). 'Moral Judgment and the Acceptance of Norms', *Ethics*, 96, 5–21.

(1990). *Wise Choices, Apt Feelings: A Theory of Normative Judgment*. Cambridge, Mass.: Harvard University Press.

Giere, Ronald N. (1988). *Explaining Science: A Cognitive Approach*. Chicago: University of Chicago Press.

Ginet, Carl (1990). *On Action*. Cambridge: Cambridge University Press.

Glück, P., and Michael Schmid (1977). 'The Rationality Principle and Action Explanations: N. Koertge's Reconstruction of Popper's Logic of Action Explanations', *Inquiry*, 20, 72–81.

Godelier, Maurice (1971). *Rationalité et irrationalité en économie*. 2 vols. Paris: Maspero.

Goldman, Alvin I. (1970). *A Theory of Human Action*. Englewood Cliffs, N.J.: Prentice-Hall.

Grandy, Richard E., and Richard Warner, eds. (1986). *Philosophical Grounds of Rationality: Intentions, Categories, Ends*. Oxford: Clarendon.

Greenspan, Patricia S. (1988). *Emotions and Reasons: An Inquiry into Emotional Justification*. New York: Routledge.

Grice, Paul (1986). 'Actions and Events', *Pacific Philosophical Quarterly*, 67, 1–35.

(1989). *Studies in the Way of Words*. Cambridge, Mass.: Harvard University Press.

Grünbaum, Adolf (1984). *The Foundations of Psychoanalysis: A Philosophical Critique*. Berkeley: University of California Press.

Guibert-Sledziewski, Elisabeth, and Jean-Louis Vieillard-Baron, eds. (1988). *Penser le sujet aujourd'hui*. Paris: Meridiens-Klincksieck.

Gunderson, Keith, ed. (1975). *Language, Mind, and Knowledge*. Minneapolis: University of Minnesota Press.

Gustafson, Donald F. (1986). *Intention and Agency*. Dordrecht: Reidel.

Habermas, Jürgen (1981). *Theorie des kommunikativen Handelns*. 2 vols. Frankfurt: Suhrkamp.

Hahn, Frank, and Martin Hollis, eds. (1979). *Philosophy and Economic Theory*. Oxford: Oxford University Press.

Haller, Rudolph, ed. (1981). *Science and Ethics*. Amsterdam: Rodopi.

Hands, Douglas Wade (1985). 'Karl Popper and Economic Methodology: A New Look', *Economics and Philosophy*, 1, 83–99.

Harding, Sandra (1982). 'Is Gender a Variable in Concepts of Rationality: A Survey of Issues', *Dialectica*, 36, 225–42.

Harman, Gilbert (1976). 'Practical Reasoning', *Review of Metaphysics*, 29, 431–63.

(1983). 'Rational Action and the Extent of Intentions', *Social Theory and Practice*, 9, 123–41.

(1986). *Change in View: Principles of Reasoning*. Cambridge, Mass.: M.I.T. Press.

Harrison, Ross, ed. (1979). *Rational Action: Studies in Philosophy and Social Science*. Cambridge: Cambridge University Press.

Harsanyi, John C. (1983). 'Basic Moral Decisions and Alternative Concepts of Rationality', *Social Theory and Practice*, 9, 231–44.

(1985). 'Does Reason Tell Us What Moral Code to Follow, and, Indeed, to Follow Any Moral Code at All?' *Ethics*, 96, 231–44.

Harsanyi, John C., and Reinhard Selten (1988). *A General Theory of Equilibrium Selection in Games*. Cambridge, Mass.: M.I.T. Press.

Heimer, Carol A., and Arthur L. Stinchcombe (1980). 'Love and Irrationality', *Social Science Information*, 19, 697–754.

Henderson David K. (1990). 'An Empirical Basis for Charity in Interpretation', *Erkenntnis*, 32, 83–103.

Hilpinen, Risto, ed. (1980). *Rationality in Science*. Dordrecht: Reidel.

Hintikka, Jaakko (1962). *Knowledge and Belief*. Ithaca: Cornell University Press.

Hogarth, Robin M. (1980). *Judgement and Choice: The Psychology of Decision*. Chichester: John Wiley.

Hogarth, Robin M., and Melvin W. Reder, eds. (1986). *Rational Choice: The Contrast between Economics and Psychology*. Chicago: University of Chicago Press.

Hollis, Martin (1977). *Models of Man: Philosophical Thoughts on Social Action*. Cambridge: Cambridge University Press.

(1979). 'Rational Man and Social Science', in *Rational Action*, ed. Harrison, 1–15.

(1987). *The Cunning of Reason*. Cambridge: Cambridge University Press.

Hollis, Martin, and Steven Lukes, eds. (1982). *Rationality and Relativism*. Cambridge, Mass.: M.I.T. Press.

Hollis, Martin, and Edward J. Nell (1975). *Rational Economic Man: A Philosophical Critique of Neo-Classical Economics*. Cambridge: Cambridge University Press.

Howell, William C., and Sarah A. Burnett (1978). 'Uncertainty Measurement: A Cognitive Taxonomy', *Organizational Behavior and Human Performance*, 22, 45–68.

Hume, David (1978). *A Treatise of Human Nature*. Ed. Peter Harold Nidditch. Oxford: Clarendon.

Janis, Irving L., and Leon Mann (1977). *Decision Making: A Psychological Analysis of Conflict, Choice, and Commitment*. New York: Free Press.

Jeffrey, Richard C. (1965). *The Logic of Decision*. New York: McGraw Hill.

Johnson-Laird, Philip N. (1983). *Mental Models: Towards a Cognitive Science of Language, Inference, and Consciousness*. Cambridge: Cambridge University Press.

Kagan, Shelly (1986). 'The Present-Aim Theory of Rationality', *Ethics*, 96, 746–59.

Kahneman, Daniel, Paul Slovic, and Amos Tversky, eds. (1982). *Judgment Under Uncertainty: Heuristics and Biases*. Cambridge: Cambridge University Press.

Kant, Immanuel (1963). *Kant on History*. Ed. and trans. Lewis White Beck. Indianapolis: Bobbs-Merrill.

Kaye, Howard L. (1986). *The Social Meaning of Modern Biology: From Social Darwinism to Sociobiology*. New Haven: Yale University Press.

Kekes, John (1987). 'Rationality and Problem-Solving', in *Rationality: The Critical View*, ed. Agassi and Jarvie, 265–79.

  (1988). 'Some Requirements of a Theory of Rationality', *Monist*, 7, 320–38.

Keynes, John Maynard (1973). *The General Theory of Employment Interest and Money*. London: Macmillan.

Knight, Frank H. (1921). *Risk, Uncertainty, and Profit*. Boston and New York: Houghton Mifflin.

Koertge, Noretta (1975). 'Popper's Metaphysical Research Program for the Human Sciences', *Inquiry*, 18, 437–62.

  (1979). 'The Methodological Status of Popper's Rationality Principle', *Theory and Decision*, 10, 83–98.

Kuhl, Julius, and Jürgen Beckmann, eds. (1985). *Action Control: From Cognition to Behavior*. Berlin: Springer.

Lagueux, Maurice (forthcoming). 'Popper et le principe de rationalité.'

Lallement, Jérôme (1987). 'Popper et le principe de rationalité', *Economies et Sociétés*, 10, 25–40.

Lash, Scott, and Sam Whimster, eds. (1987). *Max Weber, Rationality and Modernity*. London: Allen and Unwin.

Latsis, Spiro J. (1972). 'Situational Determinism in Economics', *British Journal for the Philosophy of Science*, 23, 207–45.

  ed. (1976). *Method and Appraisal in Economics*. Cambridge: Cambridge University Press.

  (1983). 'The Role and Status of the Rationality Principle in the Social Sciences', in *Epistemology, Methodology and the Social Sciences*, ed. Cohen and Wartofsky, 123–51.

Lee, Wayne (1971). *Decision Theory and Human Behavior*. New York: John Wiley.

Lepenies, Wolf (1985). 'Cold Reason and the Culture of the Feelings: Social Science Literature and the End of the Enlightenment', *Social Science Information*, 24, 3–21.

LePore, Ernest, and Brian McLaughlin, eds. (1985). *Actions and Events: Perspectives on the Philosophy of Donald Davidson*. Oxford: Basil Blackwell.

Levi, Isaac (1986). *Hard Choices*. Cambridge: Cambridge University Press.

Levin, Janet (1988). 'Must Reasons be Rational?' *Philosophy of Science*, 55, 199–217.

Lewis, David (1969). *Convention: A Philosophical Study*. Cambridge, Mass.: Harvard University Press.

(1975). 'Languages and Language', in *Language, Mind, and Knowledge*, ed. Gunderson, 3–35.

(1988). 'Desire as Belief', *Mind*, 97, 323–32.

Lindzey, Gardner, and Elliot Aronson, eds. (1983). *The Handbook of Social Psychology*. 3rd ed. New York: Random House.

Livingston, Paisley (forthcoming:b). *Models of Desire: René Girard and the Psychology of Mimesis*.

Loar, Brian (1981). *Mind and Meaning*. Cambridge: Cambridge University Press.

Locke, Don (1982). 'Beliefs, Desires, and Reasons for Action', *American Philosophical Quarterly*, 14, 241–49.

Loeb, Jacques (1964). *The Mechanistic Conception of Life*. Ed. Donald Fleming. Cambridge, Mass.: Harvard University Press.

Luce, R. Duncan, and Howard Raiffa (1957). *Games and Decisions*. New York: John Wiley.

Lukes, Steven (1967). 'Some Problems About Rationality', *Archives Européenes de Sociologie*, 7, 247–64.

Lyons, William (1980). *Emotions*. Cambridge: Cambridge University Press.

McCann, Hugh J. (1986). 'Rationality and the Range of Intention', *Midwest Studies in Philosophy*, 10, 191–211.

McLaughlin, Brian P., and Amelie Oksenberg Rorty, eds. (1988). *Perspectives on Self-Deception*. Berkeley: University of California Press.

Maclean, Douglas, ed. (1984). *The Security Gamble: Deterrence Dilemmas in the Nuclear Age*. New York: Rowman and Allanheld.

McMullin, Ernan, ed. (1988). *Construction and Constraint: The Shaping of Scientific Rationality*. Notre Dame: Notre Dame University Press.

Macnamara, John (1972). 'Cognitive Basis of Language Learning in Infants', *Psychological Review*, 79 (1979), 1–13.

Madsen, Karl B. (1974). *Modern Theories of Motivation: A Comparative Metascientific Study*. New York: John Wiley.

Manninen, Juha, and Raimo Tuomela, eds. (1976). *Essays on Explanation and Understanding*. Dordrecht: Reidel.

Margolis, Joseph, Michael Krausz, and Richard M. Burian, eds. (1986). *Rationality, Relativism and the Human Sciences*. Dordrecht: Martinus Nijhoff.

Marks, Joel, ed. (1986a). *The Ways of Desire: New Essays in Philosophical Psychology on the Concept of Wanting*. Chicago: Precedent.

(1986b). 'The Difference between Motivation and Desire', in *Ways of Desire*, ed. Marks, 133–47.

Marshall, Graeme (1981). 'Action on the Rationality Principle', *Australian Journal of Philosophy*, 59, 54–76.

Martin, Mike W., ed. (1985). *Self-Deception and Self-Understanding.* Lawrence: Kansas University Press.

Martin, Rex (1977). *Historical Explanation.* Ithaca: Cornell University Press.

Mayo, David J. (1986). 'The Concept of Rational Suicide', *Journal of Medicine and Philosophy*, 11, 143–56.

Meiland, Jack (1970). *The Nature of Intention.* London: Methuen.

Mele, Alfred R. (1987). *Irrationality: An Essay on Akrasia, Self-Deception, and Self-Control.* New York: Oxford University Press.

   (1988). 'Against a Belief/Desire Analysis of Intention', *Philosophia*, 18, 239–42.

   (1989a). 'Intention, Belief, and Intentional Action', *American Philosophical Quarterly*, 26, 19–30.

   (1989b). 'Intentions by Default', *Pacific Philosophical Quarterly*, 70, 155–66.

   (1989c). 'She Intends to Try', *Philosophical Studies*, 55, 101–6.

Merton, Robert K. (1936). 'The Unanticipated Consequences of Social Action', *American Sociological Review*, 1, 894–904.

   (1973). *The Sociology of Science: Theoretical and Empirical Investigations.* Ed. Norman W. Storer. Chicago: University of Chicago Press.

Miller, David, ed. (1967). *Popper Selections.* Princeton: Princeton University Press.

Miller, Richard W. (1987). *Fact and Method: Explanation, Confirmation and Reality in the Natural and the Social Sciences.* Princeton: Princeton University Press.

Mischel, Theodore, ed. (1977). *The Self: Psychological and Philosophical Issues.* Totowa, N.J.: Rowman and Littlefield.

Mises, Ludwig von (1949). *Human Action: A Treatise on Economics.* New Haven: Yale University Press.

Mongin, Philippe (1988a). 'Simon et la théorie néo-classique de la rationalité limité', *Cahiers du CREA*, 11, 269–310.

   (1988b). 'La Théorie du choix rationnel considérée comme morale et psychologie', in *L'Age de la science 1*, ed. Récanati, 157–95.

Mortimore, Geoffrey W. (1976). 'Rational Action', in *Rationality and the Social Sciences*, ed. Benn and Mortimore, 93–110.

Mortimore, Geoffrey W., and J. B. Maund (1976). 'Rationality in Belief', in *Rationality and the Social Sciences*, ed. Benn and Mortimore, 11–57.

Mullane, Harvey (1971). 'Psychoanalytic Explanation and Rationality', *Journal of Philosophy*, 68, 413–26.

Myers, Milton L. (1983). *The Soul of Modern Economic Man: Ideas of Self Interest.* Chicago: University of Chicago Press.

Nadeau, Robert (1990). 'Confuting Popper on the Rationality Principle', *Cahiers d'Epistémologie*, 9012, 1–20.

Nathanson, Stephen (1985). *The Ideal of Rationality*. Atlantic Highlands: Humanities.

Neumann, John von, and Oskar Morgenstern (1944). *Theory of Games and Economic Behavior*. Princeton: Princeton University Press.

Newell, Alan, and Herbert A. Simon (1972). *Human Problem Solving*. Englewood Cliffs, N.J.: Prentice-Hall.

Nussbaum, Martha Craven (1978). *Aristotle's 'De Motu Animalium'*. Princeton: Princeton University Press.

O'Neill, John, ed. (1973). *Models of Individualism and Collectivism*. London: Heinemann.

Orléan, André (1985). 'Héterodoxie et incertitude', *Cahiers du CREA*, 5, 247–75.

(1986). 'Mimétisme et anticipations rationelles: une perspective keynésienne', *Recherches Economiques de Louvain*, 52, 45–66.

(1987). 'Anticipations et conventions en situation d'incertitude', *Cahiers d'Economie Politique*, 13, 153–72.

(1988). 'L'Autoréférence dans la théorie keynésienne de la spéculation', *Cahiers du CREA*, 11, 119–44.

(1989a). 'Mimetic Contagion and Speculative Bubbles', *Theory and Decision*, 27, 63–93.

(1989b). 'Pour une Approche cognitive des conventions économiques', *Revue Economique*, 40, 241–72.

Osherson, Daniel N., and Edward E. Smith, eds. (1990). *Thinking*. Cambridge, Mass.: M.I.T. Press.

Owen, Denis (1982). *Camouflage and Mimicry*. Chicago: University of Chicago Press.

Parfit, Derek (1986). *Reasons and Persons*. Oxford: Clarendon.

Parret, Herman, and Jacques Bouveresse, eds. (1981). *Meaning and Understanding*. Berlin: Walter de Gruyter.

Partridge, P. H., Stanley I. Benn, and Geoffrey W. Mortimore (1976). 'The Rationality of Societies', in *Rationality and the Social Sciences*, ed. Benn and Mortimore, 359–83.

Patterson, Sarah (1990). 'The Explanatory Role of Belief Ascriptions', *Philosophical Studies*, 59, 313–32.

Pears, David (1984). *Motivated Irrationality*. Oxford: Clarendon.

Pépin, Benoît (1990). 'Hands on Popper: A Critique', *Cahiers d'Epistémologie*, 9011, 1–20

Perry, John, ed. (1975). *Personal Identity*. Berkeley: University of California Press.

Pettit, Philip (1986). 'Broad-minded Explanation and Psychology', in *Subject, Thought and Context*, ed. Pettit and McDowell, 17–58.

Pettit, Philip, and Huw Price (1989). 'Bare Functional Desire', *Analysis*, 49, 162–69.

Pettit, Philip, and John McDowell, eds. (1986). *Subject, Thought, and Context*. Oxford: Clarendon.

Platts, Mark (1986). 'Desire and Action', *Nous*, 20, 143–55.

Popper, Karl (1957). *The Poverty of Historicism*. London: Routledge and Kegan Paul.

(1967). 'La Rationalité et le statut du principe de rationalité', in *Les Fondements philosophiques des systèmes économiques*. Ed. Classen, 142–50. Trans. 'The Rationality Principle' (1967), in *Popper Selections*, ed. Miller, 357–65.

(1969). 'Die Logik der Sozialwissenschaften', in *Der Positivismusstreit*, ed. Adorno et al., 103–124.

Price, Huw (1989). 'Defending 'Desire-as-Belief'', *Mind*, 98, 119–27.

Pylyshyn, Zenon W. (1984). *Computation and Cognition: Toward a Foundation for Cognitive Science*. Cambridge, Mass.: M.I.T. Press.

Radnitzky, Gerald, and William W. Bartley, eds. (1987). *Evolutionary Epistemology, Theory of Rationality, and Sociology of Knowledge*. La Salle: Open Court.

Récanati, François, ed. (1988). *L'Age de la science: lectures philosophiques 1*. Paris: Odile Jacob.

Rescher, Nicholas (1968). *The Logic of Decision and Action*. Pittsburgh: University of Pittsburgh Press.

(1988). *Rationality: A Philosophical Inquiry into the Nature and the Rationale of Reason*. Oxford: Clarendon.

Richard, Mark (1990). *Propositional Attitudes: An Essay on Thoughts and How We Ascribe Them*. Cambridge: Cambridge University Press.

Rorty, Amélie Oksenberg, ed. (1980). *Explaining Emotions*. Berkeley: University of California Press.

Rose, Steven, Richard C. Lewontin, and Leon J. Kamin, (1984). *Not in Our Genes: Biology, Ideology, and Human Nature*. New York: Pantheon.

Rosenberg, Seymour, and Russell Jones (1972). 'A Method for Investigating and Representing a Person's Implicit Theory of Personality: Theodore Dreiser's View of People', *Journal of Personality and Social Psychology*, 22, 372–86.

Roth, Michael D., and Glenn Ross, eds. (1990). *Doubting: Contemporary Perspectives on Skepticism*. Dordrecht: Kluwer.

Ryle, Gilbert (1949). *The Concept of Mind*. London: Hutchinson and Co.

Sarkar, Husain (1983). *A Theory of Method*. Berkeley: University of California Press.

Satinoff, Evelyn, and Philip Teitelbaum, eds. (1983). *Motivation*. New York: Plenum.

Scheff, Thomas (1967). 'Toward a Sociological Model of Consensus', *American Sociological Review*, 32, 32–46.

Schelling, Thomas C. (1960). *The Strategy of Conflict*. Oxford: Oxford University Press.

Schick, Frederic (1984). *Having Reasons: An Essay on Rationality and Sociality*. Princeton: Princeton University Press.

Schluchter, Wolfgang (1980). *Rationalismus der Weltbeherrschung: Studien zu Max Weber*. Frankfurt: Suhrkamp.

Schmid, Michael (1988). 'The Idea of Rationality and its Relationship to Social Science: Comments on Popper's Philosophy of the Social Sciences', *Inquiry*, 31, 451–69.

Schnädelbach, Herbert, ed. (1984). *Rationalität: Philosophische Beiträge*. Frankfurt: Suhrkamp.

Schoemaker, Paul J. H. (1982). 'The Expected Utility Model: Its Variants, Purposes, Evidence and Limitations', *Journal of Economic Literature*, 20, 529–63.

Scholz, Roland W., ed. (1983). *Decision Making Under Uncertainty*. New York: Oxford.

Schotter, Andrew (1981). *The Economic Theory of Social Institutions*. Cambridge: Cambridge University Press.

Schueler, G. F. (1989). *The Idea of a Reason for Acting*. Lewiston: Mellen.

Schutz, Alfred (1967). *The Phenomenology of the Social World*. Trans. George Walsh and Frederick Lehnert. Evanston: Northwestern University Press.

Searle, John R. (1969). *Speech Acts: An Essay in the Philosophy of Language*. Cambridge: Cambridge University Press.

(1977). 'Reiterating the Differences: Reply to Derrida', *Glyph*, 1, 198–208.

(1979). *Expression and Meaning: Studies in the Theory of Speech Acts*. Cambridge: Cambridge University Press.

(1983). *Intentionality: An Essay in the Philosophy of Mind*. Cambridge: Cambridge University Press.

Sen, Amartya K. (1979). 'Rational Fools', in *Philosophy and Economic Theory*, ed. Hahn and Hollis, 87–109.

(1985). 'Rationality and Uncertainty', *Theory and Decision*, 18, 109–28.

(1987). *On Ethics and Economics*. Oxford: Basil Blackwell.

Shackle, George L. S. (1961). *Decision, Order and Time in Human Affairs*. Cambridge: Cambridge University Press.

(1972). *Epistemics and Economics: A Critique of Economic Doctrines*. Cambridge: Cambridge University Press.

Shapere, Dudley (1988). 'Discussion: Doppelt Crossed', *Philosophy of Science*, 55, 134–40.

Shaver, Kelly G. (1985). *The Attribution of Blame: Causality, Responsibility, and Blameworthiness*. New York: Springer.

Shubik, Martin (1982). *Game Theory in the Social Sciences: Concepts and Solutions*. Cambridge, Mass.: M.I.T. Press.

Siegel, Harvey (1987). *Relativism Refuted: A Critique of Contemporary Epistemological Relativism*. Dordrecht: Reidel.

Simon, Herbert A. (1957). *Models of Man*. New York: John Wiley.

(1976). 'From Substantive to Procedural Rationality', in *Method and Appraisal in Economics*, ed. Latsis, 129–48.

(1978). 'Rationality as Process and as Product of Thought', *American Economic Review*, 68, 1–16.

(1983). *Reason in Human Affairs*. Stanford: Stanford University Press.

(1986). 'Rationality in Psychology and Economics', in *Rational Choice*, ed. Hogarth and Reder, 25–40.

Skyrms, Brian (1990). *The Dynamics of Rational Deliberation*. Cambridge, Mass.: Harvard University Press.

Slote, Michael (1989). *Beyond Optimizing: A Study of Rational Choice*. Cambridge, Mass.: Harvard University Press.

Sorrentino, Richard, and E. Tory Higgins, eds. (1986). *Handbook of Motivation and Cognition: Foundations of Social Behavior*. New York: Guilford.

Stampe, Dennis W. (1987). 'The Authority of Desire', *The Philosophical Review*, 96, 335–82.

Steinbruner, John D. (1974). *The Cybernetic Theory of Decision*. Princeton: Princeton University Press.

Stich, Steven (1985). 'Can Man Be an Irrational Animal?' *Synthese*, 64, 115–35.

(1990). 'Rationality', in *Thinking*, ed. Osherson and Smith, 173–96.

Stigler, George J. (1961). 'The Economics of Information', *Journal of Political Economy*, 69, 213–25.

Stigler, George J., and Gary S. Becker (1977). 'De Gustibus Non Est Disputandum', *American Economic Review*, 67, 76–90.

Stinchcombe, Arthur L. (1986). *Stratification and Organization: Selected Papers*. Cambridge: Cambridge University Press.

Stove, David C. (1982). *Popper and After: Four Modern Irrationalists*. Oxford: Pergamon.

(1986). *The Rationality of Induction*. Oxford: Clarendon.

Suppes, Patrick (1981). 'The Limits of Rationality', in *Science and Ethics*, ed. Haller, 85–102.

Szabados, Béla (1979). 'A Note on Irrationality', in *Rationality Today*, ed. Geraets, 387–90.

Taine, Hippolyte (1883). *De l'intelligence*. 2 vols. Paris: Hachette, 4th ed.

Tamny, Martin, and K. D. Irani, eds. (1986). *Rationality in Thought and Action*. New York: Greenwood Press.

Taylor, Charles (1977). 'What is Human Agency?' In *The Self*, ed. Mischel, 103–35.

(1982). 'Rationality', in *Rationality and Relativism*, ed. Hollis and Lukes, 87–105.

Thagard, Paul (1988). *Computational Philosophy of Science*. Cambridge, Mass.: M.I.T. Press.

Thalberg, Irving (1977). *Enigmas of Agency*. New York: Humanities.

(1985). 'Analytical Action Theory: Breakthroughs and Deadlocks', in *Social Action*, ed. Seebass and Tuomela, 1–41.

Tisdell, Clement A. (1976). 'Rational Behaviour as a Basis for Economic Theories', in *Rationality and the Social Sciences*, ed. Benn and Mortimore, 196–222.

Toates, Frederick (1986). *Motivational Systems.* Cambridge: Cambridge University Press.

Toates, Frederick M., and Timothy R. Halliday (1980). *Analysis of Motivational Processes.* New York: Academic.

Tomberlin, James E., ed. (1983). *Agent, Language, and the Structure of the World: Essays Presented to Hector-Neri Castañeda, with His Replies.* Indianapolis: Hackett.

Tugendhat, Ernst (1986). *Self-Consciousness and Self-Determination.* Trans. Paul Stern. Cambridge, Mass.: M.I.T.

Tuomela, Raimo (1977). *Human Action and its Explanation: A Study on the Philosophical Foundations of Psychology.* Dordrecht: Reidel.

  (1984). *A Theory of Social Action.* Dordrecht: Reidel.

Tuomela, Raimo, and Gottfried Seebass, eds. (1985). *Social Action.* Dordrecht: Reidel.

Turner, Jonathan H. (1988). *A Theory of Social Interaction.* Stanford: Stanford University Press.

Uleman, James S., and John A. Bargh, eds. (1989). *Unintended Thought.* New York: Guilford.

Ullmann-Margalit, Edna (1977). *The Emergence of Norms.* Oxford: Clarendon.

Velleman, J. David (1989). *Practical Reflection.* Princeton: Princeton University Press.

Vermazen, Bruce, and Merrill B. Hintikka, eds. (1985). *Essays on Davidson: Actions and Events.* Oxford: Clarendon.

Wallace, R. Jay (1990). 'How to Argue about Practical Reason', *Mind,* 99, 355–85.

Walliser, Bernard (1988). 'Rationalité instrumentale et rationalité cognitive', *Cahiers du CREA,* 11, 189–233.

Watkins, John (1970). 'Imperfect Rationality', in *Explanation in the Behavioral Sciences,* ed. Borger and Cioffi, 167–217.

Weber, Max (1968a). *Economy and Society.* 2 vols. Ed. and trans. Guenther Roth and Claus Wittich. Berkeley: University of California Press.

  (1968b). *Gesammelte Aufsätze zur Wissenschaftslehre.* Tubingen: J.C.B. Mohr.

Weiner, Bernard (1980). *Human Motivation.* New York: Holt, Rinehart and Winston.

  (1986). 'Attribution, Emotion, and Action', in *Handbook of Motivation and Cognition: Foundations of Social Behavior,* ed. Sorrentino and Higgins, 281–312.

Weingartner, Paul (1983). 'Normative Principles of Rational Communication', *Erkenntnis,* 19, 405–16.

Wickler, Wolfgang (1968). *Mimicry in Plants and Animals.* Trans. R. D. Martin. New York: McGraw-Hill.

Wilensky, Robert (1983). *Planning and Understanding: A Computational Approach to Human Reasoning.* Reading, Mass.: Addison-Wesley.

Wilkerson, T. E. (1986). 'Desire, Belief, and Rational Action', *Ratio*, 28, 114–31.

Wilson, Bryan R., ed. (1970). *Rationality*. Oxford: Basil Blackwell.

Wilson, George M. (1989). *The Intentionality of Human Action*. Revised ed. Stanford: Stanford University Press.

Wollheim, Richard, and J. Hopkins, eds. (1982). *Philosophical Essays on Freud*. Cambridge: Cambridge University Press.

Wright, Georg Henrik von (1963). *The Logic of Preference: An Essay*. Edinburgh: Edinburgh University Press.

(1971). *Explanation and Understanding*. Ithaca: Cornell University Press.

(1972). 'The Logic of Preference Reconsidered', *Theory and Decision*, 3, 140–67.

(1983). *Practical Reason*. Oxford: Basil Blackwell.

Index